The Value of Humor in Educational Leadership

No Laughing Matter

Robert Palestini

ROWMAN & LITTLEFIELD EDUCATION
A division of
ROWMAN & LITTLEFIELD PUBLISHERS, INC.
Lanham • New York • Toronto • Plymouth, UK

Published by Rowman & Littlefield Education
A division of Rowman & Littlefield Publishers, Inc.
A wholly owned subsidary of The Rowman & Littlefield Publishing Group, Inc.
4501 Forbes Boulevard, Suite 200, Lanham, Maryland 20706
www.rowman.com

10 Thornbury Road, Plymouth PL6 7PP, United Kingdom

British Library Cataloguing in Publication Information Available

Library of Congress Cataloging-in-Publication Data

Palestini, Robert H.
No laughing matter : the value of humor in educational leadership / Robert Palestini.
p. cm.
Includes bibliographical references.
ISBN 978-1-61048-860-0 (cloth : alk. paper) — ISBN 978-1-61048-861-7 (pbk. : alk. paper) — ISBN 978-1-61048-862-4 (electronic) (print)
1. Educational leadership. 2. Wit and humor in education. I. Title.
LB2805.P2894 2013
371.2—dc23
2012029797

♾™ The paper used in this publication meets the minimum requirements of American National Standard for Information Sciences Permanence of Paper for Printed Library Materials, ANSI/NISO Z39.48-1992.

Printed in the United States of America

To Tom Koerner, whose longtime faith in me as an author is much appreciated.
To Judy, whose support and encouragement mean the world to me.
To Karen, Scott, Rob, and Brendan, whose presence in my life is reinvigorating.
To Liz and Wendy, for willingly providing much-needed technical assistance.

Contents

Preface

Educators are not alone in perennially seeking the best leadership practices and applying them to their own leadership behavior. What constitutes effective leadership seems to be on the minds of people everywhere. Recently, there has been some seminal work done with regard to the role of humor in leadership effectiveness. Several contemporary empirical studies corroborate some earlier research that closely linked effective leadership to whether the leader possesses a well-developed sense of humor (Priest and Swain, 2002; Hughes and Avery, 2009). Of particular interest to educational leaders would be a study that demonstrates that there are significant relationships between certain humor factors and an improvement in school climate (Ziegler, Boardman, and Thomas, 1985).

In light of this connection between possessing a keen sense of humor and leadership effectiveness, this book profiles the leadership behavior of ten proven leaders from many walks of life whose leadership style included a highly developed sense of humor. In alphabetical order they include Winston Churchill, Albert Einstein, Benjamin Franklin, John F. Kennedy, Abraham Lincoln, Golda Meir, Ronald Reagan, Theodore Roosevelt, Casey Stengel, and Harry Truman. The idea, of course, would be to look at the overall leadership behavior of these individuals, but focus especially on their symbolic frame leadership behavior in the form of humor, to determine how their behavior can inform our own particular leadership style.

In analyzing the leadership behavior of these leaders, I utilize both the Bolman/Deal and Hersey/Blanchard models of situational leadership theory. Lee Bolman and Terrance Deal posit four frames of leadership behavior: (1) structural, (2) human resource, (3) symbolic (including a sense of humor), and (4) political. I supplement their model with a fifth frame that I call the moral frame. Bolman and Deal argue that effective and impactful leaders combine and balance their use of these frames, rather than dwelling on one or two frames to the virtual exclusion of the others.

In addition to the Bolman/Deal model, I further analyze these leaders' leadership behavior through the lens of the Paul Hersey/Ken Blanchard leadership model, which stresses the *readiness* level of the leaders' followers in determining the appropriate leadership behavior to be applied. Hersey and Blanchard define readiness level as the follower's ability and willingness to accomplish a specific task; this is the major contingency that influences which leadership frame behavior should be applied. Follower readiness incorporates the follower's level of achievement motivation, ability, and willingness to assume responsibility for his or her own behavior in accomplishing specific tasks, as well as his or her education and experience relevant to the task.

So, in its simplest form, the Hersey/Blanchard model would posit that a person with a low readiness level should be dealt with by using structural frame leadership behavior (telling behavior), while a person with a very high readiness level should be dealt with using human resource and symbolic frame leadership behavior (collaborative leadership behavior).

Additionally, since we all aspire to be transformational leaders—leaders who inspire positive change in our organizations and our followers—we analyze the leaders' leadership behavior through the lens of transformational leadership theory. Transformational leaders use charisma, often in the form of humor, to inspire their followers. They talk to the followers about how essential their performance is and how they expect the group's performance to exceed expectations. A transformational leader changes an organization by recognizing an opportunity and developing a vision, communicating that vision to organizational members, building trust in the vision, and achieving the vision by motivating organizational members to attain it.

Finally, I focus on moral frame leadership behavior. As I indicated, the moral frame is my own contribution to situational leadership theory. In my view, the moral frame *completes* situational leadership theory. Without it, leaders could just as easily use their leadership skills in the pursuit of evil rather than in promoting good. Leaders operating out of the moral frame are concerned about their obligations and responsibilities to their followers. Moral frame leaders use some type of moral compass to direct their behavior. They practice what has been described as servant leadership and are concerned with those individuals and groups that are marginalized in their organizations and in society. In short, in addition to all the other leadership considerations, they are concerned about integrity, equality, fairness, and social justice.

Basically, then, this is a book about leadership. The conventional wisdom is that leaders are born, not made. I disagree! My experience and, more importantly, scholarly research indicate that leadership skills can be learned. Granted, some leaders will be superior to others because of genetics, but the basic leadership skills are learned behaviors and can be cultivated, enhanced, and honed.

The first chapter of this book speaks to the so-called science of leadership, while the second chapter deals with the "art" of administration and leadership. One needs to lead with both mind (science) and heart (art) to be truly effective. The next ten chapters are about the leadership behavior of ten proven leaders and are predicated on the belief that leadership skills can be learned and replicated. In the last chapter of the book, the leadership implications for educators and other leaders are explored.

The effective building blocks of quality leadership are the skills of communication, motivation, organizational development, management, and creativity. Mastering the theory and practice in these areas of study will produce high-quality leadership ability and, in turn, produce successful leaders; doing so with "heart" or compassion will result in not only highly successful leadership, but what author Chris Lowney calls *heroic leadership.*

There is another broadly held assumption about effective leadership and administration that I would also dispute: namely, that "nice guys (and gals) finish last." To be a successful leader, the belief goes, one needs to be firm, direct, even autocratic. Once again, scholarly research, as well as my own experience, indicates that no one singular leadership style is consistently effective in all situations and at all times. Empirical and experiential studies indicate that effective leaders vary their styles depending on the situation.

This *situational* approach is the underlying theme of this book. In the concluding chapter, we assert that truly effective leaders use both their minds, in the form of structural and political leadership behavior, and their hearts, in the form of human resource, symbolic, and moral leadership behavior, and in doing so, nice guys and gals *do* often finish first.

Some forty years ago, when I was coaching high school basketball, I attended a coaching clinic where the main clinicians were Dean Smith, then coach of the University of North Carolina, and Bobby Knight, then coach of Indiana University. Both coaches were successful then, and almost four decades later, they remain respected and, in one case at least, revered.

In the morning session Bobby Knight explained how *fear* is the most effective motivator in sports. If you want your players to listen to and obey you and want to be successful as a coach, you need to instill fear in them, Knight declared. In the afternoon session, Dean Smith explained how *love* is the most effective motivator in sports. If you want to win and be successful, you must inspire love in your players.

You can understand my sense of confusion by the end of that clinic. Here were two of the most successful men in sports giving contradictory advice. As a young and impressionable coach, I was puzzled by these apparently mixed messages. Over the intervening years, I have often thought about that clinic and tried to make sense of what I heard. After these many years, I have drawn two conclusions from this incident, both of which have had a significant impact on my philosophy of leadership and on this book.

The first conclusion has to do with the *situational* nature of leadership. Bobby Knight and Dean Smith impressed upon me the truism that there is no one singular leadership style that is effective at all times and in all situations. The second conclusion I drew, is that, despite reaping short-term success with fear, the better style for ensuring continued success is one that inspires love, trust, and respect. Just as athletes become robotic and frightened of making mistakes when fear is the only motivator, so do employees who are too closely supervised by an autocratic manager. Initiative, creativity, and self-sufficiency are all stymied by the leader who instills fear in his or her subordinates. Thus, I arrived at my ultimate conclusion that effective school administration in particular, and leadership in general, begins with love, trust, and respect, which are all moral frame leadership behaviors.

In addition to an emphasis on the nature of leadership, this book focuses on placing *theory* into practice. We should not underestimate the value and importance of theory. Without theory we have no valid way of analyzing and correcting failed practice. Without a theoretical base, we often lead by trial and error, or by the proverbial "seat of our pants." On the other hand, knowledge of theory without the ability to place it into reflective practice is of no value and will not lead to effective leadership. Thus, we suggest that leaders and aspiring leaders adopt one of the leadership theories described in this book and place it into reflective practice, modeled after the leadership behavior of the ten leaders profiled here.

This book uses the case study approach in order to facilitate placing theory into effective practice. Each chapter contains an extensive study of one of ten famous leaders. I analyze each case to demonstrate how these leaders were able to place leadership theory into effective practice. I believe that the lessons learned will prove invaluable to leaders and aspiring leaders, whether they be parents, teachers, school principals, or chief executive officers.

This book also takes an organizational development approach to producing effective leadership. Picture yourself standing in the middle of a dense forest. Suppose you were asked to describe the characteristics of the forest; what types of trees are growing in the forest; how many acres of trees are there; where are the trees thriving; where are they not? Faced with this proposition, most people would not know where to start; they would not be able "to see the forest for the trees."

Newly appointed executives and administrators often have this same feeling of confusion when faced with the prospect of having to assume a leadership role in a complex organization like a school, a school system, or a company. Where does one start? An effective place to start would be to systematically examine the components that make up an organization. Such a system of organizational diagnosis and prescription will lead to a comprehensive and integrated analysis of the organization's strengths and weaknesses and point the way toward possible improvement.

Using the leadership behaviors found among the successful leaders profiled here as a model, the final chapter of this book suggests such a sequential and systematic approach. In the appendix, there is a pair of diagnostic tools that I developed, the Heart Smart Surveys I and II, that assess the health of an organization. Utilizing them effectively can produce dramatic and useful results.

This leads me to what I refer to as the Seven Principles of Effective Leadership.

Effective leaders

- need to be able to adapt their *leadership style* to the situation, while maintaining a *sense of humor*;
- must be keenly aware of the organizational *structure and culture* (readiness level) of the institution;
- must be able to engender a sense of *trust and respect* in their followers;
- need to continuously improve their organizations and, therefore, must be *agents for change*;
- need to be *well organized and creative* and have a clearly articulated *vision*;
- must be able to *communicate* effectively; and
- must know how to *motivate* their followers and be able to *manage the conflicts* that arise.

In my view, which is supported by a prodigious amount of empirical research, if an administrator can master the knowledge and skills encompassed in these seven principles, and do it with heart and humor, he or she will be a highly effective leader.

Chapter One

Contemporary Leadership Theory

The effective functioning of social systems from the local PTA to the United States of America is assumed to be dependent on the quality of their leadership. —Victor H. Vroom

Leadership is offered as a solution for most of the problems of organizations everywhere. Schools will work, we are told, if principals provide strong instructional leadership. Around the world, administrators and managers say that their organizations would thrive if only senior management provided strategy, vision, and real leadership. Though the call for leadership is universal, there is much less clarity about what the term means.

Historically, researchers in this field have searched for the one best leadership style that would be most effective. Current thought is that there is no one best style. Rather, a combination of styles depending on the situation in which the leader finds him or herself has been found to be more appropriate. To understand the evolution of leadership theory thought, we will take a historical approach and trace the progress of leadership theory, beginning with the trait perspective of leadership and moving to the more current contingency theories of leadership.

THE TRAIT THEORY

Trait theory suggests that we can evaluate leadership and propose ways of leading effectively by considering whether an individual possesses certain personality traits, social traits, and physical characteristics. Popular in the 1940s and 1950s, trait theory attempted to predict which individuals would successfully become leaders and then whether they were effective. Leaders

1

differ from non-leaders in their drive, desire to lead, honesty and integrity, self-confidence, cognitive ability, and knowledge of the business that they are in. Scholars also found that the traits judged necessary for top, middle, and low-level management differed among leaders of different countries; for example, U.S. and British leaders valued resourcefulness; the Japanese, intuition; and the Dutch, imagination, but for lower-level and middle managers only (Kirkpatrick and Locke, 1991, p. 49).

The trait approach has more historical than practical interest for managers and administrators, even though recent research has once again tied leadership effectiveness to leader traits. Some view the transformational perspective described later in this chapter as a natural evolution of the earlier trait perspective.

THE BEHAVIORAL PERSPECTIVE

The limitations in the ability of traits to predict effective leadership caused researchers during the 1950s to view a person's behavior rather than that individual's personal traits as a way of increasing leadership effectiveness. This view also paved the way for later situational theories.

The types of leadership behaviors investigated typically fell into two categories: production oriented and employee oriented. Production-oriented leadership, also called concern for production, initiating structure, or task-focused leadership, involves acting primarily to get the task done. An administrator who tells his or her department chair to do "everything you need to get the curriculum developed on time for the start of school no matter what the consequences" demonstrates production-oriented leadership. So does an administrator who uses an autocratic style or fails to involve workers in any aspect of decision making.

In contrast, employee-oriented leadership, also called concern for people or consideration, focuses on supporting the individual workers in their activities and involving the workers in decision making. A principal who demonstrates great concern for his or her teachers' satisfaction with their duties and what is happening in their personal lives has an employee-oriented leadership style (Stogdill and Coons, 1957).

MANAGERIAL ROLES THEORY

A study of chief executive officers by Henry Mintzberg suggested a different way of looking at leadership. He observed that managerial work encompasses ten roles: three that focus on interpersonal contact—(1) figurehead,

(2) leader, (3) liaison; three that involve mainly information processing—(4) monitor, (5) disseminator, (6) spokesman; and four related to decision making—(7) entrepreneur, (8) disturbance handler, (9) resource allocator, and (10) negotiator. Note that almost all roles would include activities that could be construed as leadership that is influencing others toward a particular goal.

In addition, most of these roles can apply to non-managerial positions as well as managerial ones. The role approach resembles the behavioral and trait perspectives because all three call for specific types of behavior independent of the situation; however, the role approach is more compatible with the situational approach and has been shown to be more valid than either the behavioral or trait perspective (Mintzberg, 1979).

EARLY SITUATIONAL THEORIES

Contingency or situational models differ from the earlier trait and behavioral models in asserting that no single way of leading works in all situations. Rather, appropriate behavior depends on the circumstances at a given time. Effective managers diagnose the situation, identify the leadership style that will be most effective, and then determine whether they can implement the required style.

THEORY X AND THEORY Y

One of the older situational theories, Douglas McGregor's Theory X/ Theory Y formulation, calls for a leadership style based on individuals' assumptions about other individuals, together with characteristics of the individual, the task, the organization, and environment. Although managers may have many styles, Theories X and Y have received the greatest attention.

Theory X managers assume that people are lazy, extrinsically motivated, and incapable of self-discipline or self-control, and that they want security and no responsibility in their jobs. Theory Y managers assume people do not inherently dislike work, are intrinsically motivated, exert self-control, and seek responsibility. A Theory X manager, because of his or her limited view of the world, has only one leadership style available, that is, autocratic. A Theory Y manager has a wide range of styles in his or her repertoire. McGregor's research concluded that Theory Y management is by far the more effective approach (McGregor, 1961; Schein, 1974, p. 3).

FREDERICK FIEDLER'S THEORY

While McGregor's theory provided a transition from behavioral to situational theories, Frederick Fiedler developed and tested the first leadership theory explicitly called a contingency or situational model. He argued that changing an individual's leadership style is quite difficult, but that organizations should put individuals in situations that fit with their style. Fiedler's theory suggests that managers can choose between two styles: task oriented and relationship oriented. Then the nature of leader-member relations, task structure, and position power of the leader influences whether a task-oriented or a relationship-oriented leadership style is more likely to be effective.

Leader-member relations refer to the extent to which the group trusts and respects the leader and will follow the leader's directions. Task structure describes the degree to which the task is clearly specified and defined or structured, as opposed to ambiguous or unstructured. Position power means the extent to which the leader has official power, that is, the potential or actual ability to influence others in a desired direction owing to the position he or she holds in the organization (Fiedler and Garcia, 1987).

The style recommended as most effective for each combination of these three situational factors is based on the degree of control or influence the leader can exert in his or her leadership position. In general, high-control situations call for task-oriented leadership because they allow the leader to take charge. Low-control situations also call for task-oriented leadership because they require rather than allow the leader to take charge. Moderate-control situations, in contrast, call for relationship-oriented leadership because the situations challenge leaders to get the cooperation of their subordinates.

Despite extensive research to support the theory, critics have questioned the reliability of the measurement of leadership style and the range and appropriateness of the three situational components. This theory, however, is particularly applicable for those who believe that individuals are born with a certain management style, rather than the management style being learned or flexible (Fielder and Garcia, 1987).

CONTEMPORARY SITUATIONAL LEADERSHIP

Current research suggests that the effect of leader behaviors on performance is altered by such intervening variables as the effort of subordinates, their ability to perform their jobs, the clarity of their job responsibilities, the organization of the work, the cooperation and cohesiveness of the group, the sufficiency of resources and support provided to the group, and the coordination of work group activities with those of other subunits.

Thus, leaders must respond to these and broader cultural differences in choosing an appropriate style. A leader-environment-follower interaction theory of leadership notes that effective leaders first analyze deficiencies in the follower's ability, motivation, role perception, and work environment that inhibit performance and then act to eliminate these deficiencies (Biggart and Hamilton, 1987, pp. 429–441).

THE HERSEY/BLANCHARD MODEL

In an attempt to integrate previous knowledge about leadership into a prescriptive model of leadership style, Hersey and Blanchard cite the "readiness of followers," defined as their ability and willingness to accomplish a specific task, as the major contingency that influences appropriate leadership style (Hersey and Blanchard, 1988). Follower readiness incorporates the follower's level of achievement motivation, ability and willingness to assume responsibility for his or her own behavior in accomplishing specific tasks, and education and experience relevant to the task. The model combines task and relationship behavior to yield four possible styles, as shown in figure 1.1.

Leaders should use a telling style, and provide specific instructions and closely supervise performance, when followers are unable and unwilling or insecure (Readiness Level I). Leaders should use a selling style, and explain decisions and provide opportunity for clarification, when followers have moderate to low readiness (Readiness Level II). A participating style, where the leader shares ideas and helps facilitate decision making, should be used when followers have moderate to high readiness (Readiness Level III). Finally, leaders should use a delegating style, and give responsibility for decisions and implementation to followers, when followers are able, willing, and confident (Readiness Level IV).

Although some researchers have questioned the conceptual clarity, validity, robustness, and utility of the model, as well as the instruments used to measure leadership style, others have supported the utility of the theory. For example, the Leadership Effectiveness and Description Scale (LEAD) and related instruments developed to measure leadership style by the life cycle researchers are widely used in industrial training programs. This model can easily be adapted to educational administration as well as other types of leadership positions and be used analytically to understand leadership defi-

LEADER BEHAVIOR

Readiness Level III Participating Style	Readiness Level II Selling Style
Readiness Level IV Delegating Style	Readiness Level I Telling Style

FOLLOWER READINESS

R IV	R III	R II	R I
Seasoned veteran and/or very secure	much experience and/or secure	some experience and/or confidence	inexperienced and/or insecure

Figure 1.1.   Adopted from Hersey/Blanchard Situational Leadership Model.

ciencies and to prescribe the appropriate style for a variety of situations. We will use the follower readiness aspect of this model in analyzing the leadership behavior of the ten leaders profiled in this book.

THE BOLMAN/DEAL MODEL

Lee Bolman and Terrence Deal have developed a unique situational leadership theory that analyzes leadership behavior through four frames of reference: structural, human resource, political, and symbolic. Each of the frames offers a different perspective on what leadership is and how it operates in organizations. Each can result in either effective or ineffective conceptions of leadership (Bolman and Deal, 1991).

Structural leaders develop a new model of the relationship of structure, strategy, and environment for their organizations. They focus on implementation. The right answer helps only if it can be implemented. These leaders emphasize rationality, analysis, logic, fact, and data. They are likely to believe strongly in the importance of clear structure and well-developed management systems. A good leader is someone who thinks clearly, makes good decisions, has good analytic skills, and can design structures and systems that get the job done.

Structural leaders sometimes fail because they miscalculate the difficulty of putting their designs in place. They often underestimate the resistance that it will generate, and they take few steps to build a base of support for their innovations. In short, they are often undone by human resource, political, and symbolic considerations. Structural leaders do continually experiment, evaluate, and adapt, but because they fail to consider the entire environment in which they are situated, they sometimes are ineffective.

Human resource leaders believe in people and communicate that belief. They are passionate about "productivity through people." They demonstrate this faith in their words and actions and often build it into a philosophy or credo that is central to their vision of their organizations. They believe in the importance of coaching, participation, motivation, teamwork, and good interpersonal relations. A good leader is a facilitator and participative manager who supports and empowers others. Human resource leaders are visible and accessible. Tom Peters and Robert Waterman popularized the notion of "management wandering around," the idea that managers need to get out of their offices and interact with workers and customers. Many educational administrators have adopted this aspect of management.

Effective human resource leaders empower, that is, they increase participation, provide support, share information, and move decision making as far down the organization as possible. Human resource leaders often like to refer to their employees as "partners" or "colleagues." They want to make it clear that employees have a stake in the organization's success and a right to be involved in making decisions. When they are ineffective, however, they are seen as naive or as weaklings and wimps.

Political leaders believe that managers and leaders live in a world of conflict and scarce resources. The central task of management is to mobilize the resources needed to advocate and fight for the unit's or the organization's goals and objectives. They emphasize the importance of building a power base: allies, networks, coalitions. A good leader is an advocate and negotiator, understands politics, and is comfortable with conflict. Political leaders clarify what they want and what they can get. Political leaders are realists above all. They never let what they want cloud their judgment about what is possible. They assess the distribution of power and interests.

The political leader needs to think carefully about the players, their interests, and their power; in other words, he or she must map the political terrain. Political leaders ask questions such as: Whose support do I need? How do I go about getting it? Who are my opponents? How much power do they have? What can I do to reduce the opposition? Is the battle winnable? However, if ineffective, these leaders are perceived as being untrustworthy and manipulative.

The symbolic frame provides still a fourth turn of the kaleidoscope of leadership. In this frame, the organization is seen as a stage, a theater in which every actor plays certain roles and attempts to communicate the right impressions to the right audiences. The main premise of this frame is that whenever reason and analysis fail to contain the dark forces of ambiguity, human beings erect symbols, myths, rituals, and ceremonies to bring order, meaning, and predictability out of chaos and confusion. They believe that the essential role of management is to provide inspiration. They rely on personal charisma, a flair for drama, and a keen sense of humor to get people excited and committed to the organizational mission.

A good leader is a prophet and visionary, who uses symbols, tells stories, and frames experience in ways that give people hope and meaning. Transforming leaders are visionary leaders, and visionary leadership is invariably symbolic.

Transforming leaders use symbols to capture attention. When a female colleague of mine became principal of a middle school in Philadelphia, she knew that she faced a substantial challenge. The middle school had all the usual problems of urban public schools: decaying physical plant, lack of student discipline, racial tension, troubles with the teaching staff, low morale, and limited resources. The only good news was that the situation was so bad that almost any change would be an improvement.

In such a situation, symbolic leaders will try to do something visible, even dramatic, to let people know that changes are on the way. During the summer before she assumed her duties, my colleague wrote a letter to every teacher to set up an individual meeting. She traveled to meet teachers wherever they wanted, driving two hours in one case. She asked teachers how they felt about the school and what changes they wanted.

She also felt that something needed to be done about the school building, because nobody likes to work in a dumpy place. She decided that the front door and some of the worst classrooms had to be painted. She had few illusions about getting the bureaucracy of the Philadelphia public school system to provide painters, so she persuaded some of her family members to help her do the painting. When school opened, students and staff members immediately saw that things were going to be different, if only symbolically. Perhaps even more important, staff members received a subtle challenge to make a contribution themselves.

Each of the four frames captures significant possibilities for leadership, but each in and of itself is incomplete. In the early part of the century, leadership as a concept was rarely applied to management, and the implicit models of leadership were narrowly rational (structural frame). In the 1960s and 1970s, human resource frame leadership became fashionable. The literature on organizational leadership stressed openness, sensitivity, and participation.

In recent years, symbolic frame leadership has moved to center stage, and the literature now offers advice on how to become a visionary leader with the power to transform organizational cultures. Organizations do need vision, but it is not their only need and not always their most important one. Leaders need to understand their own frame and its limits. Ideally, they will also learn to combine multiple frames into a more comprehensive and powerful style.

It is this Bolman/Deal leadership theory on which we will base the bulk of our conclusions regarding the effective leadership behavior of the ten leaders profiled in this book. Before leaving our discussion of Bolman and Deal's approach, however, let us reinforce the point that balance needs to occur both *among* and *within* the frames. That is to say that in addition to utilizing all four frames, the effective leader needs to be careful not to behave to the extreme within any one frame. Striving for the Golden Mean is the goal.

TRANSFORMATIONAL LEADERSHIP

A charismatic or transformational leader uses charisma to inspire his or her followers and is an example of one who acts primarily in the symbolic frame of leadership outlined above. He or she talks to the followers about how essential their performance is, how confident he or she is in the followers, how exceptional the followers are, and how he or she expects the group's performance to exceed expectations.

Lee Iacocca and Jack Welch, in industry, and John Dewey and Notre Dame's former president Reverend Theodore Hesburgh, in education, are examples of this type of leader. Among the leaders that we profile in this study, virtually all of them were found to be transformational leaders. Such leaders use dominance, self-confidence, a need for influence, and conviction of moral righteousness to increase their charisma and consequently their leadership effectiveness (House, 1977).

A transformational leader changes an organization by recognizing an opportunity and developing a vision, communicating that vision to organizational members, building trust in the vision, and achieving the vision by motivating organizational members. The leader helps subordinates recognize the need for revitalizing the organization by developing a felt need for change, overcoming resistance to change, and avoiding quick-fix solutions to problems.

Encouraging subordinates to act as devil's advocates with regard to the leader, building networks outside the organization, visiting other organizations, and changing management processes to reward progress against competition also help them recognize a need for revitalization. Individuals must disengage from and disidentify with the past, as well as view change as a way of dealing with their disenchantments with the past or the status quo. The transformational leader creates a new vision and mobilizes commitment to it by planning or educating others. He or she builds trust through demonstrating personal expertise, self-confidence, and personal integrity.

The charismatic leader can also change the composition of the team, alter management processes, and help organizational members reframe the way they perceive an organizational situation. The charismatic leader must empower others to help achieve the vision. Finally, the transformational leader must institutionalize the change by replacing old technical, political, cultural, and social networks with new ones. For example, the leader can identify key individuals and groups, develop a plan for obtaining their commitment, and institute a monitoring system for following the changes.

If an administrator wishes to make an innovative program acceptable to the faculty and the school community, for example, he or she should follow the above plan and identify influential individuals who would agree to champion the new program, develop a plan to gain support of others in the community through personal contact or other means, and develop a monitoring system to assess the progress of the effort (Conger and Kanungo, 1987, pp. 637–647; Willner, 1984).

A transformational leader motivates subordinates to achieve beyond their original expectations by increasing their awareness about the importance of designated outcomes and ways of attaining them; by getting workers to go beyond their self-interest to that of the team, the school, the school system, and the larger society; and by changing or expanding the individual's needs. Subordinates report that they work harder for such leaders. In addition, such leaders are judged higher in leadership potential by their subordinates as compared to the more common transactional leader.

One should be cognizant, however, of the negative side of charismatic leadership, which may exist if the leader overemphasizes devotion to him or herself, makes personal needs paramount, or uses highly effective communication skills to mislead or manipulate others. Such leaders may be so driven to achieve a vision that they ignore the costly implications of their goals.

The superintendent of schools that overexpands his or her jurisdiction in an effort to form an "empire," only to have the massive system turn into a bureaucratic nightmare, is an example of transformational leadership gone sour. A business that expands too rapidly to satisfy the ego of the CEO and, as a result, loses its quality control is another example. Nevertheless, recent research has verified the overall effectiveness of transformational leadership style.

IMPLICATIONS FOR LEADERS

The implications of leadership theory for educational and other administrators are rather clear. The successful leader needs to have a sound grasp of leadership theory and the skills to implement it. The principles of situational and transformational leadership theory are guides to effective administrative behavior. The leadership behavior applied to an inexperienced faculty member may be significantly different than that applied to a more experienced and tested one. Task behavior may be appropriate in dealing with a new teacher, while relationship behavior may be more appropriate when dealing with a seasoned teacher.

The four frames of leadership discussed by Bolman and Deal may be particularly helpful to school leaders and leaders in general. Consideration of the structural, human relations, political, and symbolic implications of leadership behavior can keep an administrator attuned to the various dimensions affecting appropriate leadership behavior.

With the need to deal with collective bargaining entities, school boards, and a variety of other power issues, the political frame considerations may be particularly helpful in understanding the complexity of relationships that exist between administrators and these groups. Asking oneself the questions posed earlier under the political frame can be an effective guide to the appropriate leadership behavior in dealing with these groups.

SUMMARY

Recently, a plethora of research studies have been conducted on leadership and leadership styles. The overwhelming evidence indicates that there is no one singular leadership style that is most appropriate in all situations. Rather, an administrator's leadership style should be adapted to the situation so that at various times task behavior or relationship behavior might be appropriate. At other times and in other situations, various degrees of both task and relationship behavior may be most effective.

The emergence of transformational leadership has seen leadership theory come full circle. Transformational leadership theory combines aspects of the early trait theory perspective with the more current situational or contingency models. The personal charisma of the leader, along with his or her ability to formulate an organizational vision and to communicate it to others, determines the transformational leader's effectiveness.

Since the effective leader is expected to adapt his or her leadership style to an ever-changing environment, administration becomes an even more complex and challenging task. However, a thorough knowledge of leadership theory can make some sense of the apparent chaos that the administrator faces on a daily basis.

Among scholars there is an assertion that *theory informs practice and practice informs theory.* This notion posits that to be an effective leader, one must base his or her practice on some form of leadership theory. If the leader consciously based his or her practice on leadership theory, this would be an example of theory informing practice. On the other hand, when a leader utilizes theory-inspired behavior that is continually ineffective, perhaps the theory must be modified to account for this deficiency. In this case, practice would be informing or changing theory.

In this book, we will examine the leadership behavior of ten famous leaders to ascertain whether their behavior conforms to the principles of the Bolman/Deal situational leadership theory, focusing especially on their symbolic frame leadership behavior in the form of humor, and if not, does their practice need to be modified, or does the theory need to be modified to reflect effective practice? We will also suggest how these leaders' leadership practices can be applied to our own leadership behavior to make it more effective. However, before we do so, we will explore the *art* of leadership, or what I call leading with heart.

Chapter Two

Leading with Heart

Do unto others what you would have them do unto you. —The Golden Rule

How the leader utilizes the concepts contained in the preceding chapter depends largely on one's philosophy of life regarding how human beings behave in the workplace. The two extremes of the continuum might be described as, on one end, those leaders who believe that human beings are basically lazy and will do the very least that they need to do to "get by" in the workplace and, on the other, those who believe that people are basically industrious and, if given the choice, would opt for doing a quality job. I believe that today's most effective leaders hold the latter view.

I agree with Max De Pree, owner and chief executive officer of the highly successful Herman Miller furniture company. Writing in his book, *Leadership Is an Art*, he says that a leader's function is to "liberate people to do what is required of them in the most effective and humane way possible" (De Pree, 1989). Instead of catching people doing something wrong, our goal as enlightened leaders is to catch them doing something right. I would suggest, therefore, that in addition to taking a rational approach to leadership, a truly enlightened leader leads with heart.

Too often, leaders underestimate the skills and qualities of their followers. I remember Bill Faries, the chief custodian at a high school at which I was assistant principal in the mid-1970s. Bill's mother, with whom he had been extraordinarily close, had passed away after a long illness. The school was religiously affiliated and the school community went "all out" in its remembrance of Bill's mother. We held a religious service in which almost four thousand members of the school community participated. Bill, of course, was very grateful. As a token of his gratitude he gave the school a six-by-eight-foot quilt that he had personally knitted. From that point on I did not know whether Bill was a custodian who was a quilt weaver, or a quilt weaver who was a custodian.

The point is that it took the death of his mother for me and others to realize how truly talented our custodian was. So our effectiveness as leaders begins with an understanding of the diversity of people's gifts, talents, and skills. When we think about the variety of gifts that people bring to organizations and institutions, we see that leading with heart lies in cultivating, liberating, and enabling those gifts.

LEADERSHIP DEFINED

The first responsibility of a leader is to define reality through a vision. The last is to say thank you. In between, the leader must become the servant of the servants. Being a leader means having the opportunity to make a meaningful difference in the lives of those who allow leaders to lead. This summarizes what I call leading with heart. In a nutshell, these leaders don't inflict pain; they bear pain.

Whether one is a successful leader can be determined by looking at one's followers. Are they reaching their potential? Are they learning? Are they able to change without bitterness? Are they able to achieve the institution's goals and objectives? Can they manage conflict among themselves? Where the answer to these questions is an emphatic "yes" is a place where a truly effective leader resides.

I prefer to think about leadership in terms of what the gospel writer Luke calls the "one who serves." The leader owes something to the institution he or she leads. The leader is seen in this context as steward rather than owner or proprietor. Leading with heart requires the leader to think about his or her stewardship in terms of legacy, direction, effectiveness, and values.

LEGACY

Too many of today's leaders are interested only in immediate results that bolster their career goals. Long-range goals are left to their successors. I believe that this approach fosters autocratic leadership, which oftentimes produces short-term results but militates against creativity and its long-term benefits. In effect, this approach is the antithesis of leading with heart.

On the contrary, leaders should build a long-lasting legacy of accomplishment that is institutionalized for posterity. They owe their institutions and their followers a healthy existence and the relationships and reputation that enable continuity of that healthy existence. Leaders are also responsible for future leadership. They need to identify, develop, and nurture future leaders to carry on the legacy.

VALUES

Along with being responsible for providing future leaders, leaders owe the individuals in their institutions certain other legacies. Leaders need to be concerned with the institutional value system that determines the principles and standards that guide the practices of those in the organization. Leaders need to model their value systems so that the individuals in the organization can learn to transmit these values to their colleagues and to future employees. In a civilized institution we see good manners, respect for people, and an appreciation of the way in which we serve one another. A humane, sensitive, and thoughtful leader will transmit his or her value system through his or her daily behavior. This, I believe, is what Peter Senge refers to as a "learning organization" (Senge, 1990).

DIRECTION

Leaders are obliged to provide and maintain direction by developing a vision. We made the point earlier that effective leaders must leave their organizations with a legacy. Part of this legacy should be a sense of progress or momentum. An educational administrator, for instance, should imbue his or her institution with a sense of continuous progress, a sense of constant improvement. Improvement and momentum come from a clear vision of what the institution ought to be, a well-planned strategy to achieve that vision, and carefully developed and articulated directions and plans that allow everyone to participate in and be personally accountable for achieving those plans.

EFFECTIVENESS

Leaders are also responsible for institutional effectiveness by being enablers. They need to enable others to reach their potential both personally and institutionally. I believe that the most effective ways of enabling one's colleagues is through participative decision making. It begins with believing in the potential of people, believing in their diversity of gifts. Leaders must realize that to maximize their own power and effectiveness, they need to empower others. Leaders are responsible for setting and attaining the goals in their organizations. Empowering or enabling others to help achieve those goals enhances the leader's chances of attaining the goals, ultimately enhancing the leader's effectiveness. Paradoxically, giving up power really amounts to gaining power.

EMPLOYEE OWNERS

We often hear managers suggest that a new program does not have a chance of succeeding unless the employees take "ownership" of the program. Most of us agree to the common sense of such an assertion. But how does a leader promote employee ownership? Let me suggest four steps as a beginning.

1. *Respect people.* As was indicated earlier, this starts with appreciating the diverse gifts that individuals bring to your institution. The key is to dwell on the strengths of your co-workers, rather than on their weaknesses. Try to turn their weaknesses into strengths. This does not mean that disciplinary action or even dismissal will never become necessary. What it does mean, however, is that we should focus on the formative aspect of the employee evaluation process before we engage in the summative part.

2. *Let belief guide policy and practice.* We spoke earlier of developing a culture of civility in your institution. If there is an environment of mutual respect and trust, I believe that the organization will flourish. Leaders need to let their belief or value system guide their behavior. Style is merely a consequence of what we believe and what is in our hearts.

3. *Recognize the need for covenants.* Contractual agreements cover such things as salary, fringe benefits, and working conditions. They are part of organizational life and there is a legitimate need for them. But in today's organizations, especially educational institutions, where the best people working for these institutions are like volunteers, we need covenantal relationships. Our best workers may choose their employers. They usually choose the institution where they work based on reasons less tangible than salaries and fringe benefits. They do not need contracts; they need covenants. Covenantal relationships enable educational institutions to be civil, hospitable, and understanding of individuals' differences and unique charismas. They allow administrators to recognize that treating everyone equally is not necessarily treating everyone equitably and fairly.

4. *Understand that culture counts more than structure.* An educational institution that I have been associated with recently went through a particularly traumatic time when the credibility of the administration was questioned by the faculty and staff. Various organizational consultants were interviewed to facilitate a "healing" process. Most of the consultants spoke of making the necessary structural changes to create a culture of trust. We finally hired a consultant whose attitude was that organizational structure has nothing to do with trust. Interpersonal relations based on mutual respect and an atmosphere of goodwill are what create a culture of trust. Would you rather work as part of a school with an outstanding reputation or work as part of a group of outstanding individuals? Many times these two characteristics of an organization go together, but if one had to make a choice, I believe that most people would opt to work with outstanding individuals.

IT STARTS WITH TRUST, RESPECT, AND KINDNESS (HEART)

These are exciting times in education. Revolutionary steps are being taken to restructure schools and rethink the teaching-learning process. The concepts of empowerment and total quality management, the use of technology, and strategic planning are becoming the norm. However, while these activities have the potential to influence education in significantly positive ways, they must be based upon a strong foundation to achieve their full potential.

Achieving educational effectiveness is an incremental, sequential improvement process. This improvement process begins by building a sense of security within each individual so that he or she can be flexible in adapting to changes within education. Addressing only skills or techniques, such as communication, motivation, negotiation, or empowerment, is ineffective when individuals in an organization do not trust its systems, themselves, or each other. An institution's resources are wasted when invested only in training programs that assist administrators in mastering quick-fix techniques that at best attempt to manipulate and at worst reinforce mistrust.

The challenge is to transform relationships based on insecurity, adversarialism, and politics into those based on mutual trust. Trust is the beginning of effectiveness and forms the foundation of a principle-centered learning environment that places emphasis upon strengths and devises innovative methods to minimize weaknesses. The transformation process requires an internal locus of control that emphasizes individual responsibility and accountability for change and for promoting effectiveness.

TEAMWORK

For many of us, there exists a dichotomy between how we see ourselves as persons and how we see ourselves as workers. Ideally, that should not be. Perhaps the following words of a Zen Buddhist will be helpful:

> The master in the art of living makes little distinction between his work and his play, his labor and his leisure, his mind and his body, his education and his recreation, his love and his religion. He hardly knows which is which. He simply pursues his vision of excellence in whatever he does, leaving others to decide whether he is working or playing. To him he is always doing both.

Work can be and should be productive, rewarding, enriching, fulfilling, and joyful. It is often what gets us out of bed every morning. Work is one of our greatest privileges, and it is up to leaders to make certain that work is everything that it can and should be.

One way to think of work is to think of how a philosopher would lead an organization, rather than how a businessman or woman would lead an organization. Plato's *Republic* speaks of the "philosopher-king," where the king would rule with the philosopher's ideals and values.

Paramount among the ideals that leaders need to recognize in leading an organization are the notion of teamwork and the valuing of each individual's contribution to the final product. The synergy produced by an effective team is greater than the sum of its parts.

The foundation of the team is the recognition that each member needs every other member, and no individual can be successful without the cooperation of others. As a young boy I was a very enthusiastic baseball fan. My favorite player was the recently deceased Hall of Fame pitcher Robin Roberts of the Philadelphia Phillies. During the early 1950s his fastball dominated the National League. My uncle, who took me to my first ballgame, explained that opposing batters were so intimidated by Roberts's fastball that they were automatic "outs" even before they got to the plate. My uncle claimed that Robin Roberts was unstoppable. Even as a young boy I intuitively knew that no one was unstoppable by himself. I said to my uncle that I knew how to stop Robin Roberts. "Make me his catcher!"

EMPLOYEES AS VOLUNTEERS

Our institutions will not amount to anything without the people who make them what they are. And the individuals most influential in making institutions what they are, are essentially volunteers. Our very best employees can work anywhere they please. So, in a sense, they volunteer to work where they do. As leaders, we would do far better if we looked upon and treated our employees as volunteers. We made the point earlier that we should treat our employees as if we had a covenantal relationship rather than a contractual relationship with them.

Alexander Solzhenitsyn, speaking to the 1978 graduating class of Harvard College, said this about legalistic relationships: "A society based on the letter of the law and never reaching any higher, fails to take advantage of the full range of human possibilities. The letter of the law is too cold and formal to have a beneficial influence on society. Whenever the tissue of life is woven of legalistic relationships, this creates an atmosphere of spiritual mediocrity that paralyzes men's noblest impulses." And later: "After a certain level of the problem has been reached, legalistic thinking induces paralysis; it prevents one from seeing the scale and the meaning of events" (Solzhenitsyn, 1978, pp. 17–19).

Covenantal relationships, on the other hand, induce freedom, not paralysis. As the noted psychiatrist William Glasser explains, "coercion only produces mediocrity; love or a sense of belonging produces excellence" (Glasser, 1984). Our goal as leaders is to encourage a covenantal relationship of love, warmth, and personal chemistry among our employee volunteers. Shared ideals, shared goals, shared respect, a sense of integrity, a sense of quality, a sense of advocacy, a sense of caring: these are the basis of an organization's covenant with its employees.

THE VALUE OF HEROES

Leading with heart requires that an organization has its share of heroes, both present and past. We have often heard individuals in various organizations say that so and so is an "institution" around here. Heroes such as these do more to influence the organizational culture of an institution than any manual or policies and procedures handbook ever could.

The senior faculty member who is recognized and respected for his or her knowledge as well as his or her humane treatment of students is a valuable asset to an educational institution. He or she is a symbol of what the institution stands for. It is the presence of these heroes that sustains the reputation of the institution and allows the workforce to feel good about itself and about where it works. The deeds and accomplishments of these heroes need to be promulgated and to become part of the folklore of the institution.

The deeds of these heroes are usually perpetuated by the "tribal storytellers" in an organization (Bolman and Deal, 1991). These are the individuals who know the history of the organization and relate it through stories of its former and current heroes. Rather than seeing them as a threat, an effective leader encourages the heroes and tribal storytellers, knowing that they are serving an invaluable role in an organization.

They work at the process of institutional renewal. They allow the institution to continuously improve. They preserve and revitalize the values of the institution. They mitigate the tendency of institutions, especially educational institutions, to become bureaucratic. These concerns are concerns of everyone in the institution, but they are the special province of the tribal storyteller. Every institution has heroes and storytellers. It is the leader's job to see to it that things like manuals and handbooks don't replace them.

THE SIGNS OF HEARTLESSNESS

Up to now we have dwelled on the characteristics of a healthy organization. In contrast, here are some of the signs that an organization is suffering from a lack of heart:

- when there is a tendency to merely "go through the motions"
- when a dark tension exists among key individuals
- when a cynical attitude prevails among employees
- when finding time to celebrate accomplishments becomes impossible
- when stories and storytellers cease
- when there is the view that one person's gain needs to be at another's expense
- when mutual trust and respect erode
- when leaders accumulate power rather than distribute it
- when attainment of short-term goals becomes detrimental to the acquisition of long-term goals
- when individuals abide by the letter of the law, but not its spirit
- when people treat students or customers as impositions
- when the accidents become more important than the substance
- when a loss of grace, style, and civility occurs
- when leaders use coercion to motivate employees
- when administrators dwell on individuals' weaknesses rather than strengths
- when individual turf is protected to the detriment of institutional goals
- when diversity and individual charismas are not respected
- when communication is only one-way
- when employees feel exploited and manipulated
- when arrogance spawns top-down decision making
- when leaders prefer to be served rather than to serve

LEADERSHIP AS A MORAL SCIENCE

Here we address how educational administrators and other leaders should be educated and trained for their positions. Traditionally, there has been only one answer: practicing and future administrators should study educational administration in order to learn the scientific basis for decision making and to understand the scientific research that underlies proper administration.

Universities train future administrators with texts that stress the scientific research done on administrative behavior, review various studies of teacher and student performance, and provide a few techniques for accomplishing educational goals. Such approaches instill a reverence for the scientific method, but an unfortunate disregard for any humanistic and critical development of the art of administration (Foster, 1986). These approaches teach us how to lead with our minds, but not necessarily with our hearts.

We are suggesting a different approach. Although there is certainly an important place for scientific research and empirically supported administrative behavior, we suggest that educational administrators also be *critical humanists* and lead with both their minds and their hearts. Humanists appreciate the usual and unusual events of our lives and engage in an effort to develop, challenge, and liberate human souls. They are critical because they are educators and are therefore not satisfied with the status quo; rather, they hope to change individuals and institutions for the better and to improve social conditions for all. We will argue that an *administrative* science be reconstructed as a *moral* science.

An administrative science can be empirical, but it also must incorporate hermeneutic (the science of interpreting and understanding others) and critical dimensions. Social science has increasingly recognized that it must be informed by moral questions. The paradigm of natural science does not always apply when dealing with human issues. As a moral science, the science of administration is concerned with the resolution of moral dilemmas. A critical and a literary model of administration helps to provide us with the necessary context and understanding wherein such dilemmas can be wisely resolved, and we can truly actualize our potentials as administrators and leaders.

One's proclivity to be a critical humanist often depends on one's philosophy on how human beings behave in the workplace. Worth repeating here are the two extremes of the continuum: (1) those leaders who believe that human beings are basically lazy and will do the very least that they need to do to "get by" in the workplace and (2) those who believe that people are basically industrious and, if given the choice, would opt for doing the "right thing." I believe that today's most effective leaders hold the latter view.

THE CRITICAL TRADITION

A post-positivist leader combines the *humanist* tradition with *critical* theory. Dissatisfaction with current administrative approaches to examining social life stems from administrations' inability to deal with questions of value and morality and their inability to fulfill their promise.

For example, Daniel Griffiths and Peter Ribbins (1995) criticize orthodox theories because they "ignore the presence of unions and fail to account for the scarcity of women and minorities in top administrative positions." David Ericson and Richard Ellett (2002) ask, "Why had educational research had so few real implications for educational policy?" An empiricist research program modeled on the natural sciences fails to address issues of understanding and interpretation. This failure precludes researchers from reaching a genuine understanding of the human condition. It is time, we argue, to treat educational research as a moral science. The science of administration can also be a moral one—a critically moral one (Erickson, 1984, pp. 525–546).

The term "moral" is being used here in its cultural, professional, spiritual, and ethical sense, not in a religious sense. The moral side of administration has to do with the *dilemmas* that face us in education and other professions. All educators face at least three areas of dilemmas: control, curriculum, and societal. Control dilemmas involve the resolution of classroom management and control issues, particularly the issue of who is in charge and to what degree.

Control dilemmas center around four questions: (1) Do you treat the child as a student, focusing narrowly on cognitive goals, or as a whole person, focusing more broadly on intellectual, aesthetic, social, and physical dimensions? (2) Who controls classroom time? In some classrooms, children are given latitude in scheduling their activities; in others, class activities follow a strict and mandatory schedule. (3) Who controls operations or the larger context of what it means to be human and how we resolve the inevitable conflicts that go on in the classroom? (4) Who controls the standards and defines success and failure?

Similar dilemmas occur in the curricular domain and relate to whether the curriculum is considered as received, public knowledge or whether it is considered private, individualized knowledge, of the type achieved through discoveries and experiments. These curricular difficulties also depend on whether one conceives of the child as a customer or as an individual. The customer receives professional services generated from a body of knowledge, whereas the individual receives personal services generated from his or her particular needs and context.

A final set of dilemmas has to do with what children bring to school and how they are to be treated once there. One concerns the distribution of teacher resources. Should one focus more resources on the less talented, in order to bring them up to standards, or on the more talented, in order for them to reach their full potential? The same question arises in regard to the distribution of justice. Should classroom rules be applied uniformly, without regard to the differing circumstances of each child, or should family background, economic factors, and other sociological influences be considered? Should a teacher stress a common culture or ethnic differences and subculture consciousness?

Much of teaching involves resolving such dilemmas by making a variety of decisions throughout the school day. Such decisions can be made, however, in a *reflective* or an *unreflective* manner. An unreflective manner means simply teaching as one was taught, without giving consideration to available alternatives. A reflective approach involves an examination of the widest array of alternatives. Thus, reflective teaching suggests that dilemmas need not be simply resolved but can be transformed so that a higher level of teaching expertise is reached.

This same logic can be applied to administration. Administration involves the resolution of various dilemmas, that is, the making of moral decisions. As with teaching, one set of dilemmas involves control. How much participation can teachers have in the administration of the school? How much participation can parents and students have? Who evaluates and for what purpose? Is the role of administration collegial or authority centered? The area of the curriculum brings up similar questions. Is the school oriented to basic skills, advanced skills, social skills, or all three? Should the curricula be teacher made or national, state, or system mandated? Should student evaluation be based on teacher assessment or standardized tests? What is authentic assessment?

Finally, an additional set of dilemmas pertains to the idea of schooling in society. Should the schools be oriented to ameliorate the apparent deficits that some students bring with them, or should they see different cultures and groups as strengths? Should schools be seen as agents of change, oriented to the creation of a more just society, or as socializers that adapt the young to the current social structure?

Oftentimes, these questions are answered unreflectively and simply resolved on an "as needed" basis. This approach often resolves the dilemma but does not foster a real *transformation* in one's self, role, or institution. If administration and leadership encompass transformation, and we would argue that they should, then an additional lens to structural functionalism must be found through which these questions can be viewed. We suggest that the additional lens be in the form of critical humanism and the Ignatian vision. In this context, then, administrative leadership can be viewed as a moral science.

THE IGNATIAN VISION

In addition to the critical humanist lens, another lens through which we can view leadership behavior is the Ignatian vision. More than 450 years ago, Ignatius of Loyola, a young priest born to a Spanish aristocratic family, founded the Society of Jesus, the Jesuits, and wrote his seminal book, *The Spiritual Exercises* (Loyola, 2007).

In this book, he suggested a "way of life" and a "way of looking at things" that have been propagated by his religious community and his other followers for almost five centuries. His principles have been utilized in a variety of ways. They have been used as an aid in developing one's own spiritual life; they have been used to formulate a way of learning that has become the curriculum and instructional method employed in the sixty Jesuit high schools and the twenty-eight Jesuit colleges and universities in the United States; and they have been used to develop one's own administrative style. Together, these principles comprise the *Ignatian vision.*

There are five Ignatian principles that we will explore here as a foundation for developing a moral frame and an administrative philosophy and leadership style: (1) Ignatius's concept of the magis, or the "more"; (2) the process of *inquiry and discernment*; (3) the implications of his notion of *cura personalis*, or "care of the person"; (4) the development of *men and women for others*; and (5) service to the *underserved* and marginalized, or his concept of *social justice.*

At the core of the Ignatian vision is the concept of the magis, or the "more." Ignatius spent the greater part of his life seeking perfection in all areas of his personal, spiritual, and professional life. He was never satisfied with the status quo. He was constantly seeking to improve his own spiritual life, as well as his secular life as leader of a growing religious community. He was an advocate of "continuous improvement" long before it became a corporate slogan, and long before people like W. Edwards Deming used it to develop his Total Quality Management approach to management, and long before Japan used it to revolutionize its economy after World War II.

The idea of constantly seeking "the more" implies change. The magis is a movement away from the status quo; and moving away from the status quo defines change. The Ignatian vision requires individuals and institutions to embrace the process of change as a vehicle for personal and institutional improvement. For his followers, frontiers and boundaries are not obstacles or ends, but new challenges to be faced, new opportunities to be welcomed.

Thus, change needs to become a way of life. Ignatius further implores his followers to "be the change that you expect in others." In other words, we are called to model desired behavior—to live out our values, to be of ever fuller service to our communities, and to aspire to the more universal good. Ignatius had no patience with mediocrity. He constantly strove for the greater good.

The magis principle, then, can be described as the main norm in the selection of information and the interpretation of it. Every real alternative for choice must be conducive to the advancement toward perfection. When some aspect of a particular alternative is *more* conducive to reaching perfection than other alternatives, we have reason to choose that alternative. Earlier, we spoke of the "dilemmas" that educators face during every working day. The magis principle is a "way of seeing" that can help us in selecting the better alternative.

At first hearing, the magis principle may sound rigid and frightening. It is absolute, and Ignatius is unyielding in applying it, but not rigid. On the one hand, he sees it as the expression of our love of humanity, which inexorably seeks to fill all of us with a desire to not be content with what is less good for us.

On the other hand, he sees that humanity not only has its particular gifts, but also has its limitations and different stages of growth. If we were making a choice that in the abstract would be more humane than it would be in the concrete, that choice would not be seen as adhering to the magis principle. For example, tracking students according to ability can be seen as humane in the abstract, but in the concrete can be dehumanizing. Ignatius would advise us to focus on the concrete in resolving this dilemma.

In every case, then, accepting and living by the magis principle is an expression of our love of humanity. So, whatever the object for choice, the measure of our love of neighbor will be the fundamental satisfaction we will find in choosing and acting by the magis principle. Whatever one chooses by this principle, no matter how undesirable in some other respect, will always be what one would most want as a moral and ethical member of the human race.

Closely related to the principle of the magis is the Ignatian principle of *inquiry and discernment*. In his writings, he urges us to challenge the status quo through the methods of inquiry and discernment. This is very similar to one of the tenets of critical theory. In fact, the Ignatian vision and critical theory share a number of norms.

To Ignatius, to enter into inquiry and discernment is to determine God's will. However, this process is of value for the purely *secular* purpose of deciding on which "horn of a dilemma" one should come down. To aid us in utilizing inquiry and discernment as useful tools in challenging the status quo and determining the right choice to be made, Ignatius suggests that the ideal disposition for inquiry and discernment is humility. The disposition of humility is especially helpful when, despite one's best efforts, the evidence that one alternative is more conducive to the betterment of society is not compelling.

When the discerner cannot find evidence to show that one alternative is more conducive to the common good, Ignatius calls for a judgment in favor of what more assimilates the discerner's life to the life of poverty and humiliation. Thus, when the *greatest* good cannot readily be determined, the *greater* good is more easily discerned in a position of humility. These are very demanding standards, but they are consistent with both the magis principle and the tenets of critical humanism.

In addition to the magis principle norm, taking account of what has just been said and of what was said earlier about the norm of humility as a disposition for seeking the greater good, the relationship of the greater good norm to the greatest good norm can be clarified. The latter is absolute, overriding, and always primary.

The greater good norm is secondary; it can never, in any choice, have equal weight with the first magis principle; it can never justify a choice of actual poverty and humiliation over riches and honors if the latter are seen to be more in the service of humanity in a particular situation for choice, with all its concrete circumstances, including one's responsibilities to others and his or her own stage of psychological and spiritual development. In other words, if being financially successful allows one to better serve the poor and underserved, that would be preferred to actual poverty.

Ignatius presents us with several other supplemental norms for facing our "dilemmas." In choices that directly affect the individual person and the underserved or marginalized, especially the poor, Ignatius urges us to give preference to those in need. This brings us to his next guiding principle, *cura personalis*, or care of the person.

Another of Ignatius's important and enduring principles is his notion that, despite the primacy of the common good, the need to care for the individual person should never be lost. From the very beginning, the cura personalis principle has been included in the mission statement of virtually every high school and college founded by the Jesuits. It also impacts the method of instruction suggested for all Jesuit schools in the *Ratio Studiorum*, or the "course of study," in these institutions. Thus, a Jesuit education is primarily student centered rather than teacher centered.

All Jesuit educational institutions are to foster what we now refer to as a "constructivist" classroom, where the student is an active participant in the learning process. This contrasts with the "transmission" method of instruction, where the teacher is paramount and the student is a passive participant in the process. In the Ignatian vision, the care of the person is a requirement not only on a personal needs basis, but also on a "whole person" basis, which would, of course, include classroom education.

This principle also has implications for how we conduct ourselves as educational administrators. Ignatius calls us to value the gifts and charismas of our colleagues and to address any deficiencies that they might have and turn them into strengths. For example, during the employee evaluation process, Ignatius would urge us to focus on the formative or developmental stage of the evaluation far more than on the summative or employment decision stage. This would be one small way of applying cura personalis theory to practice.

The fourth principle that we wish to consider is the Ignatian concept of service. Once again, this principle has been propagated from the very outset. The expressed goal of virtually every Jesuit institution is "to develop men and women with and for others." Jesuit institutions are called on to create a culture of service as one way of ensuring that the students, faculty, and staffs of these institutions reflect the educational, civic, and spiritual values of the Ignatian vision.

Institutions following the Ignatian tradition of service to others have done so through community service programs and, more recently, service learning. Service to the community provides students with a means of helping others, a way to put their value system into action, and a tangible way to assist local communities. Although these are valuable benefits, there was no formal integration of the service experience into the curriculum and no formal introspection concerning the impact of service on the individual.

During the last twenty years there has been a movement toward creating a more intentional academic relationship. Service has evolved from a modest student activity into an exciting pedagogical opportunity. In the past, service was viewed as a cocurricular activity; today, it plays an integral role in the learning process. For example, at Saint Joseph's University in Philadelphia, accounting majors help senior citizens complete their income tax returns.

Since many institutions are situated in an urban setting, service gives them a chance to share resources with surrounding communities and allows reciprocal relationships to form between the university and local residents. Immersion into different cultures—economic, racial, educational, social, and religious—is the vehicle by which students make connections. Working side by side with people of varying backgrounds significantly impacts the students, forcing them outside of their comfort zones and into the gritty reality of how others live. Through reflection, these students have the opportunity to integrate these powerful experiences into their lives, opening their eyes and hearts to the larger questions of social justice.

Peter-Hans Kolvenbach, the former superior general of the Jesuit order, in his address on justice in American Jesuit universities, used the words of Pope John Paul II to challenge Jesuit educators to "educate the whole person of solidarity for the real world" not only through concepts learned in the classroom, but also through contact with real people (Tripole, 1994).

Upon assuming the position of superior general in 1973 and echoing the words of Ignatius, Pedro Arrupe declared that "our prime educational objective must be to form men and women for others; men and women who will live not for themselves but for others" (Ravier, 1987). In the spirit of these words, the service learning movement has legitimized the educational benefit of all experiential activity.

The term "service learning" means different things to different people, and debates on service learning have been around for decades, running the gamut from unstructured "programmatic opportunities" to structured "educational philosophies."

At Ignatian institutions, service learning is a bridge that connects faculty, staff, and students with community partners and their needs. It connects academic and student life to views about the educational value of experiential learning. It also connects students' textbooks to human reality, and their minds and hearts with values and action. The programs are built on key components of service learning including integration into the curriculum, a reciprocal relationship between the community agency and student, and structured time for reflection, which is very much related to the Ignatian principle of inquiry and discernment discussed earlier.

Participation in service by high school and college students, whether as a cocurricular or a course-based experience, correlates to where they are in their developmental process. Service work allows students to explore their skills and limitations, to find what excites and energizes them, to put their values into action, and to use their talents to benefit others, to discover who they are and who they want to become. By encouraging students to reflect on their service, these institutions assist in this self-discovery. The reflection can take many forms: an informal chat, a facilitated group discussion, written dialogue, journal entries, reaction papers, or in-class presentations on articles.

By integrating the service experience through critical reflection, students develop self-knowledge of the communities in which they live, and knowledge about the world that surrounds them. It is only after the unfolding of this service-based knowledge that the students are able to synthesize what they have learned into their lives. Through this reflection, the faculty members also have an opportunity to learn from and about their students. Teachers witness the change and growth of the students firsthand. In short, "service to others" changes lives.

The implications of "service to others" for administration are clear. Educational administrators can enhance their effectiveness not only by including the idea of service to others in their curricula, but also by modeling it in their personal and professional lives. The concept of administrators becoming the "servant of the servants" is what we have in mind here. Servant leaders do not inflict pain; they bear pain, and they treat their employees as "volunteers," a concept explored earlier.

The fifth principle, the Ignatian concept of "service," leads into his notion of solidarity with the underserved (poor) and marginalized and his principle of *social justice*. We begin with an attempt to achieve some measure of clarity on the nature and role of social justice in the Ignatian vision. According to some, Ignatius defined justice in both a narrow and a wide sense (Tripole, 1994). In the *narrow* sense, it is "justice among men and women" that is involved. In this case, it is a matter of "clear obligations" among "members of the human family." The application of this kind of justice would include the rendering of not only material goods, but also immaterial goods such as "reputation, dignity, the possibility of exercising freedom" (Tripole, 1994).

Many of his followers also believe Ignatius defined justice in a *wider* sense "where situations are encountered which are humanly intolerable and demand a remedy" (Tripole, 1994). Here, the situations may be a product of "explicitly unjust acts" caused by "clearly identified people" who cannot be commanded to correct the injustices, yet the dignity of the human person requires that justice be restored; or they may be caused by unidentifiable people.

It is precisely within the structural forces of inequality in society that injustice of this second type is found, where injustice is "institutionalized," that is, built into economic, social, and political structures both national and international, and where people are suffering from poverty and hunger, from the unjust distribution of wealth, resources, and power. The critical theorists, of whom we spoke earlier, would likely prefer this wider definition of social justice.

It is almost certain that Ignatius did not only concern himself with injustices that were purely economic. He often cites injustices about "threats to human life and its quality," "racial and political discrimination," and loss of respect for the "rights of individuals or groups" (Chapple, 1993). When one adds to these the "vast range of injustices" enumerated in his writings, one sees that the Ignatian vision understands its mission of justice to include "the widest possible view of justice," involving every area where there is an attack on human rights.

We can conclude, therefore, that although Ignatius was to some degree concerned about commutative justice (right relationships between private persons and groups) and distributive justice (the obligations of the state to render to the individual what is his or her due), he is most concerned about what is generally called today social justice, or "justice of the common good." Such justice is comprehensive, and includes a person's strict legal rights and duties, but is more concerned about the natural rights and duties of individuals, families, communities, and the community of nations toward one another as members of the common family of human beings.

Every form of justice is included in and presupposed by social justice, but with social justice, it is the social nature of the person that is emphasized, as well as the social significance of all earthly goods, the purpose of which is to aid all members of the human community in attaining their dignity as human beings. Many of Ignatius's followers believe that this dignity is being undermined in our world today, and their main efforts are aimed toward restoring that dignity.

In the pursuit of social justice, Ignatius calls on his followers to be "in solidarity with the poor." The next logical question might then be, who are the poor? The poor are usually thought to be those who are economically deprived and politically oppressed. Thus, we can conclude that the promotion of justice means to work to overcome the oppressions or injustices that make the poor, poor.

The fallacy here, however, is that the poor are not necessarily oppressed or suffering injustice, and so Ignatius argues that our obligation toward the poor must be understood to be linking "inhuman levels or poverty and injustice" and not be understood to be concerned with the "lot of those possessing only modest resources," even though those of modest means are often poor and oppressed. So we conclude that the poor include those "wrongfully" impoverished or dispossessed (Institute of Jesuit Sources, 1995).

An extended definition of the poor, one that Ignatius would espouse, would include any of these types of people:

First are those who are economically deprived and socially marginalized and oppressed, especially, but not limited to, those with whom one has immediate contact and is in a position to positively effect.

The second group includes the "poor in spirit," that is, those who lack a value system or an ethical and moral sense.

The third group includes those who are emotionally poor—those who have psychological and emotional shortcomings and are in need of comfort.

In defining the poor in the broadest way, Ignatius exhorts us to undertake social change in our role as leader—to do what we can do to bring an end to inequality, oppression, and injustice. Once again we can see the close connection between the Ignatian principles of social justice and the main tenets of critical theory.

IMPLICATIONS FOR ADMINISTRATION

Each of the principles of the Ignatian vision noted above has a variety of implications for leaders. The magis principle has implications for administrators in that it calls for us to continually be seeking perfection in all that we do. In effect, this means that we must seek to continually improve. And, since improvement implies change, we need to be champions of needed change in our institutions. This means that we have to model a tolerance for change and embrace not only our own change initiatives, but also those in other parts of the organization. In effect, the Ignatian vision prompts us to be not merely leaders but transformational leaders. The principle of cura personalis has additional implications. To practice the Ignatian vision, one must treat people with dignity under all circumstances. Cura personalis also requires us to extend ourselves in offering individual attention and attending to the needs of all those with whom we come in contact. Being sensitive to the individual's unique needs is particularly required. Many times in our efforts to treat people equally, we fail to treat them fairly or equitably. Certain individuals have greater needs than others, and many times these needs require exceptions to be made on their behalf.

For example, if an adult student does not hand in an assignment on time, but the tardiness is due to the fact that he or she is going through some personal or family trauma at the moment, the principle of cura personalis calls on us to make an exception in this case. It is likely that some would consider such an exception to be unfair to those who made the effort to complete the assignment in a timely manner, or say that we cannot possibly be sensitive to the special needs of all of our students and colleagues.

However, as long as the exception is made for everyone in the same circumstances, Ignatius would not perceive this exception as unfair. In fact, the exception would be expected if one were practicing the principle of "care of the person."

The Ignatian process of discernment requires educational administrators to be reflective practitioners. It calls on us to be introspective regarding our administrative and leadership behavior. We are asked to reflect on the ramifications of our decisions, especially in light of their cumulative effect on the equitable distribution of power and on the marginalized individuals and groups in our communities. In effect, the principle of discernment galvanizes the other principles embodied in the Ignatian vision. During the discernment process, we are asked to reflect upon how our planned behavior will manifest the magis principle, cura personalis, and service to the community, especially the underserved, marginalized, and oppressed.

The development of men and women for others requires that one have his or her own sense of service toward those with whom the leader interacts, and that one also develop this spirit of service in others. The concept of "servant leadership" requires us to encourage others toward a life and career of service and to assume the position of being the "servant of the servants." Ignatius thinks about leadership in terms of what the gospel writer Luke calls the "one who serves." The leader owes something to the institution he or she leads. The leader is seen in this context as steward rather than owner or proprietor.

The implications of Ignatius's notion of social justice are myriad for a leader. Being concerned about the marginalized among our constituencies is required. We are called to be sensitive to those individuals and groups that do not share equitably in the distribution of power and influence. Distinctions according to race, class, gender, and status should be corrected. Thus, participative decision making and collaborative behavior are encouraged among administrators imbued with the Ignatian tradition.

Equitable representation of all segments of the school community should be provided whenever feasible. Leadership behavior such as this will ensure that the dominant culture is not perpetuated to the detriment of the minority culture, rendering the minorities powerless. We will find in the succeeding chapters that the most heroic of the leaders profiled incorporate many of the Ignatian concepts into their leadership behavior.

Thus, in my view, the Ignatian vision in the form of a moral frame *completes* situational leadership theory. Left on its own, situational leadership theory is secular and amoral. Utilizing situational leadership theory alone is as likely to produce a leader in the mold of Adolf Hitler as it is to produce a leader in the mold of Abraham Lincoln. But viewing our situational leadership behavior through the additional lens of the Ignatian vision will ensure that we have more leaders like Lincoln and fewer like Hitler in our world.

SUMMARY

We began this book by suggesting that leaders are made, not born. We posited that if one could master the technical skills involved in effective leadership, one could become a successful administrator. In this chapter, however, we make the assertion that learning the skills involved in effective leadership is only part of the story. Leadership is as much an art, a belief, a condition of the heart, as it is mastering a set of skills and understanding leadership theory. A truly successful and heroic leader, therefore, is one who leads with both the *mind* and the *heart*.

When we look at the leadership behavior of the leaders included in the study, we should observe not only whether their leadership practices conform to the Bolman/Deal situational leadership model, but also whether they are leading with *heart.* I believe that we will find that those leaders that are most comfortable consistently operating out of a moral frame are most likely to be leading with heart. The most effective leaders, then, will be those who lead with both mind (structural, political frames) and heart (human resource, symbolic frames) and view their leadership behavior through the lens of the Ignatian vision or some similar moral philosophy.

Chapter Three

Benjamin Franklin

Certainty? In this world nothing is certain but death and taxes. —Benjamin
Franklin

BACKGROUND

Benjamin Franklin was born in Boston in 1706. From humble beginnings, he
became one of the most famous men in the world. He joined his brother,
James, in the newspaper business, and when he was only fifteen, he and his
brother published the first newspaper in Boston, the *New England Courant.*
After a dispute with his brother, Franklin moved to Philadelphia, where he
was to spend the remainder of his life.

In Philadelphia, Franklin eventually established his own print shop and in
time purchased and began publishing a newspaper called the *Daily Gazette.*
He not only printed the paper, but often wrote articles and editorials under
fictitious names. The *Daily Gazette* quickly became the most read newspaper
in the colonies. In 1732 he published his famous *Poor Richard's Almanac*,
and in 1737 he became the postmaster general of Philadelphia.

By the time Franklin was in his early twenties, he had become fascinated
with the idea of public service, and founded the Junto, a young professionals'
political organization dedicated to civic improvement. At around the same
time, he became active in the Masons; launched projects to pave, clean, and
light the streets; founded the Library Company and the American Philosophi-
cal Society; and helped establish Pennsylvania Hospital. He was a busy man,
indeed.

In 1736, Franklin established Philadelphia's first fire department. Since fire damage often resulted in families losing their entire life's savings, Franklin founded the Philadelphia Contribution for Insurance against Loss by Fire insurance company. In 1749, he retired from business and began devoting his time to science. He went on to invent the Franklin Stove, swim fins, a musical instrument called the glass armonica, bifocals, and, of course, his famous kite-flying experiment that revealed the nature of electricity.

Later in the next decade, Franklin became involved in politics, becoming a Pennsylvania state representative. Eventually he moved to London and became the colonial representative to Britain for Pennsylvania, Georgia, New Jersey, and Massachusetts. During this time, Franklin considered himself to be a loyal and devoted British citizen. But after the passage of the Stamp Act and other oppressive acts by Great Britain, he began to think seriously about American independence.

Upon returning from England, Franklin was elected to the Second Continental Congress and helped draft the Declaration of Independence. After signing the Declaration, Franklin sailed to Paris to take up residence as the United States' first ambassador to France. He was very popular in France, having established a worldwide reputation as a scientist and statesman. His crowning achievement as ambassador to France was the signing of the Treaty of Alliance in 1778, which secured military personnel and loans that played a critical part in the outcome of the Revolutionary War. Franklin was also on hand to sign the Treaty of Paris officially ending the war.

Franklin returned to America and served as a delegate to the Constitutional Convention and signed the U.S. Constitution. Later, he became active in the abolitionist movement, having written an anti-slavery treatise in 1789. Franklin passed away a year later, in 1790, at the age of eight-four (Morgan, 2002; workinghumor.com).

THE STRUCTURAL FRAME

We begin the analysis of Benjamin Franklin's leadership behavior with the structural frame. Structural frame leaders seek to develop a new model of the relationship of structure, strategy, and environment for their organizations. Strategic planning, extensive preparation, and effecting change are priorities for them. They are often described as firm and direct by their followers.

As a structural leader, Franklin could never stop experimenting with and studying things that he could not explain. It was said that he could not drink a cup of tea without wondering why the tea leaves formed one configuration rather than another in the bottom of the cup. He made many of his most important discoveries serendipitously. For example, from pouring oil on water in a glass, he turned to doing so on the surface of ponds and lakes and watched in wonder as a few drops of oil flattened out the ripples (Morgan, 2002).

When it dawned on Franklin that an ocean voyage between America and Europe took two weeks longer going east versus going west, he put on his structural frame hat and discovered the Gulf Stream. A Nantucket whaler helped him find its exact location on a map, and Franklin had copies engraved for the benefit of ship captains everywhere.

Franklin engaged in structural frame behavior on the evening of October 21, 1743, in Philadelphia, when he was preparing to watch a lunar eclipse predicted for nine o'clock and a rainstorm hit at eight o'clock, blackening the skies. The storm lasted two full days. In the coming week, in the newspapers from the colonies, he read of the damage inflicted by the storm up and down the East Coast. It soon became clear that the storm that blew from the northeast had come from the opposite direction—thus he had discovered the nor'easter.

In Franklin's time, everyone knew that hot air rises, but Franklin once again engaged in structural frame behavior in asking where the air came from that went up the chimney with the smoke. Once he realized that one needed a flow of air to sustain a fire, he made stoves and chimneys more efficient by providing direct access to air (the flue) on the chimneys and stoves he designed. This innovation was important enough that these more efficient stoves took on their inventor's name (the Franklin Stove).

Almost everyone knows of Franklin's use of structural frame behavior in the form of his experiments with electricity. Almost immediately, Franklin was able to distinguish between positive and negative charges of electricity, between conductors and non-conductors (terms he coined), and, within a short period of time after that, the nature of lightning. He had convinced himself that lightning was nothing more than powerful electric sparks passing between oppositely charged clouds and between clouds and the earth. His experiments not only gave the world a new understanding of electricity but also provided the insight that enabled him to invent a way to protect buildings and ships from damage—the lightning rod.

Being the structural frame leader that he oftentimes was, Franklin had always to be doing something. When he was at a meeting where the proceedings bored him, he would doodle an experimental design on a piece of notepaper. One of his more notable doodles involved the construction of parallel columns of numbers he called magic squares or circles, in which the figures all added up to the same number in every direction.

Franklin's structural frame leanings were evident in his meteoric rise in the printing business. Within two years of leaving his first employment in printing in Boston and striking out on his own in Philadelphia, Franklin had not only became the sole proprietor of a thriving printing business but had won all the official printing business for the Pennsylvania colony. He purchased the newspaper of his former employer and opened a successful stationery and bookshop. At age thirty he won the postmaster general position for Philadelphia, and by forty-two he was able to retire from business and devote the remainder of his life to public service.

Once again utilizing structural frame behavior, Franklin commandeered an empty building, constructed for disgraced Episcopal minister George Whitefield, to house the Academy of Philadelphia, which became the University of Pennsylvania, opening its doors in 1750 and ultimately developing into one of the most prestigious universities in the United States (Morgan, 2002).

Franklin used structural frame leadership behavior in helping to organize the colonies' first defenses. He proposed a voluntary association to perform the most basic function of government—the protection of its citizens. The Association gave Pennsylvania an effective armed force. But being the structural frame leader that he was, he did not stop there. As early as 1751, he had become convinced of a need for a union of the colonies to deal consistently and fairly with the Indians. Acting together, the colonies could "form a strength that the Indians may depend on for protection, in case of rupture with the French; or expect great danger from, if they break with us." This first attempt at building a colonial army was called the Albany Plan, since the meeting scheduled by Franklin with representatives of the other colonies occurred in Albany, New York (Morgan, 2002, p. 81).

After spending eleven years in England using the human resource and political frames in failed attempts at eliminating the exercise of parliamentary authority in America, Franklin engaged more intently in structural frame behavior by helping to draft and signing the Declaration of Independence, securing the American alliance with France, helping to negotiate the treaty of peace with Britain, and participating in the convention that drafted the Articles of Confederation (Morgan, 2002).

THE HUMAN RESOURCE FRAME

Human resource frame leaders believe in people and communicate that belief. They are passionate about productivity through people. Having been so integrally involved in the pursuit of human freedom, it almost goes without saying that Benjamin Franklin was extremely active in the human resource frame.

Despite his international fame and reputation, Franklin always took pains to dissuade others from granting him deference. He never traded on his reputation or acted condescendingly toward others. He took people at face value and dealt with kings and beggars on equal terms.

His use of human resource frame behavior was such that wherever Franklin went people loved him. Wherever he lived he had the facility to make close and loyal friends. His friends often had no direct connection with his life in public service; they just loved him as a person. His personal charm allowed him to make friends easily both in and out of his public life. Even as he grew older, he confessed to a friend, "I find I love company, chat, a laugh, a glass, and even a song, as well as ever" (Morgan, 2002, p. 40).

Even before he decided to devote his life to public service, Franklin was dedicated to making life better for himself and those around him. When he established the Junto, for example, he did so not only so like-minded young men would be able to form social and professional networks, but also so that they could organize to help Philadelphians and Pennsylvanians in need.

Despite Franklin's normally magnanimous use of human resource frame behavior, there is at least one instance when he fell somewhat short of the ideal. Although Franklin was generally in favor of immigration, it was only in the case of the English. When an influx of German boors to the colonies began, he questioned, "Why should Pennsylvania, founded by the English, become a colony of aliens who will shortly be so numerous as to Germanize us instead of our Anglifying them, and will never adopt our language or customs any more than they can acquire our complexion." Happily, after the Declaration of Independence was signed, Franklin made an about-face and became an advocate of immigration from all nations (Morgan, 2002, p. 77).

Generally speaking, however, Franklin exhibited human resource frame behavior throughout his long life. He was highly content to enjoy the company of other human beings anywhere, with women, young and old, with children and adolescents, and with men from all walks of life with whom he could exchange ideas, jokes, and general camaraderie.

THE SYMBOLIC FRAME

In the symbolic frame, the organization is seen as a stage, a theater in which every actor plays certain roles and the symbolic leader attempts to communicate the right impressions to the right audiences. One could argue that this was Franklin's dominant frame, especially in his frequent use of symbolic frame behavior in the form of humor.

Franklin's astute use of symbolic frame leadership behavior resulted in the historical image that we have of him. His warm smile and radiant presence cannot be witnessed, but Franklin's image reaches us through his prolific writings. People thought enough of him to save many of the letters he wrote to them, and he left us with a living legacy in the form of his memoirs that recount the first fifty-two years of his life. His image was further perpetuated by the newspaper that he ran in Boston, the one he owned in Philadelphia, and the annual publication of *Poor Richard's Almanac*.

Through his extensive use of symbolic frame behavior, Franklin burnished his image as a scientist who probed the world's wonders, and a statesman who worked tirelessly on behalf of his beloved country. Few are not familiar with the image of him flying his kite with a metal key on the end in a thunderstorm to reveal the mysteries of electricity. It is as familiar in American lore as George Washington's cutting down the cherry tree, the difference being that Franklin really did fly that kite.

Franklin's use of symbolic frame behavior in connection with publicizing his experiment with electricity made him famous throughout the world. As a result, his reputation preceded him and he was granted a respect bordering on awe by people ranging from the men and women on the street to the great kings and queens of Europe. This image helped him to no end in his political machinations on behalf of the new nation.

As we know, Franklin was famous for his use of symbolic frame behavior in the form of satire. Among the many satires composed during his long career in public service was one concerning the British practice of shipping convicts to the American colonies. Franklin's suggestion, to export a regular shipment of American rattlesnakes to Britain in return, was promulgated throughout the colonies (Morgan, 2002).

In the peace following the French and Indian War between France and Britain, Franklin's mind was active in so many directions that it would have been hard to keep track but for his concomitant use of symbolic frame behavior to keep the public informed of his activities and accomplishments. This was the time when he was acquiring his own print shop and newspaper, designing electrical experiments that differentiated between conductors and non-conductors and between positive and negative currents, and inventing the lightning rod. All of these accomplishments were recognized by the Royal Society of London with its first Copley Medal for the advancement of science. As a result, he became the best-known man in the American colonies.

Also during this period, Franklin began his life in public service by entering the Pennsylvania Assembly and writing his *Observations Concerning the Increase of Mankind*, in which he outlined his plan for America to become a major power on the world stage. He calculated that at its current birthrate of doubling the population every twenty years, it would relatively shortly overcome the population of England and the other powers in Europe. He pointed out that where warfare, disease, persecution, and emigration would reduce the population of other countries, the relative absence of these events in America would allow his adopted nation to surpass many other countries in the world.

Franklin used the symbolic frame further by reflecting America as the city on the hill. Through his writings, Franklin gave the world a glimpse of his vision in which Pennsylvanians, Virginians, and New Englanders would stand on equal footing with the English and the French. His voyage to England at age fifty-one was a symbolic act in pursuit of this vision. Because he was by that time a member of the Royal Society and had received an honorary degree from St. Andrews and Oxford universities, he was always recognized as Dr. Franklin and was accorded a respect that he seldom experienced outside of Philadelphia and Pennsylvania. In France he was even more adored. "My face is now almost as well known as that of the moon," he observed (Morgan, 2002, p. 243).

We are all familiar with Franklin's use of symbolic frame leadership behavior in one of his most famous political cartoons. Franklin had long been telling Americans that their strength lay in the union. He made his point symbolically in a cartoon that depicted a snake divided into segments, with each segment marked with the name of a colony. Above the cartoon, Franklin wrote the motto, "Join or Die" (Morgan, 2002, p. 237).

THE SYMBOLIC FRAME AND HUMOR

Benjamin Franklin often used symbolic frame leadership behavior in the form of humor. According to him, he needed a keen sense of humor to keep him from being depressed by the folly of the world in which he found himself. His quick perception of the comic weaknesses of human nature might have turned a lesser man into a brooding and cynical snob. But Franklin never considered himself above the fray. He recognized the same human weaknesses in himself and was careful to conceal his observation of others' harmless mistakes in judgment. "He's a fool that cannot conceal his wisdom," he declared. He further observed, "There is a time to wink as well as to see." It was only when men of great power acted foolishly, promoting policies that were detrimental to others, that he would abandon his restraint.

As mentioned earlier, Franklin was an unmitigated hero in France. Using his keen sense of humor to describe his enculturation into French society and how the French were dressing him up like one of them, transforming him into a Frenchman, he opined that in order to fully conform to the French image he would soon have to make love to one of his friends' wives (Morgan, 2002, p. 147).

Other instances of Franklin's use of the symbolic frame in the form of humor include the following witticisms that are attributed to him:

- Blessed is he who expects nothing, for he shall never be disappointed.
- In this world nothing is certain but death and taxes.
- Content makes poor men rich; discontentment makes rich men poor.
- God heals and the doctor takes the fee.
- Guests, like fish, begin to smell after three days.
- He that falls in love with himself will have no rivals.
- If a man empties his purse into his head, no man can take it away from him. An investment in knowledge always pays the best interest.
- Keep your eyes wide open before marriage and half-shut afterwards.
- Life's tragedy is that we get old too soon and wise too late.
- Many people die at twenty-five and aren't buried until they are seventy-five.
- Most people return small favors, acknowledge medium ones and repay greater ones—with ingratitude.
- The learned fool writes his nonsense in better language than the unlearned, but it is still nonsense.
- There are three faithful friends, an old wife, an old dog, and ready money.
- Tricks and treachery are the practice of fools that don't have brains enough to be honest.
- When you're finished changing, you're finished. (Morgan, 2002)

THE POLITICAL FRAME

Leaders operating out of the political frame clarify what they want and what they can get. Political leaders are realists above all. They never let what they want cloud their judgment about what is possible. They assess the distribution of power and interests.

Franklin used political frame behavior in defending his scientific experiments, choosing to flee rather than fight. When another scientist challenged whether lightning rods should be pointed or blunt, rather than a public defensive which may have caused an altercation, Franklin chose to let his experiments speak for themselves. He believed that to engage in a public defense of his theories would demonstrate a certain vanity that he would rather conceal.

A classical use of political frame behavior took place in Franklin's successful attempt to obtain funding from the state assembly for a hospital for the poor in Philadelphia. He knew that he would have trouble convincing the rural assemblymen that it would be in their best interests to fund a urban hospital, so he requested a matching funds grant that would only be enforced if the city of Philadelphia matched the funds acquired for the assembly. The assemblymen never anticipated that Franklin could successfully raise the matching funds, so they passed the grant petition. Of course, they were proven wrong, as Franklin quickly raised the matching funds.

Franklin was the consummate politician. He firmly believed in the virtues of a pure democracy whereby every person voted on every issue. But he also knew that it would be more practical to govern through a representative democracy. The government moved more smoothly "when people at least *think* they have some share in the direction," he declared (Morgan, 2002, p. 95).

As can be said of most political frame advocates, Franklin was a master negotiator and compromiser. Faced with the intransigence of William Penn's heirs regarding local representation in the governing of Pennsylvania, as a negotiating tool, Franklin suggested a transfer of the Pennsylvania government back to the king. In light of this threat, the Penns capitulated.

Leading up to the Revolutionary War, Franklin knew that the Stamp Act would offend Americans and erode their loyalty to the Crown, but because he was in England at the time and news did not arrive in a timely manner, he misjudged just how disturbed the American populace would be. Thus, when he heard that the Virginia House of Burgesses had declared parliamentary taxation to be illegal, unconstitutional, and unjust, he was shocked. However, in true political frame manner, once he truly grasped American opinion, he altered his strategy of equal treatment and began talking more openly about independence.

Franklin's strategy worked, as Britain repealed the Stamp Act, but his use of political frame behavior did not end there. In 1767, the chancellor of the Exchequer, Charles Townshend, decided to establish Parliament's right to tax the colonies by imposing a tax on the tea they were required to purchase from England. Of course, this move led to the famous Boston Tea Party and strengthened Franklin's resolve regarding independence. The imposition of three more taxes, collectively known as the Intolerable Acts, sent Franklin and his American compatriots over the edge. Still, Franklin stood ready to use political frame behavior and accept something short of total independence. Fortunately for the future of the United States of America, the colonists did not have to settle for that option.

Franklin repeatedly made savvy use of political frame leadership behavior. In all of his public meetings, Franklin was careful to take a backseat and allow the discussion to take its course, knowing that eventually his advice would be sought. His advice would be better received, he believed, if it came without any trace of self-aggrandizement. John Adams observed in a letter to his wife, Abigail, that "Dr. Franklin has been composed and grave and in the opinion of many gentlemen very reserved" (Morgan, 2002, p. 224).

Franklin was a realist in his application of political frame behavior. He knew, for example, that in his negotiations with France for their help in the Revolutionary War the French were pursuing their own interests in helping America, but he was still grateful. He appreciated that the risk France was taking both militarily and monetarily was significant and, unlike his fellow ambassador, John Adams, considered their support with gratitude rather than as entitlement. Because of this attitude, Franklin was much more effective in his negotiations with France than Adams was, finally able to negotiate the Treaty of Alliance of 1778, whereby France sent war materials and troops to the colonies.

Later, in negotiating a peace treaty with Britain after the Revolutionary War, Franklin had to finesse not only the still-hostile British, the friendly French, and the unpredictable Spanish, but also his impetuous colleague John Adams. But as we all know, his effective use of political frame leadership behavior resulted in the Paris Peace Treaty that officially ended the Revolutionary War and enabled the United States of America to exist and prosper (Morgan, 2002).

THE MORAL FRAME

The moral frame is my own contribution to situational leadership theory. In my view, the moral frame completes situational leadership theory. Without it, leaders could just as easily use their leadership skills for promoting evil as for promoting good. Leaders operating out of the moral frame are concerned about their obligations to their followers. Moral frame leaders use some type of moral compass to direct their behavior. They practice what has been described as servant leadership and are concerned with those individuals and groups that are marginalized in their organizations and in society. In short, they are concerned about equality, fairness, and social justice.

Franklin seems never to have doubted the existence of God, but he was never a great devotee of established religion. Nevertheless, he articulated his view on morality in his *Poor Richard's Almanac* for 1739. "Sin is not hurtful because it is forbidden," he observed, "nor is a duty beneficial because it is commanded, but it is commanded because it's beneficial" (Morgan, 2002, p. 19). Whereas most churchgoers made faith the ultimate goal of religion and good works merely a sign of faith, Franklin believed that "morality or virtue is the end, faith only a means to obtain that end. And if the end is obtained, it is no matter by what means" (Morgan, 2002, p. 21).

Franklin's list of virtues through which one sought to achieve moral perfection were published in *Poor Richard's Almanac*. They included temperance, silence, order, resolution, frugality, industry, sincerity, justice, moderation, cleanliness, tranquility, chastity, and humility (Morgan, 2002, p. 23). Why charity, which was a guiding principle in his life, is missing, we do not know. Still, it is obvious that Franklin consistently operated out of the moral frame and continually filtered his leadership behavior through a moral lens before acting.

SITUATIONAL LEADERSHIP ANALYSIS

Benjamin Franklin was the quintessential situational leader. We saw how he adapted his leadership behavior to the situation and never seemed to become fixated on any one particular leadership frame. Whereas Franklin's long-term goal of establishing an Anglo-American empire directed his first twenty-five years in public service, he was perfectly willing to abandon that goal once he realized, in 1775, that the British Parliament was not open to colonial representation. And once the Declaration of Independence was signed, Franklin became as committed an advocate of independence as he was of an empire of equals. In other words, he was very capable and willing to alter his leadership behavior in light of a new and different situation.

LEADERSHIP IMPLICATIONS AND CONCLUSION

We can all agree that Benjamin Franklin was a leader after whom we can model our leadership behavior. As noted above, he was active in all of the leadership frames, depending on the situation, and was moderate in his behavior within each frame. He also reflected the theme of this book in frequently exhibiting symbolic frame leadership behavior in the form of humor. His witticisms have endured over time and are as applicable today as they were when he first uttered them more than two hundred years ago.

It is also evident that the effectiveness of Franklin's overall leadership behavior was positively impacted by his keen sense of humor. His success as the first foreign ambassador for the new nation was clearly tied to his ability to engender a smile on his counterparts' faces through his characteristic self-deprecating humor. He is a superb example of the adage that the need for an effective leader to have a good sense of humor is indeed not a laughing matter.

Chapter Four

Abraham Lincoln

How many legs does a dog have if you call the tail a leg? Four! Calling a tail a leg doesn't make it a leg. —Abraham Lincoln

BACKGROUND

Abraham Lincoln was born in 1809 in Kentucky and served as the sixteenth president of the United States from March 1861 until his assassination in April 1865. Every child in America is familiar with the stories of the Kentucky log cabin where he was born, the nicknames "Honest Abe" and "the Railsplitter," the wondrous eloquence of the Gettysburg Address, and the courageous declaration of the Emancipation Proclamation.

In 1847, Lincoln began a term in the U.S. House of Representatives, forging a name for himself as a man of strong principles eloquently expressed. But it was not until the Kansas-Nebraska Act, sponsored by Senator Stephen Douglas, that Lincoln's attention turned to the slavery question. In 1856 he joined the new Republican Party, and two years later, he ran for the Senate against Douglas. Their seven debates became legend. Lincoln proclaimed slavery fundamentally evil, thus emphasizing the moral chasm that existed between him and Douglas. Lincoln gained the presidential nomination for the Republican Party in 1860 and defeated his old nemesis Douglas, among others, in the election. The challenges he faced upon assuming office were enormous—led by South Carolina, seven Southern states had already seceded from the Union, and the country was on the verge of civil war.

On April 12, 1861, when Confederate guns fired on Fort Sumter, the Civil War began. General George McClellan continually defied Lincoln's orders to move forward and was eventually replaced by Ulysses S. Grant, a brilliant military strategist. In 1863 Lincoln issued his great Emancipation Proclamation declaring slavery unlawful in the rebelling states. The Union forces routed the Confederate troops at Gettysburg, and by the beginning of Lincoln's second term, General Sherman was nearing the end of his devastating March to the Sea. On April 9, 1865, General Robert E. Lee surrendered to General Grant on the steps of the Appomattox Court House.

Five nights later, Lincoln was assassinated by actor John Wilkes Booth at Ford's Theatre in Washington, D.C. In most historians' minds, Lincoln ranks as one of the very best American presidents (McGovern, 2009; Felzenberg, 2008; Taranto and Leo, 2004).

THE STRUCTURAL FRAME

We begin our analysis of Lincoln's leadership behavior with the structural frame. Structural frame leaders seek to develop a new model of the relationship of structure, strategy, and environment for their organizations. Strategic planning, extensive preparation, and effecting change are priorities for them. Their followers often describe structural frame leaders as being firm and direct. The effective use of the structural frame of leadership was one of Abraham Lincoln's many strengths.

In typical structural frame leadership form, Lincoln established the goals of his presidency very early on in his administration. He was absolutely determined to preserve the Union. He was supremely committed to this goal, and he vowed to accomplish it no matter how long or costly the task. At his inauguration in March 1861, he swore a sacred oath—"registered in Heaven," he said—"to preserve, protect, and defend the Constitution" (McGovern, 2009, p. 5). He delivered his message clearly, logically, and, he hoped, persuasively, like a lawyer setting out his case before the jury.

Lincoln firmly believed that the idea of a people's democracy was civilization's greatest experiment, and if the Union were not perpetual, if dissatisfied states could secede whenever they chose, the idea of such a democracy would be reduced to the absurdity of staying united when they agreed with the majority vote and leaving when they did not. Thus, he was absolutely against allowing states to secede and practiced structural frame leadership behavior to prevent them from doing so.

One of the traits that we have all come to admire about Lincoln is his structural frame behavior in the form of his amazing capacity to live and work with a strong sense of discipline. When asked what made for a successful lawyer, he replied, "Work, work, work is the main thing" (McGovern,

2009, p. 10). He carried this work ethic to the White House, rose each day at six o'clock a.m. and stayed up late, cramming as much work into a day as he could.

Lincoln took a hands-on approach to running the war, reading volumes on military strategy, tactics, and maneuvers to make up for his lack of military training. His attention to detail resulted in a new, broader definition of the president as commander-in-chief. He was an extremely intelligent man and recognized that fact at an early age. Despite his lack of formal education, he was seldom, if ever, intimidated in the courtroom, in a political debate, or in the Oval Office.

Lincoln had many traits of a structural leader, including his towering intelligence. He was particularly quick witted and eager to learn. He had an analytical mind that seemed to be working nonstop. He read every spare moment, growing especially attached to the works of Shakespeare and Robert Burns. Ultimately, he thought that he could use his mind and forensic skills to advance his position in society and, in the long run, advance society itself.

Using his structural leadership skills of organization, preparation, and adherence to ideological principles, Lincoln had been transformed from attorney to candidate to statesman. No other American president had ever faced the challenges of disunion, rebellion, and civil war. Making prolific use of structural frame leadership behavior, Lincoln met the challenges with firm resolve. For example, in his inaugural address, he declared, "The man does not live who is more devoted to peace than I am; none who would do more to preserve it. But it may be necessary to put the foot down firmly" (McGovern, 2009, p. 54).

And put his "foot down firmly" he did. In March 1863 the Republican Congress passed the Habeas Corpus Indemnity Act, which justified Lincoln's actions and offered him the power to suspend habeas corpus throughout the United States. Lincoln's unprecedented suspension of habeas corpus has been criticized, but he believed that events of rebellion justified and vindicated his use of such strong structural frame leadership behavior. He was also the first president to authorize conscription.

Once again using structural frame thinking, Lincoln recognized that the Emancipation Proclamation had to be followed by a constitutional amendment that would legitimize the prohibition of slavery. So he lobbied hard and was successful in having the Thirteenth and Fourteenth Amendments passed.

In 1862 Lincoln began to take a far more active role in managing military affairs. He read books on military theory, consulted with his advisors, and carefully studied maps and organizational charts. These efforts enabled Lincoln to begin to formulate a basic war strategy in his own mind. He was becoming the military's commander-in-chief, and he was progressing from administration to war president.

Lincoln continued to use structural frame leadership behavior in his conducting of the Civil War. Finally, after much procrastination, General McClellan earned a narrow victory at Antietam, but he failed to pursue General Lee's army as it retreated. Lincoln had finally had enough, and he relieved McClellan of his duties in November 1862, barely one year into his command. Since McClellan was not using his army, Lincoln sarcastically noted, "he would like to borrow it" for a while (McGovern, 2009, p. 85).

In yet another display of structural frame leadership behavior, Lincoln moved to total war by 1863. This was no longer a match between two armies. Anyone, or anything, that contributed to the Southern war effort was now fair game. This approach ultimately led to Sherman's famous March to the Sea that devastated great swaths of the South. Until he could find a commander to whom he could impart his trust, he would continue to use structural frame leadership behavior and remain the major strategist of the war.

Lincoln never wavered in his conviction that, given the North's advantage in numbers of men, weapons, railways, and industrial resources, Union forces should press forward all across the lines of battle, hitting the Southern army in all theaters simultaneously. This strategy would prevent Southern generals from moving forces from places not under attack to those that were under attack.

In typical structural frame fashion, Lincoln stated firmly that the war-ending peace negotiations were to be left to him. "The President holds them in his own hands, and will submit them to no military conferences and conventions," he said (McGovern, 2009, p. 139).

THE HUMAN RESOURCE FRAME

Human resource frame leaders believe in people and communicate that belief. They are passionate about productivity through people. Another of Lincoln's strengths was his ability to apply the human touch in his interaction with others.

Government's role, he said, was to "elevate the conditions of men—to lift artificial weights from all shoulders—to clear the paths of laudable pursuit for all, to afford all an unfettered start, and a fair chance in the race of life" (McGovern, 2009, p. 5). Lincoln's remarkable quality of tolerance has been a constant source of admiration for generations of Americans. His compassion touched every area of his life. He loved his children and could not bear to discipline his sons. He often represented clients in court without charge and refused to be associated with nativist movements (Know-Nothings and the American Party). And he was convinced that the best way to deal with political adversaries was to apply friendly persuasion.

Lincoln sympathized with soldiers who fought for a noble cause. He loved meeting them, particularly those who had been held prisoner or had endured hardship, and he would often be seen sitting under the shade trees on the White House lawn, talking with the men he admired so much. He pardoned, reprieved, or extended great leniency to hundreds of soldiers who were derelict in their duties, because he believed in giving a man a second chance. He wrote achingly beautiful letters to the mothers of fallen soldiers, with words that could only come from the heart. And he felt no anger toward Southerners who took up arms against their country and commanded his generals to "let 'em up easy" (McGovern, 2009, p. 8).

Ever the humanist, Lincoln scoffed at those who defended slavery on the grounds that blacks were better off as slaves in America than as heathens in Africa or as factory workers in the North. Although he acknowledged the attempt to prove slavery an acceptable thing, he said, "we never hear of a man who wishes to take the good of it, by being a slave *himself*" (McGovern, 2009, p. 68).

Lincoln felt that many Southerners, possibly the majority, had been indoctrinated with the idea that the only way of protecting their way of life from destruction by Lincoln was by secession and war. Lincoln, therefore, held out the olive branch and wanted reconstruction to take place gently, with a measure of forgiveness. In December 1863 he issued a Proclamation of Amnesty and Reconstruction, aimed at Southern areas occupied by federal forces. He hoped that the generous terms of the proclamation would entice war-weary Southern soldiers to lay down their arms while at the same time building popular and political support in the North.

THE SYMBOLIC FRAME

In the symbolic frame, the organization is seen as a stage, a theater in which every actor plays certain roles and the symbolic leader attempts to communicate the right impressions to the right audiences. Many times, leaders utilize symbolic frame behavior in the form of humorous stories, jokes, and witticisms. One could argue that the symbolic frame was Lincoln's strongest.

Lincoln took symbolic leadership behavior very seriously. As a communicator, Lincoln availed himself of the latest technical advances. He spent countless hours at the telegraph office, keeping abreast of news from the front and sending orders to generals. He made ample use of rails and barges to move armies, supplies, and even himself to the scene of the battle. He understood that his personal presence underscored the sincerity of his commitment to the task before him and for which he asked so many others to sacrifice.

With an eye toward the finish line, and knowing that after the Civil War it would be crucial for former enemies to become friends, he symbolically got this point across by appointing to his cabinet what he called "the team of rivals." He named three of his major rivals to his cabinet, confident in his ability to check their ambitions and earn their loyalty. "Keep your enemies close," he advised (Felzenberg, 2008, p. 120).

Part of the image that Lincoln worked hard to project in a symbolic way was his humility. In running for the Illinois state legislature, he said: "I am in favor of the internal improvement system and a high protective tariff. These are my sentiments and political principles. If elected I shall be thankful; if not it will be all the same." He is also famous for saying, "You may fool all the people some of the time; you can even fool some of the people all the time; but you can't fool all the people all the time" (McGovern, 2009, p. 30).

Most of Lincoln's symbolic behavior came in the form of his inspiring speeches. In 1854, Lincoln gave his first great speech, which clearly set forth not only his arguments against the Kansas-Nebraska Act but also his personal views on slavery. He said that the institution of slavery was morally wrong and a "monstrous injustice," because it denied the "humanity of the Negro." "Bleeding Kansas," as Lincoln referred to it, became a vicious battleground as pro-slavery and anti-slavery forces clashed over which way Kansas would go. Thus, Lincoln lambasted the Kansas-Nebraska Act as "conceived in violence, passed in violence, and executed in violence" (McGovern, 2009, p. 38).

"Slavery is founded in the selfishness of man's nature—opposition to it in his love of justice," he so eloquently said during his Peoria speech in 1854 (McGovern, 2009, p. 67). Slavery, he argued, violated the promise of the Declaration of Independence and its declaration that "all men are created equal."

The second great speech of Lincoln's career was his 1858 acceptance speech at the statehouse in Springfield, Illinois. Using familiar biblical language and decrying the enactment of the Kansas-Nebraska Act, which invalidated the Missouri Compromise, he said: "We are now in the fifth year since the policy was initiated with the avowed object and confident promises of putting an end to slavery. Under the operation of the policy, that agitation has not only not ceased, but has been constantly augmented . . . 'A house divided against itself cannot stand.' I believe this government cannot endure permanently half slave and half free" (McGovern, 2009, p. 42). His words were prophetic when, two years later, the Civil War broke out.

In another display of symbolic behavior, the centerpiece of the senatorial campaign, the Lincoln-Douglas debates, became one of the seminal political events in the history of American politics. Newspapers around the country closely followed the contest between "the Little Giant" and "Honest Abe."

Lincoln's third great speech was delivered at New York's Cooper Union in 1860 and contained his position that the founding fathers had meant for slavery to fade away. Twenty-nine of the thirty-nine signers, he explained, had at some point favored congressional regulation of slavery in the territories. Those who spoke of secession were misguided. They followed a "rule or ruin" philosophy. Republicans should stay the course, he urged. "Let us have faith that right makes might, and in that faith, let us to the end, dare to do our duty as we understand it" (McGovern, 2009, p. 445).

Lincoln's inaugural address was another instance of his frequent use of symbolism. "The rights of the minority would always be protected by the majority, which was held safely in restraint by constitutional checks and balances," he declared. "That is how the national government endured. For the minority to break from the Union—to secede—simply because it found itself in the minority was," Lincoln said, "the essence of anarchy" (McGovern, 2009, p. 54).

Lincoln was determined not to start the war. When he announced that he was sending provisions only, and not armaments, to Fort Sumter, the move forced the hand of the South Carolina rebels, who predictably saw Lincoln's move as a symbolic act of aggression and fired on Sumter on April 12, 1861.

The Emancipation Proclamation was at once a symbolic, structural, human resource, and political gesture. Lincoln's order freed four million slaves with one stroke of his pen. Of those, over 150,000 joined the Union forces and gave African Americans the incentive to rebel against their Southern masters. Politically, he made sure it did not apply to border slave states like Delaware, Maryland, Kentucky, and Missouri that did not secede from the Union. He also made certain that he signed the Emancipation Proclamation, which had been written almost a year earlier, after a Union victory at Antietam.

Of course, there is the famous use of symbolic leadership behavior in the form of humor in defense of Ulysses S. Grant upon being informed of his drinking problem. Lincoln said, "Find out what he's drinking and order it for my other generals" (McGovern, 2009, p. 87).

In November 1863, Lincoln traveled by train to Gettysburg, Pennsylvania, for the dedication of a new national Soldiers Cemetery on the site of the battlefield. Lincoln's two-minute speech (272 words) remains his most famous one. He succeeded in redefining the very meaning of the war itself. The struggle was no longer simply over the survival of the Union, but for the ideals of freedom promised for all Americans in the Declaration of Independence. The Gettysburg Address, along with at least five other great speeches, made Lincoln the most masterful speechwriter of any president in our national history.

In his typically symbolic way, after being nominated for a second term, he said: "I have not permitted myself, gentlemen, to conclude that I am the best man in the country; but I am reminded, in this connection, of an old Dutch farmer, who remarked to a companion once that it was not best to swap horses when crossing streams" (McGovern, 2007, p. 104).

Upon being criticized by the Democrats and the press, Lincoln once again used symbolic behavior in his astute observation that "if the end brings me out all right, what is said against me won't amount to anything. If the end brings me out wrong, ten angels swearing I was right would make no difference" (Felzenberg, 2008, p. 120).

THE SYMBOLIC FRAME AND HUMOR

Lincoln was fond of engaging in symbolic frame leadership behavior in the form of humor. Humorous quotes attributed to Abraham Lincoln include:

- How many legs does a dog have if you call the tail a leg? Four. Calling a tail a leg doesn't make it a leg.
- I am rather inclined to silence, and whether that be wise or not, it is at least more unusual nowadays to find a man who can hold his tongue than to find one who cannot.
- I don't know who my grandfather was; I am much more concerned to know what his grandson will be.
- I happen temporarily to occupy this big White House. I am living witness that someday one of your children may look to come here as my father's child has.
- I have stepped out upon this platform that I may see you and that you may see me, and in the arrangement I have the best of the bargain.
- If I were two-faced, would I be wearing this one?
- It is said an Eastern monarch once charged his wise men to invent him a sentence to be ever in view, and which should be true and appropriate in all times and situations. They presented him the words: "And this, too, shall pass away."
- My experience has taught me that a man who has no vices has damned few virtues.
- No man has a good enough memory to make a successful liar.
- The best way to get a bad law repealed is to enforce it strictly. (McGovern, 2009)

THE POLITICAL FRAME

Leaders operating out of the political frame clarify what they want and what they can get. Political leaders are realists above all. They never let what they want cloud their judgment about what is possible. They assess the distribution of power and interests. Lincoln would not be listed among the most effective presidents in American history if he had not been facile in his use of the political frame of leadership.

Unlike the radical abolitionists, Lincoln believed that if the slave system could be confined to the Southern states, it would eventually be exhausted and face economic doom. And when the free territories became free states, the national political balance would shift inexorably toward freedom. Thus, in order to avoid war, he was very willing to practice political frame leadership behavior and wait out the inevitable, even if it took a considerable amount of time. Of course, the Southern states were not content to let the inevitable happen, and their inflexibility and their attempts to extend slavery to the territories led to the Civil War.

Lincoln was a political man by nature. He was a shrewd, masterful politician who knew and appreciated the tactical and strategic demands of down-to-earth politics. In fact, it was a political decision that drew him back into public service after losing a senatorial election. He was "thunderstruck" and "astounded" as the Kansas-Nebraska Act was passed, allowing a state vote on slavery and, in effect, nullifying the Missouri Compromise, which outlawed slavery in the new territories and which Lincoln believed had "settled the slavery question forever" (McGovern, 2009, p. 37).

With his nomination assured, Lincoln immediately engaged in political frame behavior in appointing his presidential rival and secretary of the Treasury Salmon Chase to the Supreme Court. For Chase to advance his ambitions, Lincoln argued, he would have to succeed on the court. Also, he could count on Chase not to thwart emergency measures the way deceased Chief Justice Roger Taney, who presided over the Dred Scott decision, did.

In joining and ultimately becoming the standard-bearer of the newly established Republican Party in 1856, Lincoln used political leadership behavior and made some demands. The party must oppose slavery but must respect the Constitution's protection of slavery where it existed. The party had to avoid "dangerous extremes," such as the radical abolitionists demanded, and stake out the middle ground. To attract foreign-born voters, the party must officially advocate religious toleration, and to appease the Know-Nothings, it must oppose state funding of parochial schools as a violation of the First Amendment.

Recognizing that his party consisted of differing interest groups, Lincoln tried to strike an unusual balance, selecting men who had been his chief rivals for the Republican nominations. Recently, Doris Kearns Goodwin wrote about Lincoln's cabinet in her book *Team of Rivals*. In true political frame style, Lincoln believed in the concept of keeping your friends close and your enemies even closer.

Lincoln also tried to utilize political frame behavior to delay the onset of the Civil War. He authorized a series of informal peace talks, all of which he knew would prove fruitless, but he believed that his willingness even to enter into such talks sent the right message to the public.

In the campaign for reelection against General McClellan, Illinois, Indiana, New Jersey, Delaware, Rhode Island, Nevada, and Oregon did not allow field votes; soldiers from those states had to gain leave and return home to vote. Once again using political leadership behavior, Lincoln made sure that the leave was granted because he knew he had the support of the great majority of the soldiers.

In the process of passing the Thirteenth Amendment, which abolished slavery, Lincoln was particularly astute in employing political frame behavior in using his talents as a master politician to work tirelessly to gain the necessary votes. Lincoln offered federal jobs to congressmen of both parties and their family members in exchange for votes. At the instant it was passed, he engaged in a little symbolic behavior and kicked off a hundred-gun salute that rocked the city of Washington. And he was proud of the fact that the very first state to ratify the amendment was his home state of Illinois.

THE MORAL FRAME

The moral frame is my own contribution to situational leadership theory. In my view, the moral frame completes situational leadership theory. Without it, leaders could just as easily use their leadership skills for promoting evil as for promoting good. Leaders operating out of the moral frame are concerned about their obligations to their followers. Moral frame leaders use some type of moral compass to direct their behavior. They practice what has been described as servant leadership and are concerned with those individuals and groups that are marginalized in their organizations and in society. In short, they are concerned about equality, fairness, and social justice.

Although Lincoln never belonged to an established religion, he came to acknowledge, and even depend upon, a higher power; indeed, it seemed that the connection between Lincoln and the Almighty enabled him to take on the great challenges he faced as president. He saw himself as an instrument of God's will. He had been charged with a vast and sacred trust, which carried responsibilities from which he had no moral right to shrink. He spoke of Providence, and the idea of exact retribution. He believed that God might punish the nation for the sin of slavery, the North for allowing the evil institution to exist, and the South for the institution itself.

So Lincoln had strong standards of morality and ethics. He charged that the institution of slavery was morally wrong and a "monstrous injustice" because it denied the "humanity of the Negro." He also described it as "the eternal struggle between right and wrong—throughout the world" (McGovern, 2009, p. 37).

Lincoln's Emancipation Proclamation fundamentally and dramatically transformed the character of the Civil War. Now there was added a moral, humanitarian force to the Union cause, and the humanistic struggle to expand the domain of freedom would transcend the original war effort to preserve the Union.

SITUATIONAL LEADERSHIP ANALYSIS

Situational models of leadership differ from earlier trait and behavioral models in asserting that no single way of leading works in all situations. Rather, appropriate behavior depends on the circumstances at a given time. Effective managers diagnose the situation, identify the leadership style or behavior that will be most effective, and then determine whether they can implement the required style.

Lincoln was a prototypical situational leader. For example, when he issued the Emancipation Proclamation, he convened a cabinet meeting, informed the attendees of his decision, and declared that he did not wish their "advice about the main matter," which, he said, he had already "determined for himself" (Felzenberg, 2008, p. 123). He then sought their input on style, the manner of implementation, and legal issues.

Further demonstrating his flexibility regarding the use of leadership behavior, Lincoln began his administration promising not to disturb slavery where it existed. Later on, he tried to persuade slaveholders to accept compensated emancipation. Finally, when nothing else proved effective, he banned slavery altogether.

Basically an ethicist, Lincoln was also an artist in the Machiavellian use of power. It was a combination of qualities that made Lincoln's contribution to the anti-slavery movement so demonstrably effective. Lincoln was nothing less than a relentless foe of slavery, biding his time to strike it at the most opportune and promising moment—the timing of the Emancipation Proclamation to coincide with a major victory, for example. In addition, we saw that Lincoln had a keen sense of humor and utilized symbolic frame behavior in the form of humor rather frequently. Whether consciously doing so or not, Lincoln was an expert in placing situational leadership theory into effective practice.

LEADERSHIP IMPLICATIONS AND CONCLUSION

In Abraham Lincoln we see the essence of situational leadership. He used symbolic behavior to inspire a people and an army and used structural behavior to sustain and support them. He often used symbolic frame behavior in the form of humor, as when he asked those who criticized General Grant for his alleged alcoholism to "tell me what brand of whiskey that Grant drinks. I would like to send a barrel of it to my other generals" (McGovern, 2009, p. 80). He mobilized and energized the nation by appealing to the best and highest of ideals (moral frame behavior); that is, he convinced the nation that "a more perfect Union"—a Union of justice and freedom—was worth the fight. As a human resource frame leader, he wished for the "kindly spirit" of America, "a Union of hearts and minds as well as of States" (McGovern, 2009, p. 147).

Lincoln holds perhaps the highest place in American history. General William Tecumseh Sherman said, "Of all the men I ever met, he seemed to possess more of the elements of greatness, combined with goodness, than any other" (McGovern, 2009, p. 249). He is the president against whom all others will forever be measured. We hope we and our leaders can be more like he was. By manifesting the many lessons in situational leadership that Lincoln modeled, perhaps we can all come to reflect his ideals of leadership in our own inimical ways.

Chapter Five

Theodore Roosevelt

A man who has never gone to school may steal from a freight car; but if he has a university education, he may steal the whole railroad. —Theodore Roosevelt

BACKGROUND

Theodore Roosevelt was born in 1858 in New York City and was the twenty-sixth president of the United States. If ever there was a president who embodied the characteristics of our national identity, especially in the early 1900s, it was Teddy Roosevelt. Interestingly enough, Roosevelt was a frail and asthmatic child who took up boxing to develop stamina. He was a brilliant scholar, graduating Phi Beta Kappa from Harvard and afterward matriculating at Columbia Law School.

Roosevelt was only twenty-three when elected to the New York state assembly and twenty-six when appointed chairman of the state delegation to the Republican National Convention in 1884. In that same year, tragedy struck when his beloved wife, Alice, two days after giving birth, died. Retreating to the vast ranch he owned in the Badlands of the Dakota Territory, he found relief from his mourning by working as a cowboy and acting as deputy sheriff.

From 1889 to 1895, Roosevelt served as civil service commissioner under President Benjamin Harrison. From there he moved to New York City as police commissioner and was often to be found patrolling the streets alongside his patrolmen. In 1897 President William McKinley appointed him assistant secretary of the navy. As relations with Spain worsened, Roosevelt recruited some of his cowboy friends and former college athletes for the First United States Volunteer Cavalry Regiment, known in history as the Rough

Riders. We are all familiar with images of Roosevelt astride his mount, with a polka-dot scarf tied to his hat, leading the victorious charge up San Juan Hill.

In 1898 Roosevelt was elected governor of New York. Conservative Republicans nominated him as McKinley's vice president in hopes of ending his career in what was up to then a mostly dead-end job. This strategy backfired when McKinley was fatally shot, and Theodore Roosevelt became the youngest U.S. president in American history.

Known as an activist president, Roosevelt went on a trust-busting rampage, winning twenty-five indictments. When a United Mine Workers strike promised to drag on, he forced the mine owners to submit to mediation, becoming the first president to intervene in a labor dispute. He established the Department of Commerce and Labor, and expanded the military in keeping with his celebrated motto, "Speak softly and carry a big stick."

Roosevelt was easily reelected in 1904, running on a platform called the Square Deal. Always concerned with consumers, he endorsed the Pure Food and Drug Act. He signed the Elkins Act aimed at railroad corruption, and doubled the number of national parks, increasing America's forest reserve by 150 million acres. In 1904 he oversaw the purchase of the Panama Canal, and he won the Nobel Peace Prize. He is consistently rated by historians as one of the most effective U.S. presidents (Auchincloss, 2001; Felzenberg, 2008; Taranto and Leo, 2004).

THE STRUCTURAL FRAME

We begin our analysis of Theodore Roosevelt's leadership behavior with the structural frame. Structural frame leaders seek to develop a new model of the relationship of structure, strategy, and environment for their organizations. Strategic planning, extensive preparation, and effecting change are priorities for them. We will find that Theodore Roosevelt was strong in all five leadership frames, including the structural frame.

President McKinley appointed Theodore Roosevelt assistant secretary of the navy under John Long, an easygoing gentleman who was delighted to let his more forceful assistant handle most of the work. Showing his structural frame leadership tendencies, Roosevelt immediately got to work to increase the number of U.S. warships and made the existing ones more efficient. He saw in America's deteriorating relations with Spain over Cuba an opportunity to prove U.S. superiority at sea in both oceans by sinking the Spanish fleet.

In one of Long's frequent absences, Roosevelt took it upon himself to cable Commodore George Dewey to mobilize his fleet in case of war. Long was far from thrilled by Roosevelt's premature action, but it eventually facilitated Dewey's dramatic victory over the Spanish in Manila Bay.

Roosevelt's strong structural frame leanings helped enable him to accomplish a great deal as president. His major legislative accomplishments during his two terms of office can be summed up as these: the Elkins Act against the railroads' practice of giving rebates to favored customers like John D. Rockefeller; the creation of the Department of Commerce and Labor with its Bureau of Corporations, which grew to regulate every business that crossed state lines; the Hepburn Bill, which amended and vitalized the Interstate Commerce Act and gave government the power to set railroad rates; the Pure Food and Meat Inspection laws, which remedied some of the scandals of the meatpacking industry, as exposed by Upton Sinclair's novel *The Jungle*; and the Employers' Liability and Safety Appliance laws, which limited the working hours of employees.

Roosevelt further displayed his structural frame tendencies during the 1902 United Mine Workers strike called under the leadership of John Mitchell. The strike shut down the anthracite coal mines in West Virginia and Pennsylvania. Roosevelt announced that if an accord was not reached, federal troops would take over the mines and run them as a receivership. At this point the operators agreed to binding arbitration, but without a union member on the panel. This time Roosevelt used political leadership behavior along with structural frame behavior and once again stepped in and broke the impasse by suggesting a union man who was also an eminent sociologist.

Over time, Roosevelt gained a reputation for being a strong structural frame leader. In his negotiations with Panama over the building of the canal, he wanted to take advantage of the openness of the newly established government there, so he immediately granted them recognition. Referring to his having recognized the new government of Panama without waiting for Congress to be in session, he stated in typical structural frame fashion: "I took the Canal Zone and let Congress debate" (Auchincloss, 2001, p. 58).

Roosevelt utilized structural frame leadership behavior well before he became president. As undersecretary of the navy he improved the navy status from fifth in the world in size to second only to Great Britain. "I do believe there is enough chance of war with Japan to make it extremely wise to secure against it by building a navy as to forbid Japan's hope of success," he declared (Auchincloss, 2001, p. 70).

In yet another display of structural frame behavior, Europe and Latin America learned that Roosevelt's interpretation of the Monroe Doctrine would not tolerate any European attempt to collect debts in the Northern Hemisphere by force. America's neighbors had the obligation to behave responsibly. When the government of Santo Domingo fell apart, Roosevelt assumed virtual control of the republic and made sure that it continued to pay its debts.

When post-presidency ideological differences occurred between Roosevelt and William Howard Taft, Roosevelt once again used structural frame behavior and decided to run on the Progressive ticket because of his increasing conviction that his mission in life had not been fulfilled, and that several reforms that he had been able to bring about might be annulled by a conservative successor.

Roosevelt's structural frame tendencies were always evident. After all, he had been in turn a brash, young reformer in the New York State Assembly; a rough-riding frontier rancher; an unsuccessful New York City mayoral candidate; a progressive U.S. Civil Service commissioner; a crusading police commissioner; a whirlwind of a navy assistant secretary who argued, schemed, and prepared for war with Spain; a nationally celebrated military hero of the same war; governor of New York; and vice president of the United States even before becoming the reform-oriented twenty-sixth president.

THE HUMAN RESOURCE FRAME

Human resource frame leaders believe in people and communicate that belief. They are passionate about productivity through people. Although Theodore Roosevelt is depicted by some historians as egocentric, there is much evidence that he was concerned with the welfare of others as much as he was with his own.

First of all, he was a devoted father and never missed some sort of interaction with his offspring every evening, even on the busiest days. But beyond his love for his family was his real affection for humankind. For example, early in his first term, Roosevelt invited Booker T. Washington to dine at the White House, which aroused a howl of protest in newspapers throughout the South. "As things have turned out I am very glad that I asked him," he said, "for the clamor aroused by the act makes me feel as if the act was necessary" (Auchincloss, 2001, p. 63).

Roosevelt could be impetuous, intemperate, egotistical, and too self-confident. He personalized political differences, attributing all manner of base motives to his opponents. They were all cowards or scoundrels. But he was incorruptible, courageous, resolute, just, and visionary. He believed that the moral obligations that concerned individuals should concern government as well. This attitude prompted him to operate out of the human resource frame of leadership behavior quite often.

THE SYMBOLIC FRAME

In the symbolic frame, the organization is seen as a stage, a theater in which every actor plays certain roles and the symbolic leader attempts to communicate the right impressions to the right audiences. Many times, leaders operating out of this frame utilize symbolic behavior in the form of humorous stories, jokes, and witticisms. One could argue that this was Theodore Roosevelt's strongest frame.

Theodore Roosevelt is one of the few presidents whose life is even more important historically than his accomplishments as the country's chief executive. What survives in the panorama of history, even more than his trustbusting, or his building of the Panama Canal, or his negotiation of the Russo-Japanese War peace treaty, which were all accomplished via structural frame and political frame leadership behavior, is the symbolic vision of the intrepid Rough Rider who charged up San Juan Hill, the fearless antagonist of political vice and corruption, and the wielder of the "big stick" who sent his "Great White Fleet" around the globe to impress the alien powers with the spectacle of America's might.

Roosevelt acted in the symbolic frame when he promptly resigned his post as assistant secretary of the navy and joined the fighting forces, leading to his great victory commanding his Rough Riders in the Battle of San Juan Hill during the Spanish-American War. He was nominated for the Medal of Honor for his efforts, but his earlier exposés about the lack of readiness of the army earned him enough enemies in the military to thwart his receiving the medal. It was only in 2001 that Congress finally awarded the Medal of Honor to him posthumously.

Roosevelt used symbolic frame behavior in his very creative way of coining terms. For example, during his trustbusting days he referred to the tycoons with whom he was dealing as the "malefactors of great wealth." When he declared his candidacy for president in 1912, he used the occasion to coin the phrase, "My hat is in the ring." And, during his second term, he described his new socially progressive principles as his "Square Deal." Twenty-five years later his cousin "borrowed" the term and altered it slightly in naming FDR's New Deal (Auchincloss, 2001, p. 62).

Symbolic leadership behavior was once again used by Roosevelt during his second term, when he sent his newly constructed Great White Fleet around the world in a show of force to the world powers that the United States was in a position to back up its word. And again, in 1906, he used symbolic behavior by donating his prize money to charity when he received the Nobel Peace Prize for helping to negotiate a peace treaty between Russia and Japan after their war.

Roosevelt once again utilized symbolic frame leadership behavior when he chaired a conference on world peace, in which thirteen nations assembled in Spain in 1906 to discuss the dispute between Britain, France, and Germany over Morocco. The kaiser had asked Roosevelt to chair the session, and he reluctantly did so in the interest of world peace. He did not want the United States too involved with European affairs in that he foresaw the coming of World War I. The eight years of peace that followed the treaty were at least a small victory, and the world owed them at least in part to Theodore Roosevelt.

In another symbolic frame move, Roosevelt ceremoniously appointed Gifford Pinchot, the great forest conservationist, to head up his conservation efforts almost immediately after taking office as president. Pinchot, throughout Roosevelt's two terms, was a power in the land. He never obtained cabinet status, but he had constant access to the president, who almost always listened to him. Despite strong opposition, Roosevelt increased the national forests from 42 to 172 million acres and created fifty-one wildlife preserves.

In 1912 Roosevelt was shot in the chest by a would-be assassin while making a speech in Milwaukee. In a typical display of symbolic frame behavior, he said: "Friends, I shall ask you to be as quiet as possible. I don't know whether you fully understand that I have been shot; but it takes more than a bullet to kill a bull moose" (Auchincloss, 2001, p. 122). It was another dramatic performance in a lifetime of dramatic performances.

Being the symbolic frame leader that he was, he firmly believed that one of his great misfortunes lay in not having a war during his presidency in which he could act upon his beliefs. His worst time was after the outbreak of World War I, which he viewed as a perfect historical occasion for his kind of heroic and symbolic leadership. As a result, he opposed President Woodrow Wilson's cautionary approach every step of the way.

In his view, it was he who should have been the hero of the script. It was a role for the Rough Rider, for the man who built the great canal, who had engineered peace in the Far East, who had confronted the criminals in the streets of New York and faced the charging elephants and lions in Africa. And what did the country have instead? A dry scholar, a university professor, a man who had never heard a shot fired in anger.

In one last grasp for glory, Roosevelt volunteered to raise a company similar to the Rough Riders and go to France to fight in World War I. However, President Wilson denied the request. In voicing his discouragement to the president's aide, Colonel House, Roosevelt said: "After all, I'm only asking to be allowed to die." House is supposed to have replied: "Oh? Did you make that quite clear to the President?" (Auchincloss, 2001, p. 132).

THE SYMBOLIC FRAME AND HUMOR

Theodore Roosevelt was particularly fond of engaging in symbolic frame leadership behavior in the form of humor. Humorous quotes attributed to Roosevelt include:

- A man who has never gone to school may steal from a freight car; but if he has a university education, he may steal the whole railroad.
- A typical vice of American politics is the avoidance of saying anything real on real issues.
- A vote is like a rifle; its usefulness depends upon the character of the user.
- Absence and death are the same; only that in death there is no suffering.
- Appraisals are where you get together with your team leader and agree what an outstanding member of the team you are, how much your contribution has been valued, what massive potential you have and, in recognition of all this, would you mind having your salary halved.
- Believe you can and you're halfway there.
- Big jobs usually go to the men who prove their ability to outgrow small ones.
- Don't hit at all if it is honorably possible to avoid hitting; but never hit soft.
- Every reform movement has a lunatic fringe.
- For unflagging interest and enjoyment, a household of children, if things go reasonably well, certainly all other forms of success and achievement lose their importance by comparison. (Auchincloss, 2001; workinghumor.com)

THE POLITICAL FRAME

Leaders operating out of the political frame clarify what they want and what they can get. Political leaders are realists above all. They never let what they want cloud their judgment about what is possible. They assess the distribution of power and interests. Roosevelt was a master at engaging in political frame leadership behavior.

Theodore Roosevelt was a political idealist who had the wisdom to know that only by astute and well-considered compromise in the legislative process could he hope to see enacted even a fraction of the social and military programs that he deemed essential to the welfare of the nation.

At the 1884 Republican Convention both Roosevelt and his lifelong friend Henry Cabot Lodge were against the nomination of the corrupt James G. Blaine as the party's standard-bearer, but despite his nomination, Roosevelt remained in the Republican Party. He adhered to Benjamin Disraeli's famous growl: "Damn your principle! Stick to your party" (Auchincloss, 2001, p. 19). This came to be a wise decision on Roosevelt's part when he was declared the party's nominee for vice president in 1900.

Roosevelt had second thoughts about taking the dead-end job of vice president under McKinley, but out of party loyalty he took it. But when McKinley was assassinated, Roosevelt became president. Mark Hanna, who was instrumental in convincing the party to offer him the vice presidency to "get him out of the way," wailed: "Look what we've got! That damned cowboy is president of the United States" (Auchincloss, 2001, p. 38).

In a particularly radical use of political frame leadership behavior, Roosevelt encouraged a civil war in Panama. When his patience ran out over negotiating with Colombia regarding the rights to build the Panama Canal, Roosevelt supported an insurgency group of Panamanians who would eventually defeat Colombia. Roosevelt then purchased the Canal Zone from the friendly insurgents.

In the Russo-Japanese War of 1904, Roosevelt favored Japan but did not want it to gain too sweeping a victory for fear that its newfound power would someday endanger the United States, which of course it did. He decided to use political frame behavior and capitalize on his considerable standing in the international community by coaxing the two sides into a settlement, for which he received the Nobel Peace Prize.

Toward the end of Roosevelt's second term the opposition to his conservation policies, which had long festered, became fierce. A bill was introduced in Congress to deprive the president of his power to create national forests from the public domain in various western states. Knowing it was sure to pass, Roosevelt sent Pinchot to map out areas that he could nominate as forestland while he still had the power to do so. Pinchot laid out thirty-three such areas, and the president operated out of the political leadership frame and added sixteen million acres to forestland—to the fury of the lumber lobby (Auchincloss, 2001).

THE MORAL FRAME

The moral frame is my own contribution to situational leadership theory. In my view, the moral frame completes situational leadership theory. Without it, leaders could just as easily use their leadership skills for promoting evil as for promoting good. Leaders operating out of the moral frame are concerned about their obligations and responsibilities to their followers. Moral frame leaders use some type of moral compass to direct their behavior. They practice what has been described as servant leadership and are concerned with those individuals and groups that are marginalized in their organizations and in society. In short, they are concerned about equality, fairness, and social justice.

There are many instances in Theodore Roosevelt's life that indicate that he possessed a strong sense of morality. For example, the National Association for the Advancement of Colored People declared, "That he [Roosevelt] was our friend proves the justice of our cause, for Roosevelt never championed a cause that was not in essence right" (Felzenberg, 2008, p. 28). Roosevelt envisioned his role as head of the federal government as that of a disinterested moral "umpire," mediating disputes between two organized minorities on behalf of an impacted but unorganized majority.

Earlier in his life, in considering whether to marry Edith after his first wife died, he suffered greatly from his sense of guilt in betraying the memory of Alice. This attitude was characteristic of Roosevelt, who tended to see life in terms of good and evil.

As a deeply moral man, Roosevelt was first and foremost taken up in a lifelong and enthusiastic fight against lawbreakers; he was a policeman at heart, which was obviously why he did so well as a police commissioner in New York. And as a trustbuster, he was not so much against big corporations—in fact, he admired their efficiency—but against their breaking of the law to gain a competitive advantage.

With Roosevelt the crux of almost every great decision was a moral one. As pointed out above, he was not against big business per se; he was just against the businesses that practiced selfish greed under the leadership of men like Jay Gould and J.P. Morgan. To Roosevelt there were good trusts and bad trusts. "Of all forms of tyranny," he posited, "the least attractive and most vulgar is the tyranny of mere wealth" (Auchincloss, 2001, p. 50). He felt so strongly that he instructed his attorney general, Philander Knox, to prosecute Northern Securities and its directors as conspirators in restraint of trade without ever consulting his cabinet.

Because of his strong moral frame leanings, Roosevelt had never been much drawn to the study of law. He had always been repelled by the legal doctrine of caveat emptor (buyer beware), which flew in the face of what to him was the revered code of a gentleman's honor.

Roosevelt's patriotism professed a faith in America's pioneer ethos, the moral virtues that had won the West and inspired Americans to believe in themselves as the New Jerusalem, bound by sacred duty to suffer hardship and risk danger to protect the values of their civilization and impart them to humanity. "We cannot sit huddled within our own borders," he warned, "and avow ourselves merely an assemblage of well-to-do hucksters who care nothing for what happens beyond" (Taranto and Leo, 2004, p. 127).

SITUATIONAL LEADERSHIP ANALYSIS

Situational models of leadership differ from earlier trait and behavioral models in asserting that no single way of leading works in all situations. Rather, appropriate behavior depends on the circumstances at a given time. Effective managers diagnose the situation, identify the leadership style or behavior that will be most effective, and then determine whether they can implement the required style.

As we have seen, Theodore Roosevelt was very much the situational leader and was active in all five leadership frames. We saw how he operated out of the structural frame in gaining the reputation for "speaking softly but carrying a big stick." His image as the Rough Rider and trustbuster was garnered from his effective use of symbolic leadership behavior. As we have also seen, he possessed a keen sense of humor.

Roosevelt's well-known concern for the "little guy" is evidence of his use of human resource behavior. His peace negotiations that led to the end of the Russo-Japanese War were but one indication of his facility in utilizing political frame leadership behavior. And his social justice concerns lead us to believe that his unique version of a moral compass guided his leadership behavior.

Theodore Roosevelt's ranking as one of the most effective U.S. presidents in history is well earned. His leadership style reflected a balance both among and within the five leadership frames. He left as part of his legacy a road map for leaders and aspiring leaders, which, if followed, could be a pragmatic and useful guide in our journey to become the best leaders we can be.

LEADERSHIP IMPLICATIONS AND CONCLUSION

Theodore Roosevelt used structural leadership behavior in liberally interpreting the constitutional authority of the Oval Office to redress the imbalance of power between the executive and legislative branches, which had tilted decisively toward Congress in the fifty years after the Civil War. He fought party bosses who valued political privileges more than just government. He wrenched reforms from legislators who thought their power to award patronage positions was the purpose of elective office.

He used human resource behavior and fought for the common person by calling for the elimination of corporate campaign contributions because he knew they influenced elected officials to favor the wealthy few at the expense of the less advantaged many. He investigated the notoriously unsanitary meatpacking industry, and with the enactment of the Pure Food and Drug Act, he placed public health before industry profits.

But he was not a radical reformer. He used political leadership behavior in seeking not to destroy the great wealth-creating institutions of capitalism, but to save them from their own excesses. He proposed sensible and incremental regulations on commerce. Nor was he the zealot who disdained the compromises essential to lawmaking. He wanted to get things done, and through the use of astute political frame behavior, he did.

Many leaders in his age and ours tend to be preoccupied with extending their own power. Self-aggrandizement is part of human nature, and Roosevelt had his share. He gave up the presidency at the end of his second term, but wanted it back four years later for personal as well as altruistic reasons. Yet the very thought that he would seek high office for self-aggrandizement rather than to serve others deeply offended both his idea of morality and his self-esteem.

As we have noted, Roosevelt was particularly adept in symbolic frame behavior. He had a well-developed sense of humor and used humor to defuse a number of situations and to disarm his critics. However, as much as he craved the limelight, and however great his personal ambitions, he could not satisfy his ego unless he served the higher purpose of his nation's moral greatness. And that deeply personal and spiritual sense of patriotism made him the man many admire still—and the man whose effective situational leadership behavior would be worth emulating in our own personal and professional lives.

Chapter Six

Albert Einstein

Life is like riding a bicycle. To keep your balance you must keep moving. —
Albert Einstein

BACKGROUND

Albert Einstein was born in Ulm, Germany, in 1879. He was a child prodigy,
having mastered many of the mysteries of science by the time he was ten
years old. He was also proficient at the piano and the violin.

After graduating from high school, Einstein spent two frustrating years
searching for a teaching position, finally settling for a patent office job in
Bern, Switzerland. While working in the patent office, he attended the University
of Zurich, where he earned his doctoral degree in 1905. As part of his
doctoral dissertation, he published four groundbreaking papers on the photoelectric effect, Brownian motion, special relativity, and the equivalence of
matter and energy. So spectacular was his output in 1905 that it became
known as Einstein's *annus mirabilis* (miracle year).

Ten years later, Einstein completed his General Theory of Relativity, and
shortly thereafter he was awarded the Nobel Prize in Physics. He also received the Copley Medal from the Royal Society of London in 1925, by
which time he had become the most famous living scientist in the world.

In 1933, when Hitler rose to power in Germany, Einstein immigrated to
the United States. He took up residence in Princeton, New Jersey, and became a professor in the Institute for Advanced Study headquartered there. He
remained with the institute until his death.

In 1939, on the eve of the outbreak of World War II, Einstein warned President Franklin Roosevelt that the Germans were experimenting with uranium and chain reactions in an effort to build an atomic bomb. As a result, the United States initiated the Manhattan Project, with the goal of building an atomic weapon before Germany did. While working on the Manhattan Project, in 1940, Einstein became an American citizen.

Einstein was a civil rights advocate and an active member of the National Association for the Advancement of Colored People (NAACP). He corresponded with W.E.B. Du Bois regarding a strategic plan to end the disease of racism in America. Einstein passed away of an aortic aneurysm in 1955. U.S. industry eventually used his theoretical principles to develop the television, remote control devices, automatic door openers, lasers, and DVD players.

THE STRUCTURAL FRAME

We begin our analysis of Albert Einstein's leadership behavior with the structural frame. Structural frame leaders seek to develop a new model of the relationship of structure, strategy, and environment for their organization. Strategic planning, extensive preparation, and effecting change are priorities for them. It is not surprising that Albert Einstein, being the world-renowned scientist that he was, made frequent use of structural frame leadership behavior.

Einstein's structural frame tendencies began early in life. Since there was no Jewish day school in his neighborhood, he ended up being the only Jew among the seventy students in his class at the local Catholic school. Einstein displayed structural frame behavior by being the best student in his class, even helping his slower classmates master the Catholic studies course that they were all required to take.

Again demonstrating his structural frame capacities early in life, Einstein produced his first piece of scholarly work in elementary school, when he submitted a paper on the capillary effect, which, among other things, causes water to cling to the side of a straw and curl upward. More important than the topic of the paper was his embracing of the concept, novel at the time, that molecules and their atoms actually exist, and that many of the phenomena of nature can be explained by how these atoms interact with one another.

Later, when he had just turned twenty-one, Einstein combined structural and symbolic frame behavior and produced his first published work, *Annalen der Physik*, for Europe's leading scientific journal. "I started from the simple idea of attractive forces among the molecules, and I tested the consequences experimentally," he wrote. "I took gravitational forces as an analogy." His unsuccessful attempt at drawing an apodictic conclusion led him to observe:

"The question of whether and how our forces are related to gravitational forces must therefore be left completely open for the time being" (Isaacson, 2007, p. 57).

As we saw in the background section, Einstein was unsuccessful in his use of structural frame behavior to obtain a job in his field of interest. But his structural frame persistence paid off in 1902, when a session of the Swiss Council officially elected him as a technical expert, class III of the Federal Office for Intellectual Property, with an annual salary in excess of what a junior professor at a university would make.

So it was that through his dogged display of structural frame behavior, Einstein would end up spending the most creative seven years of his life in the usually mundane job of examining patent applications. "I am frightfully busy," he confided in a friend. "Every day I spend eight hours at the office and at least one hour of private lessons, and then in addition, I do some scientific work" (Isaacson, 2007, p. 78). His boss was a benign sort and ignored the sheets of paper on scientific experiments that cluttered Einstein's desk.

Einstein engaged in structural frame behavior in his persistent pursuit of his doctoral degree. Einstein's earlier papers would revolutionize science but, ironically, they were not enough in the mainstream to be acceptable for a doctoral dissertation. Realizing the need to do a study on a safe topic rather than a radical one like quanta or relativity, he settled on a work titled *A New Determination of Molecular Dimensions*, which finally earned him his doctorate at the University of Zurich.

Never one to let grass grow under his feet, eleven days after finishing his dissertation, Einstein continued his use of structural frame behavior by publishing yet another paper exploring evidence of things unseen. As he had been doing from the start, he used mathematical data acquired from the analysis of the visible effects of particles to predict their invisible makeup. He used this process to explain the Brownian effect that had been eluding scientists for almost a century, that is, why small particles suspended in a liquid like water seem to bounce around. His explanation that the movement was the result of atoms and molecules interacting proved that these particles, though unseen, actually did exist.

Einstein had the unique ability to conduct what amounted to thought experiments. His use of structural frame behavior in this form to discover the law of relativity was a result of this rare gift and a decade of intellectual and personal experiences as well as his deep understanding and knowledge of theoretical physics. In just such an experience, he remembered sitting in a chair in the patent office in Bern when the thought occurred to him that "if a person falls freely, he will not feel his own weight." This realization launched him on his journey that ended in the discovery of his special theory of relativity and gravitation (Isaacson, 2007, p. 145).

Einstein used structural frame behavior in improving his teaching performance. He was never a polished lecturer, but he used his informality to his advantage by relating more warmly with his students. Instead of prepared notes, Einstein used a car-sized strip of paper, and students got to watch him develop his thoughts spontaneously. One of his students remarked: "We obtained some insight into his working technique. We certainly appreciated this more than any stylistically perfect lecture" (Isaacson, 2007, p. 160).

Einstein's use of the structural frame even extended to his personal life. When he was going through an estrangement with his wife, Mileva Maric, he proposed a cease-fire agreement in the form of a contract. His cold scientific approach led to a contract that read:

a.   You will make sure

     a.   That my clothes and laundry are kept in good order;
     b.   That I will receive my three meals regularly in my room;
     c.   That my bedroom and study are kept neat, and especially that my desk is left for my use only.

He goes on to demand that "you will renounce all personal relations with me insofar as they are not completely necessary for social reasons," and "you will undertake not to belittle me in front of our children, either through words or behavior" (Isaacson, 2007, p. 185).

After Einstein formulated his special theory of relativity in 1905, he knew it was incomplete in that it held that no physical interaction could propagate faster than the speed of light, which conflicted with Newton's theory of gravity, and it applied only to constant-velocity motion and not to variable-velocity motion. Thus, he continued to utilize structural frame behavior for the next decade in addressing these deficiencies. This led to the development of an equivalence principle, which would guide his research to generalize relativity. "I realized that I would be able to extend or generalize the principle of relativity to apply to accelerated systems in addition to those moving at a uniform velocity," he explained. "And in doing so, I expected that I would be able to resolve the problem of gravitation at the same time" (Isaacson, 2007, p. 190).

As with most structural frame leaders, part of Einstein's genius was his tenacity and perseverance. He clung to his ideas even in the face of apparent contradictions. He also had a deep faith in his intuition and instincts. In the scientific world, where working by oneself is often the rule rather than the exception, he was even more solitary than his counterparts. He was so engrossed in his work that he often forgot to each lunch.

Einstein's solitary nature and systematic use of structural frame behavior led him to many of his greatest insights and discoveries. In contemplating the nature of the universe, for example, he began by observing that an absolutely infinite universe filled with stars and other objects was unthinkable. On the other hand, a finite universe floating at some location in space was also implausible. So he developed a third option: a finite universe, but one without boundaries.

Einstein reasoned that the masses in the universe caused space to curve, and further, caused space to curve completely in on itself. "The system is closed and finite, but there is no end or edge to it," he declared (Isaacson, 2007, p. 252). However, unlike the development of the theory of relativity, which was largely the product of Einstein's working alone, he showed his adaptability by using structural and human resource frame leadership behavior in assembling a team of scientists in the development of quantum mechanics.

For nearly three hundred years, the mechanical universe of Sir Isaac Newton, based on definite and unchanging principles, had dominated scientific thought and informed the psychological foundation of the Enlightenment. Its reliance on the social order, with its rigid belief in cause and effect, was replaced by Einstein's idea of relativity, where the definitions of time and space were situational. His conclusions, arrived at through the effective use of structural frame behavior, changed the world. No longer was there metaphysical certitude about anything. Everything was now relative (Isaacson, 2007).

THE HUMAN RESOURCE FRAME

Human resource frame leaders believe in people and communicate that belief. They are passionate about productivity through people. Although, as we saw above, Einstein liked the solitary life, there are abundant instances in which he operated out of the human resource frame.

An example of Einstein's human resource frame tendencies occurred when he was seeking citizenship in another country after renouncing his German citizenship upon the rise to power of Hitler's anti-Semitic regime. Each month he put aside a part of his salary to pay the fee necessary to become a Swiss citizen, admiring their system of democracy and respect for individuals and their differences. "I like the Swiss because, by and large, they are more humane than the other people among whom I have lived," he said (Isaacson, 2007, p. 58).

Another human resource frame practice in which Einstein engaged was his routine outings with his students after his lectures. At the end of class he would often ask, "Who's coming to the Café Terrasse?" There, he would sometimes hold court, interacting with his students into the wee hours of the morning (Isaacson, 2007, p. 160).

Einstein's human resource frame tendencies came to the fore after his divorce from his wife, Mileva Maric. The prospect of parting from his children was debilitating to him. He became deeply depressed as he imagined life without his two sons. "I have carried these children around the world innumerable times day and night," he confided to his sister, "taken them out in the pram, played with them, romped around and joked with them. They used to shout with joy when I came; the little one cheered even now, because he was still too small to grasp the situation. Now they will be gone forever, and their image of their father is being spoiled" (Isaacson, 2007, p. 187).

Although he shunned public advocacy, Einstein's human resource frame tendencies prevailed in his preference for socialism as a form of government and in his commitment to pacifism. The irrationality of war made Einstein believe that in his role as a scientist, he had a special obligation to foster internationalism and decry nationalism. Unfortunately, many scientists did not adopt Einstein's ideology in this regard, especially those involved in using their genius in support of the Nazi regime in Germany.

To Einstein, socialism was a way of bringing about social justice by removing the stigma attached to class, gender, and race. He believed that it would lead to a more equitable economic system. When compared to Communism and other political and economic systems that ignore individual rights, Einstein's human resource frame tendencies led him to much prefer those systems more concerned with the individual.

In typical human resource frame fashion, Einstein was famous for his love of children. In one telling anecdote, an eight-year-old neighbor rang his doorbell and asked for help with a math problem. She carried a plate of homemade fudge as a bribe. "Come in," he said. "I'm sure we can solve it." He helped explain the math to her, but made her do her own homework. In return for the fudge, he gave her a cookie. Later, Einstein famously told another girl who complained about her problems in math, "Do not worry about your difficulties in mathematics; I can assure you that mine are even greater" (Isaacson, 2007, p. 440).

THE SYMBOLIC FRAME

In the symbolic frame, the organization is seen as a stage, a theater in which every actor plays certain roles and the symbolic leader attempts to communicate the right impressions to the right audiences. Many times, leaders utilize symbolic frame behavior in the form of humorous stories, jokes, and witticisms.

Einstein instinctively knew that to solidify his reputation as the greatest scientific mind in his era he needed to do more than be hyperactive in the structural frame. In addition to discovering new theories in physics, he needed to get the word out by engaging in frequent and effective symbolic behavior. He did so with his prolific writing and his ability to express complex theories in rather simple terms. Thus, he was able to coin many a phrase. Knowing, for example, the primacy of imagination and creativity among one's abilities, he coined the often-repeated observation that "imagination is more important than knowledge."

Likewise, knowing society's tendency to embrace conformity, he said: "Long live impudence! It is my guardian angel in this world." Later in his life, when many thought his reluctance to accept quantum mechanics meant that he had lost his edge, he declared: "To punish me for my contempt for authority, God made me an authority myself" (Isaacson, 2007, p. 7).

As we will see in more detail later, Einstein was particularly adept at using the symbolic frame in the form of humor. He was especially fond of telling the joke about his agnostic uncle, the only member of his family who went to synagogue. When asked why he did so, he said: "Ah, but you never know" (Isaacson, 2007, p. 15).

Einstein spent much of his time using the symbolic frame in casting himself as a nonconformist. His independent streak was demonstrated when his professor mentioned a mild disciplinary measure that the school administrators had just taken. Einstein mightily objected, pointing out very aggressively that the fundamental requirement for learning was the "need for intellectual freedom" (Isaacson, 2007, p. 49).

Then came the most nonconformist and revolutionary statement that Einstein ever wrote, suggesting that light was made up of discrete particles rather than continuous waves: "According to the assumption to be considered here, when a light ray is propagated from a point, the energy is not continuously distributed over an increasing space but consists of a finite number of energy quanta which are localized at points in space and which can be produced and absorbed only as complete units" (Isaacson, 2007, p. 98).

Einstein often used symbolic frame behavior in the form of stories to explain sophisticated scientific phenomena. Explaining the speed of light, he imagined that a ray of light was sent along the embankment of a railroad track. A man on the embankment could measure its speed at 186,000 miles per second as it passed by him. Now imagine a woman riding in a very fast train that is racing away from the light source at a speed of 2,000 miles per second. We would assume that the light beam would be traveling past her at only 184,000 miles per second (186,000 minus 2,000), since the velocity of propagation of a ray of light relative to the carriage thus comes out smaller.

The formula that Einstein used to describe the relationship between light and speed was a form of symbolic frame behavior and strikingly simple. If a body emits the energy, E, in the form of radiation, its mass decreases by the velocity of light, *m squared.* Thus the memorable equation: E=mc2. Einstein continued in his use of the symbolic frame by explaining in layman's terms the enormity of the energy he was talking about in squaring the speed of light. The speed of light by itself is very, very fast. Squaring it makes it unbelievably faster. This is why a relatively small amount of matter when converted into energy is enormous. Expressing it more vividly, Einstein asserted that the energy in the mass of one raisin could supply a large city's energy needs for an entire day.

Years later, when his younger son asked him why he was so famous, Einstein again engaged in symbolic frame behavior, and replied with a simple image to describe his great insight that gravity was the curving of the fabric of space and time: "When a blind beetle crawls over the surface of a curved branch, it doesn't notice that the track it has covered is indeed curved," he said. "I was lucky enough to notice that the beetle didn't notice" (Isaacson, 2007, p. 196).

Using symbolic frame leadership behavior once again, Einstein published a popular book on relativity, *Relativity: The Special and General Theory*, which explained in layman's terms the complex relationship between light and energy. It was translated into several languages and became a worldwide best seller.

Of course, Einstein had exactly the right personality to be transformed into an international superstar. Reporters, knowing that the time was right immediately after World War I for an international celebrity, were delighted that this newly identified genius was not a typical, stick-in-the-mud intellectual. Instead, they found themselves promoting a charming young man with a burst of disheveled hair, twinkling eyes, a disarming informality, and a penchant for uttering witty quips and memorable quotes. A willing participant in promoting his image, Einstein was often seen cavorting in public with other celebrities, like his good friend Charlie Chaplin.

Through his astute application of symbolic frame leadership behavior, Einstein became an inspiration to many of his contemporaries even when they did not understand him. This was particularly true of artists who joined him in his revolutionary concept of being free from the order of time. As Proust put it in the closing of *Remembrance of Things Past*, "How I would love to speak to you about Einstein. I do not understand a single word of his theories, not knowing algebra. Nevertheless it seems we have analogous ways of defining time" (Isaacson, 2007, p. 280).

Although it took Einstein a while to come out of his anti-nationalist shell, he finally used symbolic frame leadership behavior in his support of an independent Jewish state. "I am, as a human being, an opponent of nationalism," he declared, "but as a Jew, I am from today a supporter of the Zionist effort." He was most enthusiastic in his support of the establishment of a Jewish university in Palestine, which ultimately became the Hebrew University of Jerusalem (Isaacson, 2007, p. 282).

Einstein even used symbolic frame behavior in his acceptance speech upon receiving the 1921 Nobel Prize. Although it had been awarded to him for his work on the photoelectric effect and not for his work on relativity and gravitation, he set the record straight as to which of his discoveries he believed were the most important by talking not at all about the photoelectric effect, but about relativity and his new passion of finding a unified field theory that would reconcile general relativity with electromagnetic theory and quantum mechanics.

In addition to using the symbolic frame to establish and perpetuate his image (he appeared on the cover of *Time* magazine a record five times), Einstein used it to further his most ardent causes. One of his most memorable speeches, for example, was a pacifist call for an uncompromising anti-war position and a refusal to enlist for military service. Then he issued what became known as his call for the brave 2 percent: "The timid might say, 'What's the use? We shall be sent to prison.' To them I would reply: Even if only 2 percent of those assigned to perform military service should announce their refusal to fight, governments would be powerless. They would not dare send such a large number of people to jail" (Isaacson, 2007, p. 371).

Einstein also became a strong advocate of racial harmony. When Marian Anderson, the great African American opera star, came to his hometown of Princeton for a concert in 1937, one of the local hotels refused her a room. So Einstein invited her to stay at his home in what was a deeply personal and publically symbolic gesture. In 1940, Einstein once again engaged in symbolic frame behavior by becoming a naturalized citizen. To the amazement of all, including Einstein, ten thousand people attended, and Einstein dramatically exclaimed to the assemblage, "I am an American today!" (Isaacson, 2007, p. 507).

THE SYMBOLIC FRAME BEHAVIOR AND HUMOR

Unlike most scientists, who were stereotypically pictured as being very serious, Albert Einstein distinguished himself through his very keen sense of humor. And this sense of humor was enormously effective in creating and preserving the Einstein mystique. Following are some of the humorous quotes attributed to Albert Einstein:

- A question that sometimes drives me hazy: Am I or are the others crazy?
- Anyone who has never made a mistake has never tried anything new.
- Do not worry about your problems with mathematics; I assure you mine are far greater.
- Everybody is a genius. But if you judge a fish by its ability to climb a tree, it will live its whole life believing that it is stupid.
- Gravitation is not responsible for people falling in love.
- I want to know God's thoughts, the rest are details.
- Intellectuals solve problems; geniuses prevent them.
- It gives me great pleasure indeed to see the stubbornness of an incorrigible nonconformist warmly acclaimed.
- Only two things are infinite, the universe and human stupidity, and I'm not sure about the former.
- Put your hand on a hot stove for a minute, and it seems like an hour. Sit with a pretty girl for an hour, and it seems like a minute. THAT'S relativity.
- Reality is merely an illusion, albeit a very persistent one.
- Science is a wonderful thing if one does not have to earn one's living at it.
- Setting an example is not the main means of influencing others; it is the only means.
- The hardest thing in the world to understand is income tax.
- The most incomprehensible thing about the world is that it is comprehensible.
- The only reason for time is so that everything doesn't happen at once.
- Things should be as simple as possible, but not simpler.
- When the solution is simple, God is answering. (Isaacson, 2007; workinghumor.com)

THE POLITICAL FRAME

Leaders operating out of the political frame clarify what they want and what they can get. Political leaders are realists above all. They never let what they want cloud their judgment about what is possible. They assess the distribution of power and interests before acting. Like all effective leaders, Albert Einstein spent a fair amount of time behaving out of the political frame.

Einstein learned about the value of political frame behavior at an early age. In an effort to please his mother, he became a charming son at his parents' grand hotel in Switzerland. He found the patrons to be pompous and officious but dutifully played his violin for them at his mother's request. He made conversation with them and feigned a cheerful mood. "My popularity among the guests pleases her and my music successes act as a balm on my mother's heart," he recalled (Isaacson, 2007, p. 53).

Einstein used political frame behavior when negotiating a divorce settlement with his wife, Mileva Maric. "You would gain from change," he said convincingly. And in an effort to "sweeten the pot," he would increase to 6,000 marks the amount he would set aside for his children's education and increase Maric's alimony payments to 5,600 marks. "By making myself such a frugal bed of straw, I am proving to you that my boys' well-being is closest to my heart, above all else in the world," he declared (Isaacson, 2007, p. 228).

Then he used still more political frame behavior and added an extraordinary new inducement to persuade Maric to capitulate. He was convinced that he would eventually receive the Nobel Prize in Physics, so he made his final offer to Maric. "The Nobel Prize, in the event of the divorce and in the event that it is bestowed upon me, would be ceded to you in full" (Isaacson, 2007, p. 235). A few days later she decided to settle.

In dealing with his new wife, Elsa, and her opposition to moving from Berlin to Zurich, Einstein once again displayed political frame behavior. He compromised and backed away from a full-time move to Zurich; he retained his position in Berlin but became a guest lecturer in Zurich, making month-long visits twice a year, creating what he believed was a win-win situation.

As mentioned earlier, Einstein was against all forms of nationalism. But he was willing to compromise his principles when required. He abandoned his postulate that all forms of nationalism were bad and made room in his thinking to embrace Zionism and the movement to acquire an independent Jewish homeland in Palestine. His vision would finally come to fruition in the late 1940s, when the state of Israel was established.

Upon a visit to the Riverside Church in New York, Einstein found that the church had been built with contributions from John D. Rockefeller Jr. Einstein immediately donned his political frame hat and arranged a meeting with the famous businessman and philanthropist to discuss certain restrictions that the Rockefeller Foundation had been contemplating putting on research grants. "The red tape encases the mind like the hands of a mummy," he claimed. While he had Rockefeller's ear, he also discussed economics and social justice in light of the Great Depression. Einstein suggested that working hours be decreased rather than people getting laid off as a more just way of cutting costs. He also suggested lengthening the school year to delay seniors going into the workforce. When Rockefeller questioned whether such measures would unduly infringe on individual freedoms, Einstein replied that the current economic conditions justified measures like those taken in wartime.

Perhaps Einstein's most meaningful application of political frame leadership behavior was in reaction to atomic weapon proliferation. Believing that politicians were oblivious to the real danger of atomic weapons, he lobbied his fellow scientists to pressure political leaders to look toward internationalizing military power. For the remainder of his life, Einstein's passion for establishing a unified governing structure for the world would rival his passion for finding a way to govern all the forces of nature. We will see more of Einstein's leadership behavior with regard to nuclear weapons when we take a look at his moral frame leadership behavior (Isaacson, 2007).

THE MORAL FRAME

The moral frame is my own contribution to situational leadership theory. In my view, the moral frame completes situational leadership theory. Without it, leaders could just as easily use their leadership skills for promoting evil as for promoting good. Leaders operating out of the moral frame are concerned about their obligations to their followers. Moral frame leaders use some type of moral compass to direct their behavior. They practice what has been described as servant leadership and are concerned with those individuals and groups that are marginalized in their organizations and in society. In short, they are concerned about equality, fairness, and social justice.

Einstein's development of his personal moral compass was greatly influenced by the Jewish philosopher Baruch Spinoza. Like Spinoza, Einstein embraced the concept of an amorphous God reflected in the awe-inspiring rationality of the universe and its inspiring beauty. He did not, however, believe in a personal God who rewarded and punished and intervened in our daily lives. Nevertheless, Einstein used this belief in God to develop his ethical and moral bearings.

Einstein was mortified upon finding that popular opinion mistakenly associated his theory of general relativity with a new relativism in morality, art, and politics. There was less faith in absolutes, not only of time and space, but also of truth and morality. Einstein fretted that "the foundations of all human thought have been undermined" by this misuse of his theory. "Relativity is a purely scientific matter and has nothing to do with religion," he exasperatedly declared (Isaacson, 2007, p. 278).

His sense of morality led him to be suspicious of authority because it had a tendency to interfere with Einstein's most fundamental moral principle: that freedom and individualism are necessary for creativity and imagination to flourish. "I believe that the most important mission of the state is to protect the individual and to make it possible for him to develop into a creative personality," he said (Isaacson, 2007, p. 379).

Asked if he was religious, Einstein responded, "Yes, you can call it that. Try and penetrate with our limited means the secrets of nature and you will find that beyond all the discernible laws and connections, there remains something subtle, intangible, and inexplicable. Veneration for this force beyond anything that we can comprehend is my religion. To that extent, I am, in fact, religious" (Isaacson, 2007, p. 385).

Einstein's religious feelings of awe and humility before nature also informed his sense of social justice. They impelled him to abhor the trappings of wealth and class, to admonish excess materialism, and prompted him to dedicate his life to solidarity with the poor and oppressed.

Unlike his contemporaries Sigmund Freud, Bertrand Russell, and George Bernard Shaw, Einstein never denigrated religion or those who believed in a personal God. Instead, he tended to be critical of atheists. "What separates me from most so-called atheists is a feeling of utter humility toward the unattainable secrets of the harmony of the cosmos," he said. This belief system manifested itself in Einstein's generally being kind, good-natured, gentle, and unpretentious (Isaacson, 2007, p. 393).

Einstein's moral frame behavior further manifested itself in a profound concern for humanity. He declined Louis B. Mayer and MGM's offer to make a motion picture on the development of the atomic bomb because MGM's past work was too militaristic. As a guest on his friend Eleanor Roosevelt's radio show on the future of nuclear weapons, he made his position clear: "Each step appears as an inevitable consequence of the one that went before," he said of the arms race. "And at the end, looming ever clearer, lies general annihilation" (Isaacson, 2007, p. 501). It seems pretty obvious from the above that Albert Einstein had a moral compass that directed his leadership behavior.

SITUATIONAL LEADERSHIP ANALYSIS AND CONCLUSION

We can readily see that Albert Einstein adhered to the tenets of both situational and transformational leadership theory. He was a situational leader who was comfortable operating out of all five leadership frames and did so in pursuit of a transformational vision—discovering the law of general relativity. He was also adept at accurately determining the readiness level of his followers. In examining his leadership behavior, we observed his ability to be flexible in his application of the five leadership frames and to behave moderately within each frame. Einstein's leadership style, including its humorous dimension, enabled him to become perhaps the most recognized name in science in the world's history. He was able to place situational leadership theory into effective practice in a way that can be an inspiration and a model for leaders and aspiring leaders not only in science but in any field of endeavor.

Chapter Seven

Winston Churchill

History will be kind to me for I intend to write it. —Winston Churchill

BACKGROUND

Winston Churchill was born to an aristocratic family in 1874. He was a British politician and statesman primarily known for leading Britain and its allies to victory over Germany in World War II. He served as Britain's prime minister twice, from 1940 to 1945 and from 1951 to 1955. A renowned orator and writer, he is the only British prime minister to have won the Nobel Prize in Literature.

As a young army officer, Churchill saw action in India, the Sudan, and the Second Boer War. He became famous as a war correspondent and later went into politics. For fifty years, he remained at the forefront of British politics, serving in a number of political and cabinet posts. During World War I, he served as the first lord of the Admiralty until the British defeat at Gallipoli. He returned to government as chancellor of the Exchequer, but lost power because of his opposition to increased home rule in India and his support of Prince Edward VIII in his marriage to divorcee Wallis Simpson.

Churchill became an ardent critic of Adolf Hitler and pressured the British government to rearm. Upon the outbreak of the World War II, he was once again appointed first lord of the Admiralty. Following the resignation of Neville Chamberlain in the spring of 1940, Churchill became prime minister. His persistent refusal to consider appeasement, compromise, or defeat rallied British resistance to Hitler's Germany. He was particularly known for his

inspirational radio broadcasts to the British people and, with the help of the
Lend-Lease program with the United States, was able to lead Britain to
victory over Nazi Germany.

After the Conservative Party lost the postwar election, he was forced to
resign as prime minister and became leader of the Opposition. He again
became prime minister in 1951 before retiring in 1955. He remained active in
British society until his death in 1965, at the age of ninety (Lukacs, 2002).

THE STRUCTURAL FRAME

Structural frame leaders seek to develop a new model of the relationship of
structure, strategy, and environment for their organizations. Strategic planning, extensive preparation, and effecting change are priorities for them.
Their followers often describe them as being direct, authoritative, and hands-
on managers. As we will observe, Winston Churchill spent a fair amount of
his time operating out of the structural frame.

Most of the recorded instances of Churchill's use of leadership behavior
took place in preparation for and during World War II. He frequently used
structural frame leadership behavior in the form of a take-charge attitude
during those years. For example, in 1940, when Britain had the opportunity
to negotiate a peace treaty with Hitler, he decided that Hitler's track record
was not one that inspired confidence, so there would be no further negotiation or appeasement. Instead, he decided that war was inevitable and went
about mobilizing the forces necessary to be successful. In typical structural
frame fashion, Churchill was adamant that as long as he governed Britain,
Hitler would not win his war.

Churchill had had a structural frame attitude and a prescience about a
possible war even at an early age. When he was only twenty-five, he wrote in
his book *The River War*: "I hope that if evil days should come upon our
country, and the last army which a collapsing Empire could interpose between London and the invader was dissolving in rout and ruin, that there
would be some—even in these modern days—who would not care to accus-
tom themselves to the new order of things, and tamely survive the disaster"
(Lukacs, 2002, p. 4).

In a combination of structural and political frame behavior, Churchill
proposed what came to be known as his percentages agreement in a 1944
conference with Joseph Stalin in Moscow. Churchill argued that the governance of the various countries currently occupied by Russia should be shared
in the following way: Romania: Russia 90 percent; Great Britain 10 percent;
Greece: Russia 10 percent; Great Britain 90 percent; Yugoslavia: 50-50;

Hungary: 50-50; Bulgaria: Russia 75 percent; Great Britain 25 percent. His strategy in using such arbitrary percentages was to divert Stalin's attention from wanting to govern these countries totally.

Churchill was keenly aware that with Stalin's belligerent attitude there could very well have been a World War III immediately after the conclusion of World War II. Responding with his structural frame instincts, he went so far as to order General Montgomery and other British commanders to collect German arms, holding them in reserve for a possible confrontation with the Russians, especially in their anticipated attempt to occupy some countries in Western Europe.

After Churchill gave his Iron Curtain speech in 1946 in Fulton, Missouri, President Harry Truman advised Churchill that it might be prudent to tone down his rhetoric. In true structural frame style, Churchill would have none of it. He held steadfast to his disdain for Stalin, Communism, and the Soviet Union. And despite capitulating to Stalin on Poland and allowing Russia to occupy it after the war, Churchill had his victories in saving Greece from Soviet occupation and at least ensuring that Poland would continue to exist, thus allowing it to ultimately gain independence from Soviet domination.

Churchill used structural frame thinking in his longstanding vision of a permanent U.S.-Anglo partnership that would dominate the Western world. His unrealized vision went well beyond the end of World War II in that he looked ahead to a time when the two English-speaking democracies of the United States and Great Britain would govern the future of most of the world. "If we win victory, we shall have to assume the major responsibility for the new world order," he wrote (Lukacs, 2002, p. 54).

Still other structural frame leadership manifestations include Churchill's efforts in the development of the tank as a weapon of war during World War I, the reintroduction of the gold standard when he was the chancellor of the Exchequer in 1924, and his creation with Franklin D. Roosevelt of the novel concept of Lend-Lease during World War II. Suffice it to say that Winston Churchill made good and frequent use of structural frame leadership behavior.

THE HUMAN RESOURCE FRAME

Human resource frame leaders believe in people and communicate that belief. They are passionate about productivity through people. Although he was an aristocrat by birth and bearing, Churchill frequently utilized human resource frame leadership behavior.

One of Churchill's first uses of human resource frame behavior on a grand scale took place immediately after World War I, when he was one of those rare persons to speak up against mistreating the German people. He welcomed the 1925 Treaty of Locarno, which helped heal some of the wounds of the Versailles Treaty and proved that his image as the uncompromising bulldog was only partially accurate.

In perhaps his most notorious display of human resource frame behavior, Churchill was in the distinct minority in supporting King Edward VIII's intent to marry divorcee Wallis Simpson in 1936. Although English law prohibited a king from marrying a divorced woman, Churchill felt deeply for the king, much to his own political peril. Edward eventually abdicated and married Simpson.

Many historians suggest that perhaps Churchill's greatest virtue was his magnanimity. He easily forgave, letting bygones be bygones, and was often unapologetically moved to tears. In perhaps his greatest tribute, his daughter wrote of him: "It is hardly in the nature of things that your descendants should inherit your genius—but I earnestly hope that they may share in some way the qualities of your heart" (Lukacs, 2002, p. 154).

THE SYMBOLIC FRAME

In the symbolic frame, the organization is seen as a stage, a theater in which every actor plays certain roles and the symbolic leader attempts to communicate the right impressions to the right audiences. One could argue that with the possible exception of the political frame, Winston Churchill spent most of his time operating out of the symbolic frame.

Churchill's effective use of the symbolic frame was facilitated by his extraordinary way with words. For example, he, more than any of his contemporaries, foresaw the threatening rise of Nazism in Germany as early as 1924 and was able to articulate his concern in a way that attracted his counterparts' attention. "The enormous contingents of German youth growing to military manhood year by year are inspired by the fiercest sentiments, and the soul of Germany smolders with dreams of war of liberation or revenge," he wrote (Lukacs, 2002, p. 5).

By 1940, Churchill reduced the prewar situation into two unattractive alternatives: either Germany dominates all of Europe, or Russia dominates the Eastern portion of Europe and the other countries govern Western Europe. In other words, there was a choice between two evils: Germany and Russia. In his inimitable way, Churchill was able to express his slight preference for Russia in symbolic frame terms. "If Hitler invaded Hell," he declared, "I would at least make a favorable reference to the Devil in the House of Commons" (Lukacs, 2002, p. 12).

Churchill's ability to turn a phrase and/or coin a term was never more evident than in his so-called Iron Curtain speech, which he delivered at the behest of President Truman in a 1946 political fundraiser in Fulton, Missouri. Having seen his earlier prophecy of the dominating European presence of Russia in the form of the Soviet Union materialize, he described the Soviet Union as having hung an iron curtain across Central Europe. To reinforce this concept, he further utilized the symbolic frame by titling the last volume of his war memoirs *Triumph and Tragedy* because of the unnatural division of Europe and the Cold War that it spawned.

Churchill understood Stalin and Russia far better than most of his contemporaries and was also far better able to use symbolic frame leadership behavior to articulate his understanding. Of course, he abhorred Communism from the very beginning. He strenuously advocated Allied intervention in the Russian Civil War of 1919, believing that Communism needed to be "strangled in the cradle." He believed that the Bolsheviks were still weak enough to be overcome by their White Russian opponents. However, even after the Bolsheviks prevailed, he never gave up his belief that Communism was a seriously flawed economic and political system. In 1953, he prophetically said: "If I live my normal span I should assuredly see Eastern Europe free of Communism." Having lived until 1965, he was not off by much. He was, in fact, correct about the ultimate fate of Hitler and Nazism, and astonishingly correct about the fate of Stalin and Communism (Lukacs, 2002, p. 14).

Although he accurately predicted Communism's demise and considered Stalin more of a national than an international revolutionary, Churchill nevertheless considered Stalin and the Soviet Union a mystery. In yet another use of the symbolic frame, he is famous for saying: "I cannot forecast to you the action of Russia. It is a riddle wrapped in a mystery inside an enigma" (Lukacs, 2002, p. 25).

Churchill again used symbolic frame behavior in one of his letters to Franklin Roosevelt in trying to convince him to enter the war in Europe. He pointed out that if Britain were to be defeated, the resultant United States of Europe under Nazi command would be far stronger an opponent of the United States of America than it currently was. Thus, the time was right for the United States to enter the war, not to save Britain so much as to save itself. To pound in his point, he famously declared that Britain was fighting "by ourselves alone, but not *for* ourselves alone" (Lukacs, 2002, p. 95).

Churchill's use of symbolic frame behavior in the form of rhetoric hardened public opinion against a peaceful resolution to the Nazi advance and prepared Britain for a long and grueling war, convincing the British that they were about to enter their "finest hour." And at the height of the Battle of

Britain, he uttered another of his inspiring and enduring exhortations: "Never in the field of human conflict was so much owed by so many to so few" (Lukacs, 2002). So effective was Churchill in projecting his image through symbolic means, that the Russians were the first to refer to him as "the British Bulldog"—a nickname that stuck.

THE SYMBOLIC FRAME AND HUMOR

Many times, effective leaders utilize symbolic frame behavior in the form of humorous stories, jokes, and witticisms. Winston Churchill was particularly fond of engaging in this form of symbolic frame leadership behavior. Humorous quotes attributed to him include:

- A lie gets halfway around the world before the truth has a chance to get its pants on.
- A fanatic is one who can't change his mind and won't change the subject.
- Ending a sentence with a preposition is something up with which we will not put.
- Golf is a game whose aim is to hit a very small ball into an even smaller hole, with weapons singularly ill-designed for the purpose.
- History will be kind to me for I intend to write it.
- However beautiful the strategy, you should occasionally look at the results.
- I like pigs. Dogs look up to us. Cats look down on us. Pigs treat us as equals.
- I'm just preparing my impromptu remarks.
- Now this is not the end. It is not even the beginning of the end, but it is, perhaps, the end of the beginning.
- The Americans will always do the right thing . . . after they've exhausted all the alternatives.
- The problems of victory are more agreeable than the problems of defeat, but they are no less difficult.
- There is nothing more exhilarating than to be shot at without result.
- This report, by its very length, defends itself against the risk of being read.
- When I am abroad I always make it a rule never to criticize or attack the government of my country. I make up for lost time when I am at home. (Lukacs, 2002; workinghumor.com)

THE POLITICAL FRAME

Leaders operating out of the political frame clarify what they want and what they can get. Political leaders are realists above all. They never let what they want cloud their judgment about what is possible. They assess the distribution of power and interests. Of course, being the consummate politician that he was, Winston Churchill made frequent and mostly effective use of the political frame.

It was Churchill's vision of a postwar Russian danger that prompted his use of political frame behavior in urging the United States to devise an Anglo-American strategy in the last year of the war to advance as far east in Europe as possible so as to thwart the forward thrust of the Russian armies into Western Europe. He had the prescience to know that Stalin would want to include all the conquered lands in the new Russian empire.

Churchill knew, however, that even with the abundant sea and air military resources of the Anglo-American forces, they would not be able to defeat Nazi Germany alone. They desperately needed the primitive might of Communist Russia. Thus, Churchill engaged in political frame leadership behavior and acceded to Russian demands so that Russia would join the United States and Britain in the war against the Axis powers. And the reality was that Hitler's unsuccessful invasion of Russia eventually led to an Allied victory and the survival of Churchill's beloved Britain.

As pointed out earlier, Churchill believed that half of Europe was better than none, so he went about using political frame leadership behavior to ensure that the alternative to Germany, namely Russia, joined the Allies. Nevertheless, strategies like that mentioned above were developed so that the Russians would be able to claim the least amount of postwar territory possible. But his political frame designs were somewhat thwarted when the Allied supreme commander, General Dwight D. Eisenhower, unilaterally informed Stalin that the Allied armies would not advance any further in Europe in deference to the Russians.

In response to what he saw as a betrayal by Eisenhower, Churchill once again engaged in political frame leadership behavior and called for a summit between the British, the Americans, and the Russians to resolve the issue before it got out of hand. Upon hearing of the summit, Eisenhower objected, because he believed that such a meeting would project weakness. But Churchill challenged Eisenhower's objection by stating that "appeasement from weakness and fear is . . . fatal. Appeasement from strength is magnanimous . . . and might be the surest way to peace" (Lukacs, 2002, p. 81).

Churchill and Eisenhower had their share of disagreements both during and after the war, but Churchill was always careful to utilize political frame behavior because both the United States and Eisenhower were essential to

Britain's welfare. For example, in 1953, when Churchill was again prime minister and Eisenhower was president, he wrote to Eisenhower, saying: "But, now that you have assumed supreme political office in your country, I am most anxious that nothing should be published which might seem to others to threaten our current relations in our public duties or to impair the sympathy and understanding which exists between our countries. I have therefore gone over the book [his *Memoirs*] in the last few months and have taken great pains to ensure that it contains nothing which might imply that there was in those days any controversy or lack of confidence between us" (Lukacs, 2002, p. 70).

THE MORAL FRAME

The moral frame is my own contribution to situational leadership theory. In my view, the moral frame completes situational leadership theory. Without it, leaders could just as easily use their leadership skills for promoting evil as for promoting good. Leaders operating out of the moral frame are concerned about their obligations to their followers. Moral frame leaders use some type of moral compass to direct their behavior. They practice what has been described as servant leadership and are concerned with those individuals and groups that are marginalized in their organizations and in society. In short, they are concerned about equality, fairness, and social justice.

There is much evidence that Winston Churchill filtered his leadership behavior through a moral frame. One stark example of this was in his dealings with Russia vis-à-vis Poland after World War II. Churchill felt a moral commitment to Poland in that Hitler's invasion of Poland was the reason that Britain declared war on Germany. In addition, after Hitler occupied the country, nearly one hundred thousand Poles migrated to Britain and fought bravely as part of the British army. But Britain's alliance with Poland did little in dissuading Stalin from continuing to occupy Poland after the war. The best Churchill could do was prevent the official annexation of Poland by the Soviets, allowing it to remain independent—albeit a Soviet puppet regime. Still, that status made it easier for Poland to eventually gain real independence than it would have been if it were absorbed by Russia after the war.

The Poland situation was but one of the many instances of Churchill's adherence to moral and ethical standards. In contrast to two of his contemporaries, Adolf Hitler and Joseph Stalin, Churchill's constant use of a moral frame through which to filter his leadership behavior was exemplary.

SITUATIONAL LEADERSHIP IMPLICATIONS AND CONCLUSION

Situational models of leadership differ from earlier trait and behavioral models in asserting that no single way of leading works in all situations. Rather, appropriate behavior depends on the circumstances at a given time. Effective managers diagnose the situation, identify the leadership style or behavior that will be most effective, and then determine whether they can implement the required style.

We have seen that Winston Churchill was active among all five leadership frames and for the most part behaved moderately within each frame—and he invariably did so while maintaining an unfailing sense of humor. He was such a disciple of situational leadership theory that many historians accuse him of double standards. For example, he fought bitterly and persistently against the appeasement of Hitler, but was perfectly willing to continually appease Stalin. He also attacked his own government for abandoning Czechoslovakia to Germany, but in contrast was a willing participant in abandoning Poland to Russia. Of course, all of these instances occurred in different situations, thus requiring different responses. Britain depended on Russia's allegiance for its very survival. So it made sense to behave differently toward it as compared to its deadly enemy, Germany. Churchill knew exactly what he was doing and with whom he was dealing, observing that "the Soviets were like crocodiles, one never knew when to pat their heads or hit them" (Lukacs, 2002, p. 34).

Churchill further demonstrated the situational nature of his leadership behavior during the course of his political career. He began his parliamentary career as a Conservative in 1900, but even then he was no party stalwart. Over time, he switched to the Liberal Party, only to switch back again toward the end of his career to the Conservative Party.

In 1931, he again showed how situational he could be even in regard to his love for democracy. He publicly declared that under certain circumstances a dictatorial regime may be timely. In 1932 he wrote about universal suffrage: "Why at this moment should we force upon the untutored races of India that very system, the inconveniences of which are now felt even in the most highly developed nations, the United States, Germany, France and in England itself?" (Lukacs, 2002, p. 137).

Again being situational, he clearly preferred Fascism to Communism. In Parliament in 1937 he said: "I will not pretend that if I had to choose between Communism and Nazism, I would choose Communism." But when it came to choosing between Nazi Fascism and Communism, he chose Communism. To sum up his situational leadership leanings, he famously said: "An unchanging mind is an admirable possession—a possession which I devoutly hope I shall never possess" (Lukacs, 2002, p. 139). In conclusion, Winston Churchill is a leader whom leaders and aspiring leaders would do well to emulate.

Chapter Eight

Harry Truman

If you can't stand the heat, get out of the kitchen. —Harry Truman

BACKGROUND

Harry S. Truman was born in 1884 in Lamar, but ultimately settled in Independence, Missouri. He worked on his family farm during his early years and attended local public schools, where he was an excellent student and especially liked history and government. He was also an excellent piano player. Because of family circumstances, Truman never graduated from college, but he did attend two years of law school.

Truman worked at a variety of jobs after high school graduation and later went back home to help his family make ends meet by working on the family farm, which lasted until the outbreak of World War I. Truman enlisted in the National Guard, and in 1917 he volunteered for frontline service. He fought in France as a commander of a field artillery unit. He was part of the Meuse-Argonne campaign and was at Verdun at the end of the war.

After the war, Truman opened a haberdashery, but the business went bankrupt after only two years. Truman was then elected administrative judge of his local county. From 1935 to 1945 he served as a Democratic United States senator from Missouri. In 1945, he was chosen as the vice presidential running mate of Franklin D. Roosevelt.

After succeeding to the presidency upon the death of Franklin Roosevelt, Truman ran and was elected to a second term in 1948. He was opposed by Republican Thomas E. Dewey and surprisingly won reelection by a slim margin. During his presidency he made the decision to use the atomic bomb to end the war with Japan. He was also president during the Korean War and the beginning of the so-called Cold War with the Soviet Union. He was also responsible for the Truman Doctrine, which promised U.S. support of free peoples resisting attempted subjugation by armed minorities or outside pressures.

Truman also joined Great Britain in resisting the Soviet blockade of Berlin by airlifting supplies to the city's residents. One of his greatest achievements was the endorsement of the Marshall Plan to help rebuild Europe after the war, spending over $13 billion in the effort. And in 1948, when the state of Israel was created, the United States under Truman was among the first countries to recognize the new nation. After a lifetime of dedicated public service, Truman passed away at the age of eighty-eight (McCullough, 1992).

THE STRUCTURAL FRAME

Structural frame leaders seek to develop a new model of the relationship of structure, strategy, and environment for their organizations. Strategic planning, extensive preparation, and effecting change are priorities for them. They are often described as firm and direct by their followers. We will find that Harry Truman was very active in the structural frame.

Even though he never went to college, like most structural frame leaders, Truman was conspicuously studious, spending hours in the library. He was fond of telling reporters that he and his boyhood friend, Charlie Ross, had vowed to read every book in their town library. He claimed that they had been faithful to that vow. He was particularly drawn to the life of Benjamin Franklin and the humor of Mark Twain.

He established his structural frame tendencies in his first job, as a clerk in a bank vault. His supervisor described him as an ideal employee. "He is a willing worker, almost always here and tries hard to please everybody. We never had a boy in the vault like him before. He watches everything very closely and by his watchfulness, detects many errors which a careless boy would let slip through. His appearance is good and his habits and character are of the best" (McCullough, 1992, p. 69).

Operating out of the structural frame, Truman got himself appointed a deacon in the local branch of the Masons. The next year, he established a new lodge in a room over a store on Main Street. By age twenty-six he was firmly established as an important figure in the community. He continued his structural frame behavior in the military. In less than a year after his first command responsibility, he had transformed what had been commonly thought of as the worst battery in the regiment into what was regarded as one of the best.

Most of Truman's frontline experience in World War I was in the Meuse-Argonne campaign. The effectiveness of his structural frame leadership behavior can be assessed by noting that the 129th Field Artillery as a whole lost 129 men in the battle, while the battery that Truman led suffered only three men wounded, and none dead. "Well, part of it was luck and part of it was good leadership," said one of Truman's privates. "Some of the other batteries didn't have that kind of leadership" (McCullough, 1992, p. 135).

Invariably, some of a leader's structural frame behavior is not successful, and Truman was no exception. Despite his thoughtful planning in partnering with his lifelong friend Eddie Jacobson in the purchase of a haberdashery business, the shop went bankrupt within two years. Looking back, however, Truman admitted that he had not employed enough structural frame behavior, noting that the decision to purchase the business was made rather impulsively and may have been designed to impress his fiancée, Bess, and her mother.

Once he became a U.S. senator from Missouri, Truman continued in his use of the structural frame. Noting that there seemed to be excessive and inefficient spending on defense contracts in preparation for a possible entrance into World War II, Truman proposed the establishment of a special committee to examine the awarding of these contracts. His obscurity neared an end when the committee was dubbed the Truman Committee. The committee, officially named the Senate Special Committee to Investigate the National Defense Program, was ultimately responsible for saving the federal government more than $500 million. Engaging in a little symbolic frame behavior, Truman stood by quietly and allowed it to be informally named after him.

Truman once again utilized structural frame leadership behavior in negotiating with Joseph Stalin after World War II. At the Yalta Treaty negotiations, the Russians insisted on a puppet government in Poland. Truman remarked that it seemed that any agreements with the Russians were a one-way street. If the Russians did not want to cooperate in a more collaborative way, he declared, they could all "go to hell." He was later talked out of taking such an apodictic position and convinced to employ some political frame behavior and compromise with the Soviets over Poland.

Perhaps Truman's most famous (or infamous) use of structural frame leadership behavior was in the decision to drop the atomic bomb on Hiroshima and Nagasaki. "Although I reached my decision independently," he pointed out, "I felt that to extract a genuine surrender from the Emperor and his military advisors, there must be administered a tremendous shock which could carry convincing proof of our power to destroy the Empire. Such an effective shock would save many times the number of lives, both American and Japanese, that it would cost" (McCullough, 1992, p. 394).

Knowing that the atomic bomb was in the last stages of development, Truman once again utilized structural frame behavior, but with a human resource frame touch. He signed the Potsdam Declaration warning the Japanese that if they did not concede to an unconditional surrender, he would "prosecute the war against Japan until she ceases to exist." It was Truman's last-ditch effort to offer the Japanese an opportunity to save the lives of their own citizens. In his heart of hearts he knew that it would be an exercise in futility, since during the entire war, even when faced with certain death, not a single Japanese unit had ever surrendered (McCullough, 1992, p. 436).

Truman's structural frame behavior continued after the war; his very first postwar message to Congress presented a very controversial twenty-one-point social program that increased unemployment compensation, raised the minimum wage, established the Fair Employment Practices Committee, reformed the income tax code, established crop insurance for farmers, and proposed a national compulsory health insurance program. In effect, it was a follow-up to Roosevelt's New Deal. Using symbolic frame leadership behavior, he dubbed the twenty-one-point program the Fair Deal, and engaging in some political frame behavior, he presented his progressive agenda to Congress in one big package rather than piecemeal.

Truman's other programs that were the result of his frequent use of structural frame leadership included the Berlin Airlift; the Marshall Plan, which helped redevelop Europe after World War II; the Truman Doctrine, whereby the United States would aid countries striving toward democracy; and the recognition of the state of Israel.

For one last example of Truman's use of structural frame leadership behavior, we can look to the Korean War. In what was always referred to as a police action rather than a full-fledged war, Truman used structural frame behavior in endorsing General Douglas MacArthur's bold plan to attack the rear flank of the North Korean army at Inchon. The plan's success became the turning point of the war, allowing the South Koreans to reclaim all the territory they had lost. However, when MacArthur arbitrarily carried the war north of the thirty-eighth parallel, the Chinese entered the war and routed the South Koreans. Truman used structural frame leadership behavior once again and unceremoniously fired MacArthur (McCullough, 1992).

THE HUMAN RESOURCE FRAME

Human resource frame leaders believe in people and communicate that belief. They are passionate about productivity through people. Being the people person that he was, Harry Truman spent much of his time operating out of the human resource frame.

Truman's concern for others was demonstrated in his response to his fiancée, Bess, whose reaction to his enlisting was to suggest that they get married before he left for Europe. Displaying human resource frame behavior, he almost instinctively responded, "No!" Bess should not be made to tie herself to a man who could return home a cripple, or worse yet, not at all, he said. They would have to wait until he returned home in one piece.

One of Truman's fellow officers during World War I gave a firsthand account of his frequent use of the human resource frame. "He was not in any way the arrogant, bossy type, or Prussian type of officer," he commented. "And he was a disciplinarian but he was very fair. I don't know, I can't describe what the personal magnetism was except that he had it" (McCullough, 1992, p. 118).

Truman once again engaged in human resource frame behavior in World War I when he let a soldier with a severely twisted ankle ride his horse, which was against protocol. His superior officer flew into a rage and demanded that the soldier dismount. Truman intervened and told the officer that as long as he was in charge of the battery, the injured soldier would ride his horse.

Truman demonstrated his human resource frame tendencies in his position on civil rights. In 1940, as Senator Harry Truman from Missouri, he was considered a radical because of his strong stance against racial discrimination. In one of his speeches he declared: "I believe in the brotherhood of man; not only the brotherhood of white men, but the brotherhood of all men before the law. Negroes have been preyed upon by all types of exploiters, from the installment salesmen of clothing, pianos, and furniture to the vendors of vice. The majority of our Negro people find but cold comfort in shanties and tenements. Surely, as freedmen, they are entitled to something better than this" (McCullough, 1992, p. 247).

On his first tour of the White House as president, Truman showed his human resource side in being annoyed to find that the photographers were treated as second-class citizens among the press corps. Unlike the writers, who were provided with the comforts of a pressroom, the photographers were confined to a cramped, windowless space in the bowels of the White House. Truman would not allow this discrimination to continue and ordered that the photographers have the same privileges as the reporters.

In another display of human resource frame behavior, Truman brought the despised former president, Herbert Hoover, out of retirement and provided him with the opportunity to reconstruct his image by putting him in charge of famine relief in Europe after World War II. Having been successful in this type of activity after World War I, Hoover efficiently managed the famine relief program and was, in fact, somewhat able to restore his public image.

As the result of his human resource behavior, those around Truman were extremely loyal to him. In the years after his exit from the White House, none of those who worked for him would ever speak or write anything negative about him or belittle him in any way. There would be no vindictive "tell all" books written about him by his employees or others closest to him.

Other instances of Truman's devotion to the human resource frame include the establishment of the Marshall Plan to rebuild Europe after the war, his introduction of state and federal laws against lynching and poll taxes, restitution for the Japanese Americans who were confined during World War II, his support for a Jewish homeland, and his progressive domestic agenda that included a proposal for universal health care. Suffice it to say, Harry Truman was quite active in the human resource frame.

THE SYMBOLIC FRAME

In the symbolic frame, the organization is seen as a stage, a theater in which every actor plays certain roles and the symbolic leader attempts to communicate the right impression to the right audiences. As we shall see, Harry Truman spent a fair amount of time operating out of the symbolic frame, especially in the form of jokes, humorous stories, and witticisms.

Interestingly enough, among Truman's earliest memories of growing up in Missouri was a childhood filled with laughter. He remembered chasing a frog around the yard, laughing each time it jumped. According to his grandmother, who had reared her share of children, young Harry had an extraordinary sense of humor for a two-year-old. Another source of laughter was the memory of his mother dropping him from an upstairs window into the outstretched arms of his very muscular Uncle Harry. Of course, this all happened in 1887, when the standard of care was evidently not quite what it is today.

Truman became aware of the positive effect the use of symbolic frame behavior could have on one's image early on, when he had an opportunity to avoid playing a part in World War I. He was thirty-three at the outset of the war, two years beyond the age limit set for the military draft. He had long since been discharged from the National Guard, and his eyesight was significantly below that needed for a deferment. He was the sole provider for his mother and sister and could have stayed on the farm, producing food for his family and the war effort—which was considered patriotic at the time. But out of a strong sense of duty, he enlisted in the army immediately upon hearing the radio broadcast in which Woodrow Wilson urged Congress to declare war on Germany.

In his first action on the front lines, Truman used symbolic frame leadership behavior when, while others were panicking and retreating from the German onslaught, he courageously stood his ground. His uncharacteristic outburst of profanity during his charge toward the enemy stunned his men into action. For years afterward, at reunions, the survivors would joke about Battery D's so-called Battle of Who Run (McCullough, 1992, p. 122).

Like most symbolic frame leaders, Truman was acutely aware of the image he was projecting. He was notoriously fastidious about his dress and his comportment and loved being called "Judge," when he was in actuality a county administrator reviewing, overseeing, and awarding building contracts. Nonetheless, he enjoyed the prestige of the job and the way people greeted him with respect as he made his way to the courthouse each morning.

Even with his concern for his appearance, however, he was more concerned that he appear competent and honest. Instead of borrowing county funds from Kansas City banks at 6 percent, as was the custom of his predecessors, he used both symbolic and political frame behavior and went to Chicago and St. Louis to negotiate loans at 4 percent, and later 2.5 percent. Charged by the Democratic establishment with inflicting unjust punishment on the Kansas City bankers and their stockholders, he responded by pointing out that maybe the county taxpayers had some rights in the matter too.

Ever the symbolic frame leader, Senator Truman, who was by now a colonel in the Army Reserve and knew how scarce experienced officers were, dramatically went to Army Chief of Staff General George Marshall's office to enlist for duty in World War II. General Marshall had the good sense to tell Truman that he would be of far greater service to his country if he remained in the Senate. The two of them became lifelong friends, and Marshall went on to serve in the Truman administration.

The 1944 Democratic Convention was anything but business as usual in its choice of a vice presidential candidate. The stakes were particularly high in that the conventional wisdom was that Franklin Roosevelt would not live to carry out his full term. So the unspoken agreement was that they were in fact choosing two presidential candidates. Truman ultimately prevailed for the vice presidential nomination as "the Missouri Compromise" and "the Common Denominator." Ever the symbolic leader, however, Truman famously deferred to Dwight Eisenhower until Eisenhower decided not to run.

Truman used symbolic frame behavior to galvanize his image as a loyal and forthright man. The notorious Missouri party boss Tom Prendergast had been instrumental in Truman's climb up the political ladder. When Prendergast was sent to prison for graft, Truman, then vice president, continued to support him. Upon hearing of Prendergast's death, Truman immediately announced his intention of attending the disgraced party boss's funeral. Using symbolic leadership behavior, he dressed for the day with his customary care and donned his "uniform" to express loyalty to an old friend no matter the political consequences.

Truman expressed himself symbolically in both word and deed. Upon becoming president upon Franklin Roosevelt's death, he declared: "There have been few men in all of history the equal of this man into whose shoes I am stepping. I pray to God I can measure up to the task." And, being no friend of J. Edgar Hoover, he was not intimidated to use symbolic frame behavior toward him: "We want no Gestapo or Secret Police. The FBI is tending in that direction. They are dabbling in sex-like scandals and plain blackmail . . . This must stop," he declared (McCullough, 1992, p. 367).

The appointment of General George Marshall as secretary of state was one of Truman's more significant uses of the symbolic frame. The reaction on virtually all fronts was immediate approval of the popular World War II general. Truman's public approval rate immediately grew to its highest level during his administration. He also made good use of the symbolic frame in his renewal of Theodore Roosevelt's Good Neighbor policy by making an unscheduled visit to Mexico City's historic Chapultepec Castle, where, with this one gesture celebrating Mexico's independence from Spain, he did more for Mexican-American relations than any president in a century.

Another instance of Truman's use of the symbolic frame came with his Truman Doctrine speech before Congress in 1947. In effect, he was committing the United States to supporting democracies throughout the world in their resistance of Communism. Greece and Turkey were the first countries to receive such aid. "I believe that it must be the policy of the U.S. to support free peoples who are resisting attempted subjugation by armed minorities or by outside pressures," he declared. "Should we fail to aid Greece and Turkey in this fateful hour, the effect will be far reaching to the West as well as the East" (McCullough, 1992, p. 548).

Truman was famous for showing humility in a symbolic way. For example, even though it was mostly his brainchild, he gave full credit for the Marshall Plan to the World War II general. When Clark Clifford suggested that it be called the Truman Plan, he dismissed the idea out of hand. Ultimately, the Marshall Plan contributed $17 billion toward the rebuilding of war-torn Europe.

Truman promoted his pro-union principles through the astute use of symbolic frame behavior. When the Republican-controlled Congress passed the anti-union Taft-Hartley Act, he vetoed it even though he knew that Congress could and would override his veto. But by vetoing it he demonstrated that he would live up to his principles despite the political ramifications. He again used symbolic frame leadership behavior in support of his principles when he called for federal action against lynching, against the imposition of a poll tax, against inequality in education and employment, and against racial discrimination. His position was completely unexpected coming from a Missouri politician, but consistent with the man who coined the phrase, "If you can't stand the heat, get out of the kitchen" (McCullough, 1992).

Truman wanted to do something symbolically to support the rights of the Jewish survivors of the terrible Holocaust. As a senator, he had promised the Jews that he would fight for a homeland for them in Palestine. As president, he began his push for a Jewish homeland as early as 1945, wanting it to be part of the negotiated peace after World War II. Finally, in 1947, Truman and the Jews saw their dreams materialize in the form of the state of Israel. Of course, the United States was one of the first foreign countries to recognize the independent state of Israel. So happy were the Jewish people that the chief rabbi of Israel, Isaac Halevi Herzog, was moved to declare of Truman: "God put you in your mother's womb so you would be the instrument to bring the rebirth of Israel after two thousand years" (McCullough, 1992, p. 620).

In 1948, when Russia blockaded all rail, highway, and water traffic in and out of Berlin, Truman once again used the symbolic frame in conjunction with the structural and political frames and responded with the Berlin Airlift, which became one of the most significant logistical achievements of the postwar era and one of Truman's proudest moments. It raised the morale of the entire free world in its Cold War fight against Communism.

Truman used symbolic frame leadership behavior to help him win the 1948 presidential campaign. Facing almost insurmountable odds in the person of New York governor Thomas Dewey, Truman set out on what has become known as his Whistle-Stop Campaign, whereby he would travel some twenty-two thousand miles by rail, crisscrossing the United States and stopping at each town along the way. "Give 'em hell, Harry!" someone yelled from the crowd, which immediately became Truman's battle cry. He replied, "I never gave anybody hell, I just told the truth and they thought it was hell" (McCullough, 1992, p. 664).

Immediately upon reelection, Truman once again engaged in symbolic frame behavior and announced what he called the Point Four Program. With it he promised to continue to support the United Nations and the Marshall Plan, join a new defense relationship among freedom-loving nations (the North Atlantic Treaty Organization, or NATO), and make the benefits of American technology available to third-world countries. Ultimately, the plan became known as the Fair Deal.

Truman engaged in symbolic frame behavior in dealing with Senator Joseph McCarthy during the Communist scare in the late 1940s. When a State Department employee, Alger Hiss, was convicted of being a Communist spy, Senator McCarthy famously held up a list in front of newspaper reporters, which he said contained the names of 205 known Communists who worked in the State Department. Truman responded in his typically colorful style: "I think the greatest asset that the Kremlin has is Senator McCarthy" (McCullough, 1992, p. 763).

When the North Koreans invaded South Korea in 1947, Truman, fearing a domino effect, authorized what he called a police action, sending munitions and troops to aid the South Koreans. In typical symbolic frame fashion, he declared: "I remembered how each time that the democracies failed to act it encouraged the aggressors to keep going." Later, after losing virtually all of South Korea, General MacArthur proposed a risky attack on the rear flank of the North Koreans at the port of Inchon. But after winning that battle, he arbitrarily carried the war north of the thirty-eighth parallel and was intent on invading China, whereupon Truman used both structural and symbolic frame leadership behavior and assertively replaced him with General Matthew Ridgway (McCullough, 1992, p. 776).

THE SYMBOLIC FRAME AND HUMOR

Harry Truman was particularly fond of engaging in symbolic frame leadership behavior in the form of humor. For example, at a Gridiron Club dinner in 1946, Truman declared that General William Tecumseh Sherman had been wrong. Rather than war being so, "I'm telling you I find peace is hell" (McCullough, 1992, p. 476). And when finally firing the insubordinate, but popular, Secretary of Commerce Henry Wallace, the last New Dealer still in the cabinet, his chief of staff commented that Truman would rather be right than be president. Truman clarified the statement by saying, "I would rather be *anything* than President" (McCullough, 1992, p. 518). Other humorous quotes attributed to Truman are as follows:

- A politician is a man who understands government and it takes a politician to run a government. A statesman is a politician who's been dead ten or fifteen years.
- All the president is, is a glorified public relations man who spends his time flattering, kissing, and kicking people to get them to do what they are supposed to do anyway.
- Any man who has had the job I've had and didn't have a sense of humor wouldn't still be here.
- I don't give a damn about "The Missouri Waltz" but I can't say it out loud because it's the song of Missouri. It's as bad as "The Star-Spangled Banner" so far as music is concerned.
- I have found the best way to give advice to your children is to find out what they want and then advise them to do it.

- I never give them hell. I just tell the truth and they think it's hell.
- If you can't stand the heat, get out of the kitchen.
- It's a recession when your neighbor loses his job; it's a depression when you lose yours.
- My choice early in life was either to be a piano-player in a whorehouse or a politician. And to tell the truth, there's hardly any difference.
- Suppose you were an idiot. And suppose you were a Republican. But I repeat myself.
- The only things worth learning are the things you learn after you know it all.
- The White House is the finest prison in the world.
- When you get to be President, there are all those things, the honors, the twenty-one gun salutes, all those things. You have to remember it isn't for you. It's for the Presidency. (McCullough, 1992; workinghumor.com)

THE POLITICAL FRAME

Leaders operating out of the political frame clarify what they want and what they can get. Political leaders are realists above all. They never let what they want cloud their judgment about what is possible. They assess the distribution of power and interests. By definition, career politicians like Harry Truman spend a great deal of their time in the political frame.

In political frame behavior that came back to haunt him, Truman befriended "Big Jim" Prendergast and in doing so became part of the Kansas City, Missouri, Democratic political machine. Big Jim's younger brother, Tom, became one of Truman's best friends as he rose up the political ladder in his home state. But after Prendergast was imprisoned for voter fraud and graft, Truman's connection shadowed him throughout his career. As a member of the U.S. Senate, Truman became deridingly known as the "Senator from Prendergast."

In a rather belated application of political frame behavior, upon becoming county judge, Truman initially was convinced by some of his political friends to join the Ku Klux Klan. But when he found that membership required him to never hire a Catholic, Jew, or Negro, he remembered that he had commanded a mostly Catholic battery in France, and renounced his membership.

At the Potsdam Conference after World War II, Truman used political frame leadership behavior in his negotiations with Joseph Stalin. Although Stalin held the upper hand because his armies occupied much of Eastern Europe, he did not get all that he wanted. For example, Truman was able to keep the Soviets from having a trusteeship over Italy's former colonies in Africa, a naval base on the Bosphorus, and total control over Germany's industrial Ruhr Valley. In order to gain these concessions, however, Truman and the Allies had to agree to allow Russia to occupy and/or set up puppet regimes in many of the countries of Eastern Europe.

When Patrick Hurley resigned his position as ambassador to China because he believed that the State Department was in bed with Communist China, Truman engaged in political frame leadership behavior and avoided the criticism that his administration was sympathetic to Communism by immediately appointing the well-known anticommunist General George Marshall to the position.

After enduring national steel and coal strikes, Truman's support of unionism started to wane. So when the nation's first railroad strike began, in 1946, he decided to employ a little political frame behavior and threatened to go to Congress to tell them that he had decided to draft the striking rail workers into the army. The proposal was ultimately defeated in the Senate by an overwhelming vote, but Truman had made his point: that he was perfectly willing to employ draconian measures to avoid the continuation of the strike—and, in fact, his threats brought a quick end to the strike.

In addition to being symbolic, support for a Jewish homeland was, of course, politically motivated. Truman's employment of political frame behavior in this case resulted in his carrying the states of Pennsylvania, Illinois, and New York in the 1948 presidential election. Over four million Jews resided in those three states combined.

During that same presidential campaign, Truman further engaged in a combination of political frame and symbolic frame behavior when the Republican-controlled Congress continued to stonewall his legislative agenda. He dramatically called Congress back into session from its summer recess. "I am going to call Congress back and ask them to pass laws to halt rising prices, to meet the housing crisis—which they are saying they are for in their platform," he declared. "I shall ask them to act upon . . . aid to education, which they say they are for . . . civil rights legislation, which they say they are for." It was no surprise to Truman that the two-week special session of Congress accomplished very little, but he made it clear to the American electorate that it was the Republicans that were standing in the way of social progress (McCullough, 1992, p. 643).

In one last instance of Truman's use of political frame leadership behavior, he lobbied for what became the first-ever government allowance for a former president. In 1958, Congress passed a law providing former presidents with a $25,000 annual pension, money for staff office space, and free mailing privileges (McCullough, 1992).

THE MORAL FRAME

The moral frame is my own contribution to situational leadership theory. In my view, the moral frame completes situational leadership theory. Without it, leaders could just as easily use their leadership skills for promoting evil as for promoting good. Leaders operating out of the moral frame are concerned about their obligations to their followers. Moral frame leaders use some type of moral compass to direct their behavior. They practice what has been described as servant leadership and are concerned with those individuals and groups that are marginalized in their organizations and in society. In short, they are concerned about equality, fairness, and social justice. There are a number of instances that indicate that Harry Truman had a strong moral code.

Truman's belief in the importance of having a moral frame through which a leader can filter his or her leadership behavior is evident from some of the leaders in history that he admired. He was particularly fond of Andrew Jackson and Robert E. Lee. Truman was fond of quoting Lee's views on honesty and courage. "You must be frank with the world; frankness is the child of honesty and courage. Say just what you mean to do on every occasion, and take it for granted that you mean to do good. Never do anything wrong to make a friend or keep one; the man who requires you to do so is clearly purchased at a sacrifice," Lee declared. Truman himself adopted the motto, "I think there's more to acting than in talking" (McCullough, 1992, p. 44).

As a judge, Truman was scrupulous about money, treating the public money as if it were his own. When a road bond issue was passed, for example, Tom Prendergast was outraged to hear that Truman actually meant to keep his promise to voters and preclude favoritism being practiced in the contracting process. "The Boss wanted me to give a lot of crooked contractors the inside and I couldn't," he wrote (McCullough, 1992, p. 184).

Truman always considered the decision to drop the atomic bomb on Hiroshima and Nagasaki a moral decision. On the morning of the day that the first bomb was dropped, he attended a Catholic mass, after already having been at an earlier Protestant service. To his wife, Bess, who accompanied him to the Catholic service, Truman remarked: "I've already been to a Protestant service so I guess I should stand in good with the Almighty for the coming week—and my how I'll need it" (McCullough, 1992, p. 436).

SITUATIONAL LEADERSHIP ANALYSIS AND CONCLUSION

Situational models of leadership differ from earlier trait and behavioral models in asserting that no single way of leading works in all situations. Rather, appropriate behavior depends on the circumstances at a given time. Effective managers diagnose the situation, identify the leadership style or behavior that will be most effective, and then determine whether they can implement the required style.

We saw that Truman was active at various times in all the leadership frames and behaved moderately both among and within the various frames. At Yalta, for example, the new president decided to use some decidedly structural frame behavior, saying: "I am here to make decisions, and whether they prove right or wrong, I'm going to make them." However, he instructed his top advisor, Harry Hopkins, to use either a diplomatic approach with Stalin or a baseball-bat approach, whichever would work better (McCullough, 1992, p. 384).

We also saw how he moved from one frame to another in his union relationships. The change in Truman from a pro-union Democrat to a conservative Democrat was evident as his presidency progressed. There was the flare-up with the United Mine Workers president, John L. Lewis, in 1947. With yet another coal strike on the horizon, Truman took Lewis to court for allegedly violating the Smith-Connally Act, which prohibited strikes against government-owned facilities, the coal miners at the time being temporarily under government seizure. This resulted in a $3 million fine imposed upon the United Mine Workers.

Truman was particularly effective acting out of the symbolic frame, especially in displaying a well-developed sense of humor. He is remembered not only as the first president to recommend Medicare and for his courage in ardently supporting civil rights, but also for his ability to retain his sense of humor in even the most turbulent times. His Whistle-Stop Campaign was remembered as one of the most affirming moments of his times. His decision to drop the atomic bomb to end World War II and his decision not to use atomic weapons in the Korean War were testaments to his flexible leadership style. He was the kind of president that the founding fathers had envisioned, being a man from and for the people. He rose up from humble beginnings to become the most powerful leader in the world. We can all learn a great deal about leadership by studying and emulating the leadership behavior of Harry S. Truman.

Chapter Nine

Casey Stengel

My advice to you players is to buy stock in Pennsylvania Railroad, because if you don't start playing better ball there's gonna be so many of you riding trains outta here that railroad stocks are a cinch to go up. —Casey Stengel

BACKGROUND

Casey Stengel was a legendary baseball manager, most notably with the New York Yankees. He was born in Kansas City in 1890; he acquired his nickname, Casey, when he began his major league career and his teammates began referring to him as K.C. after his hometown. The "K.C." eventually evolved into "Casey." In the 1950s the sportswriters bestowed yet another nickname on him, "the Old Perfessor," for his sharp wit and his tendency to deliver long, sometimes unintelligible, soliloquies on baseball.

Stengel was a very good athlete but had no particular illusions of sports as a long-term profession, and he initially had aspirations of a career in dentistry. However, during his dentistry training he was drafted by the Brooklyn Dodgers. After a requisite stint in the minor leagues, he was brought up to the Dodgers, and his career flourished.

Stengel was an outfielder on several teams in the National League. He played in three World Series and finished his career with a very respectable batting average of .284 in fourteen major league seasons.

Stengel earned his reputation from managing rather than playing. His first managerial positions with the Brooklyn Dodgers and Boston Braves, however, were not very successful. Nevertheless, Stengel eventually proved that he could be a successful manager if his team had some talent. In 1944, Stengel was hired as the manager of the minor league Milwaukee Brewers, over the strenuous objections of club owner Bill Veeck. Veeck was proven wrong as Stengel led the Brewers to the American Association pennant that year. After managing the Oakland Oaks to the Pacific Coast League championship, he became manager of the New York Yankees.

As the Yankees' manager, he proceeded to set records, becoming the only person to manage a team to five consecutive World Series championships. He ultimately won a total of seven world championships and ten American League pennants with the Yankees. Nevertheless, after losing to the Pittsburgh Pirates in the 1960 World Series on a dramatic game-winning home run by Bill Mazeroski, Stengel was forced to retire because, at seventy, he was thought too old to be a manager.

After one season in retirement, however, Stengel was hired to manage the fledgling New York Mets. Although spectacularly unsuccessful with the "Amazin' Mets," Stengel still had the personal charisma to fill the stadium day after day. He managed the Mets for five years, until he fell and broke his hip and had to retire from baseball. He was inducted into the Baseball Hall of Fame in 1966. In 1975, Stengel was diagnosed with cancer of the lymph glands. He died at age eighty-five (Creamer, 1984).

SITUATIONAL LEADERSHIP ANALYSIS

Situational models of leadership differ from earlier trait and behavioral models in asserting that no single way of leading works in all situations. Rather, appropriate behavior depends on the circumstances at a given time. Effective managers diagnose the situation, identify the leadership style or behavior that will be most effective, and then determine whether they can implement the required style.

As we shall see, Casey Stengel was a master at using situational leadership and balancing his leadership behavior among the four frames of Bolman and Deal. He used the symbolic frame to establish himself as "Stengel the Clown." Humor became an important component of his leadership behavior. He was known as a very funny man, a quick-witted wisecracker, a physical comic, a natural mime who was very facile at imitating others. Yet he was always serious about the game of baseball and about how it should be played. He moved from symbolic to structural leadership behavior in placing a great emphasis on having his players thoroughly schooled in the fundamentals of the game.

John McGraw, the Hall of Fame manager of the New York Giants in the early part of the twentieth century, was Stengel's hero. He patterned his managerial behavior after that of McGraw. Beyond winning, McGraw imposed his personality on his team and on the game. In his mind, he was the best, his team was the best, and he used symbolic frame leadership behavior to get everybody else to know it. He also used structural frame behavior, at times to excess, in being ill tempered, sneering, bullying, and unpleasant. His structural frame leadership behavior also established him as a baseball genius, a tactician whose sense of the progress of the game was uncanny, a strategist who could see impending strengths and weaknesses in his own and other clubs before anyone else. But at the same time, he was known to utilize human resource frame behavior in being warmhearted, generous, and even charming at times. And Stengel wanted to be just like him—and as we will see, to a great extent, he was.

An astute awareness of change helped make Stengel and his mentors great managers. Stengel came into baseball when it was a low-scoring, singles-hitting game. He was still a player when home runs and high batting averages took over. He managed three decades later, when it was a home-runs and low-batting-average league. Watching McGraw, Stengel learned about change at the same time he learned what was immutable. He learned, for example, that you not only have to have the players, you have to know how to handle them, to keep them motivated. In short, he learned that he had to utilize a variety of leadership frames in order to remain effective as the situation changed. When he was managing the Yankees, he used a much different approach than when he had managed the Brooklyn Dodgers and the Boston Braves earlier in his career. When asked about his lack of disciplinary rules for his Yankees, he responded: "If you have men who make you set rules, then you have rules. If they don't need rules, then you don't have to make rules" (Creamer, 1984, p. 223).

Phil Rizzuto, the great Yankee shortstop, took note of Stengel's changing leadership style in a less than positive way. He claimed that Stengel was a changed man after winning the pennant in 1949 with a flawed team. He became loud and sarcastic, took too much credit for the good things the team did, criticized his players when things went wrong, and got too chummy with the press. According to Rizzuto, the subdued Stengel who had patched up the underrated 1949 team and held it together to win the pennant was gone, and a garrulous, confident know-it-all had taken his place. Actually, it was Stengel practicing situational leadership—albeit in questionable fashion.

However, as astute as Stengel was as a situational leader in most cases, he was not able to reach the proper balance among the leadership frames with perhaps his most gifted pupil, Mickey Mantle. Stengel was never quite able to get Mantle to conform to his wishes. It was simply not in Mantle's nature to openly defy an authority figure like Stengel. Rather, the defiance came in the form of not listening, of not paying attention, of not doing, like a passive-aggressive and intractable teenager. On the other hand, Stengel knew what buttons to push with Billy Martin. Once, when Martin was fuming over Stengel pulling him for a pinch hitter, Stengel walked by Martin saying,

"Widdle Bilwy mad at me?" (Creamer, 1984, p. 258). That kind of back-and-forth was impossible with Mantle. Stengel's anger toward Mantle subsided with the years, and they got along well enough after Stengel accepted the inevitable—Mantle wasn't going to change.

THE STRUCTURAL FRAME

We begin our analysis of Casey Stengel's leadership style with the structural frame. Structural frame leaders develop a new model of the relationship of structure, strategy, and environment for their organizations. Strategic planning, extensive preparation, and effecting change are priorities for them. Despite his reputation for being a "character," which would imply the frequent use of symbolic behavior, Casey Stengel was equally recognized as "the Perfessor" for his dedication to teaching the fundamentals of the game and for being a supreme strategist—both traits of the structural frame leader.

The paradox that was Casey Stengel was encapsulated in the following observation, made in 1942 by Dave Egan, a reporter for the *Boston Herald*: "He's a funny guy, always funny at somebody else's expense, always funny in his cruel and malicious way. And he was not at all reluctant to enjoy another's discomfort. Some of his players, including Joe DiMaggio and Phil Rizzuto, hated him for that, but Stengel never seemed to mind their antipathy" (Creamer, 1984, p. 13). In fact, it was a reflection of his extreme use of structural frame behavior.

As a further indication of his use of structural frame leadership behavior, Stengel always saw a lot of things in baseball that others did not. He was remarkably intelligent, although with little formal education beyond the minimum forced on him in elementary and high school and what he picked up during his two semesters at dental school. He had a prodigious memory and a startling ability to recall relevant detail. In baseball he had the kind of understanding of a situation that is often described as intuitive, but that is probably just rapid-fire, computer-speed deduction derived from long years of experience.

Stengel was schooled in his use of structural frame behavior by a number of mentors, including Norman Elberfeld, his manager in the minor leagues, who taught him the intricacies of the hit and run, hitting behind the runner, and hitting to vacated areas. He also showed him how to stand close to the plate to get hit by a pitched ball and how to move up in the batter's box to be better able to hit a curveball. As a result, Stengel was always sharing his knowledge, always teaching—sometimes out of self-defense. "What else are you gonna do when you get a second-division ball club," he said. "You only have a couple of youngsters to work with. You keep on them. You ask them why they didn't make that throw? You ask them why they played that man there?" (Creamer, 1984, p. 185).

He learned to utilize structural frame behavior early in his career when he was managing the minor league Milwaukee Brewers. One of his players there, Ed Levy, remembered that of all the managers that he played for, there was never one that was smarter and keener regarding the intricacies of baseball than Stengel. Another of his players, second baseman Tommy Nelson, indicated that Stengel had taught him more about playing second base than he ever dreamed there was to learn. Still another of his players, Heinz Becker, said that he was the greatest manager in the game when it came to keeping his players thinking. Becker never knew a manager to spend so much time with his players trying to get smart baseball across to them, trying to prepare them so that when their time came to go to the big leagues, they would be ready.

Although Stengel benefited from the Yankees' deep pockets and ability to sign great players, he was a hands-on, structural frame manager. For example, the 1949 Yankees were riddled with injuries, and Stengel's platooning abilities played a major role in their championship run. Platooning also played a major role in the team's 1951 World Series run. With Joe DiMaggio declining rapidly and Mickey Mantle yet to become a superstar, the Yankees were weak offensively. Stengel, leaving his solid pitching alone, moved players in and out of the lineup, putting good hitters in the lineup in the early innings and replacing them with better defensive players later in the game. The strategy worked and the Yankees won both the pennant and the World Series that year.

In his first year with the Yankees, Stengel engaged in more structural frame leadership behavior and initiated what he called his "seminar-type" instruction, where he divided the players and had his superstars share their knowledge of the game in small groups. Nothing like this had ever been seen in a Yankee camp before, and there was considerable skepticism among the sportswriters and some of the players. But Stengel defended the method, saying he would have loved to have been schooled by a player with Joe DiMaggio's skills as a kid learning the game of baseball. He was constantly creating new ways of looking at things, always evaluating, discovering inadequacies, locating strengths. As a result, he was one of the first to use the platoon system to maximize strengths and minimize weaknesses.

After winning his first World Series in the late 1940s, Stengel decided to use even more structural frame behavior to keep his team from becoming complacent. He had no illusions. He knew that winning a second championship could be even more difficult than winning the first, and that he had a lot of work to do. That year he was more direct and forceful in running the team, much to the chagrin of his star shortstop, Phil Rizzuto. But Stengel didn't worry about Rizzuto's view because in his mind Rizzuto was a follower, not a leader. On that same team was Joe Page, his great reliever in 1949, who was a manager's bane, a night person with a cavalier attitude toward authority. Stengel put up with it in 1949, but no longer. Page was Joe DiMaggio's personal troubleshooter, a role that Billy Martin would assume when Page was traded away that year. When DiMaggio slumped in 1950, Stengel dropped him to fifth in the batting order—no more deference was given. Page protested the move on behalf of DiMaggio. Stengel promptly traded him. Page was not missed, DiMaggio ended up hitting over .300, and Rizzuto batted .324 and blossomed in the field and was voted Most Valuable Player. Thus, Stengel's stronger structural leadership frame behavior worked. In addition, that year he brought up his protégé, Billy Martin, who was noisy and cocky in the Stengel tradition.

As Stengel became more successful as a manager, he gained confidence and began to increase his use of structural frame behavior. He began to use sarcasm more often as a motivating device. For example, when rookie outfielder Gene Woodling lost a ball in the sun and the Yankees lost a shutout, Stengel came out of the dugout to replace Whitey Ford, and while on the mound did a mocking pantomime of Woodling staggering under the fly ball. This curious performance angered some, like Woodling, while amusing others. That he could openly criticize one of his own players before a crowd of nearly 70,000 people demonstrated how far Stengel had come in asserting his dominance over the ball club.

Stengel's new position of strength and his urge to teach led the Yankees early in 1951 to accede to his request that they establish an "instructional school" for young players, to run two or three weeks before spring training began to expose the young players to the wisdom and knowledge of Stengel and the other coaches. The reporters immediately dubbed him "the Perfessor," purposely misspelling the term to conform to Stengelese. Mickey Mantle turned out to be the prized "graduate" of the school.

THE HUMAN RESOURCE FRAME

Human resource frame leaders believe in people and communicate that belief. They are passionate about productivity through people. Despite his all-too-frequent use of sarcasm aimed at his players, there are numerous instances in which Casey Stengel operated out of the human resource frame of leadership.

Al Bridwell, who knew Stengel when he played for the New York Giants, noted that "it wasn't so much knowing baseball. All of them know that. What makes the difference is knowing each player and how to handle him"

(Creamer, 1984, p. 141). When Stengel had the players to work with, as he had with the Yankees, he held them to a high level of performance for a dozen years. To keep a team playing that well for that long is more than luck. It is the astute use of human resource frame behavior, along with the other frames of leadership behavior.

Stengel learned most about the appropriate application of human resource frame behavior from his New York Giants manager, the legendary John McGraw. McGraw had become genuinely fond of Stengel. He often invited Stengel out to his new home in Pelham, in the New York suburbs, where he and Stengel would sit in the kitchen talking baseball until all hours of the night. Stengel later built this same kind of relationship with Billy Martin.

Billy Martin remembered that when Stengel managed him in the minors, he hit grounder after grounder to him, showing him different ways to make the double play, growled at him, laughed at him, bawled him out, praised him, and constantly tried to help the young Martin develop into the ballplayer he knew he could be. Stengel was like a father to him. He particularly liked Martin's "fire," because it reminded him of himself.

Also, when he managed in the minor leagues, he started the tradition of rewarding his players when they won both ends of a doubleheader. He would bring them into the locker room and say, "You fellas did pretty well today and it's up to me to buy you each a three-dollar dinner" (Creamer, 1984, p. 203). The next day he would pass out $3 apiece to twenty-seven men. This was back in 1946, when $3 could buy a gourmet dinner.

Another player that Stengel showered with human resource frame behavior was his Hall of Fame catcher, Yogi Berra. Stengel did more than just coach Berra. Aware, as no one before him had been, that Berra was a truly sensitive young man who was hurt by many of the quips made about him yet had the courage to smile through them, Stengel acted as a buffer between Berra and those who poked fun at him.

Stengel was especially astute in applying human resource frame leadership behavior to the young and impressionable players. Al Lopez, the Cleveland Indians manager, observed that Stengel was unique in sticking with a young player and nursing him along. Stengel would sit and talk to his players by the hour. He never had any children of his own, so they became his surrogate children. Of all the players Stengel managed in New York, none better exemplified the kind of individual he was trying to develop than the talented, professional, and versatile infielder Gil McDougald. McDougald was one among many that Stengel groomed into good players and, as importantly, good citizens.

THE SYMBOLIC FRAME

In the symbolic frame, the organization is seen as a stage, a theater in which every actor plays certain roles and the symbolic leader attempts to communicate the right impressions to the right audiences. One could easily argue that Casey Stengel's dominant frame was the symbolic one. Over time, he built an image of himself that was recognized internationally. He was a master storyteller who spoke in his own unique language, which was labeled "Stengelese."

His use of symbolic frame behavior began early on in his career. In 1919, Stengel was playing for the Pittsburgh Pirates and was being taunted mercilessly by fans of the Brooklyn Dodgers, his former team. Somehow Stengel got hold of a sparrow and used it to turn the crowd in his favor. With the bird tucked gently beneath his cap, Stengel strutted to the plate amidst a chorus of boos. He turned to the crowd, tipped his hat and out flew the sparrow. The jeers turned to cheers, and Stengel became an instant celebrity.

In another instance that added to the fast-developing legend, Stengel pulled a similar stunt. Wilbert Robinson, his Hall of Fame manager in Brooklyn, thought up an opening-day gimmick where one of his players would catch the ceremonial first pitch in the form of a baseball dropped out of an airplane flying over Ebbets Field. Stengel put the pilot up to dropping a grapefruit instead of a baseball, and the "big splatter" occurred as the grapefruit fell off the catcher's mitt and hit the ground. Based on past experience, everyone involved had a good idea of who was responsible for the prank.

Stengel once posed as a farmer in the stands when his team was playing the Philadelphia Athletics. He taunted the A's players, who invited him out onto the field to "do better." Of course, he did, hitting balls out of the stadium. They soon discovered it was Stengel, putting on a show for the crowd yet again. On another occasion he put his uniform on backward, prompting Phillies manager Gavvy Cravath to say: "You've done everything else backward here, you might as well wear your pants that way too" (Creamer, 1984, p. 131).

As a result of these antics, despite the triumphant end to the 1934 season, his first as a major league manager, Stengel was still considered a clown by most people during the years he managed the Dodgers—a humorous throwback hired to lead the latest edition of the "Daffiness Boys." He contributed to that image, of course, playing the comedian in the coach's box during games. For example, whenever Nick Tremark, a tiny, five-foot-five-inch outfielder, got on base, Stengel would make a great show of looking for him through mock binoculars, which always broke up the crowd. We saw earlier, however, how he eventually dispelled his "clown" image by using structural frame behavior and ultimately became known as "the Perfessor." Stengel finally got fired by the Dodgers, but in an indication of the broad popularity he had commanded, he was given a going-away party and a gift. Steve Owens, then coach of the New York Giants football team, said, "This must be the first time anyone was given a party for being fired" (Creamer, 1984, p. 189).

After Brooklyn, Stengel managed the Boston Braves with limited success, but he continued building his image by the frequent use of symbolic frame behavior. Still, it wasn't until he had his monumental success with the Yankees that his image as a baseball genius fully blossomed. One of his great stars with the Boston Braves, the Hall of Fame pitcher Warren Spahn, who later played for Stengel when he managed the Mets, astutely commented: "I played for Casey before and after he was a genius" (Creamer, 1984, p. 195).

Stengel's flamboyant image prompted others to treat him in kind. For example, Stengel was hit by a car and hospitalized in 1943, when he was managing the Boston Braves. Frankie Frisch, then managing Pittsburgh, sent a telegram to the hospital that read: "Your attempt at suicide fully understood. Deepest sympathy you didn't succeed." That same season, Dave Egan of the *Boston Herald* wrote: "The man who did the most for baseball in Boston in 1943 was the motorist who ran Stengel down two days before the opening game and kept him away from the Braves for two months" (Creamer, 1984, p. 195). The next year, the *Sporting News* took a poll of 151 sportswriters rating the funniest managers. Stengel had four times as many votes as second-place Jimmy Dykes and six times as many as third-place Charlie Grimm. Stengel was now officially the "king of the clowns."

Stengel became a master publicist and promoter of both himself and his teams. He was a captivating raconteur and, especially during the years of success with the Yankees, had the media eating out of his hands. He became as much of a public figure as many of his star players. He appeared on the cover of national magazines such as *Time, Look,* and *Life.* His stream-of-consciousness monologues on all facets of baseball history and tactics became known as Stengelese to the sportswriters, who nicknamed him "the Old Perfessor."

But he still had his dissenters. When hired as manager of the Yankees, some of the writers could not believe that the dignified Yankees were hiring the "clown of baseball." Dave Egan of the *Boston Herald* once again took a tongue-in-cheek shot at Stengel when he wrote: "Well, sirs and ladies, the Yankees have now mathematically eliminated themselves from the 1949 pennant race. They did so when they engaged 'Perfessor' Casey Stengel to mismanage them for the next two years, and you may be sure that the perfessor will oblige to the best of his unique ability." Stengel, however, fought back in his typical symbolic style. Trying to establish himself as a good manager, rather than just a clown, he presented a serious image at the Yankees press conference. But he could not keep himself from uttering a final quip. "I've been hired to win," he said, "and I think I will. There is less wrong with the Yankees than with any other club I've ever had" (Creamer, 1984, p. 223).

Some of Stengel's quotes became nationally known. When speaking about his own hitting prowess, he said: "I was such a dangerous hitter I even got intentional walks during batting practice." Then there was the quote with which we began this chapter. As manager of Toledo in the minor leagues, he said: "My advice to you players is to buy stock in Pennsylvania Railroad, because if you don't start playing better ball there's gonna be so many of you riding trains outta here that railroad stocks are a cinch to go up." Then, in 1953, after the Yankees had won four straight World Series victories, he made the following observation: "If we're going to win the pennant, we've got to start thinking we're not as smart as we think we are." And when, in his seventies, he became manager of the Mets, mocking his well-publicized advanced age, he said: "It's a great honor to be joining the Knickerbockers," a New York baseball team that had seen its last game around the time of the Civil War (Creamer, 1984, p. 178).

The Mets proved to be so incompetent that they gave Stengel plenty of fresh Stengelese material for the New York City newspaper writers. "Come see my Amazin' Mets," Stengel said. "I've been in this game a hundred years, but I see new ways to lose I never knew existed before." On his three catchers he commented: "I got one that can throw but can't catch, one that can catch but can't throw, and one who can hit but can't do either." Referring to their rookies Ed Kranepool and Greg Goossen in 1964, Stengel observed, "See that fellow over there? He's twenty years old. In ten years he has a chance to be a star. Now, that fellow over there, he's twenty, too. In ten years he has a chance to be thirty." When Marvelous Marv Throneberry hit a triple, but was called out for not touching first base, an enraged Stengel challenged the umpire, who said, "I hate to tell you but he missed second base, too." Stengel responded by saying, "Well, I know he touched third base because he's standing on it." Commenting on the brand-new Shea Stadium, Stengel said, "It's lovely, just lovely. The park is lovelier than my team." After a seven-game losing streak, he said, "If anybody wants me, tell them I'm being embalmed." Perhaps his most famous comment came after another exasperating Mets loss, when he complained, "Can't anybody here play this here game?" (Creamer, 1984).

In typical symbolic leadership style, Stengel was incessantly talking and performing. During a game, when he ventured out of the dugout to talk to his pitcher or to argue with an umpire, the crowd would sit up and pay attention because anything could happen. When speaking at banquets or luncheons or just sitting around a table, he performed with his body as well as with his words, making his odd little gestures, lifting his head this way and that. His speeches rambled incredibly, moving from one topic to another in midsentence as one thought cascaded into another. Once, in response to a reporter's question, he talked for forty minutes. When the reporter complained that he had still not answered the question, he replied, "Don't rush me" (Creamer, 1984, p. 262).

Stengel oftentimes made light of his player's failures to make his point more palatable to them. Once, when Babe Phelps, his Brooklyn Dodgers catcher, was catching for knuckleballer Dutch Leonard, someone hit a ninth-inning homer off Leonard to win the game. Stengel asked Phelps what pitch he had called, to which Phelps replied, "A fastball." Stengel asked why he didn't call for his best pitch, which was a knuckler. "His knuckler's tough to catch," Phelps said. "If his knuckler is so hard to catch, don't you think it might be a little tough to hit, too?" Stengel declared (Creamer, 1984, p. 187).

In building his image, Stengel became supremely successful in his time with the New York Yankees. After having won pennants and World Series in the late 1940s and early 1950s, if he could win the pennant again in 1952 he would tie John McGraw's string of four straight sets of the 1920s, which Joe McCarthy had matched a decade later. When he did so, it was no longer a matter of proving he could manage. He was in fast company now, and when Joe DiMaggio retired in 1951, the Yankees were no longer DiMaggio's Yankees, they were Stengel's Yankees. Five straight pennants and five straight World Series allowed Stengel to stand alone, beyond McGraw, beyond McCarthy, beyond everyone.

On his deathbed, he was watching a baseball game on television and listening to the national anthem, and in one last symbolic gesture, he swung his legs out of bed, got to his feet, and stood at attention with his hand over his heart like a Kansas City schoolboy. On Monday, September 29, the day after the 1975 baseball season ended, he died. He had lived eighty-five illustrious years (Creamer, 1984).

THE SYMBOLIC FRAME AND HUMOR

As we have already seen, Casey Stengel was fond of utilizing symbolic frame leadership behavior in the form of humor. The following are some additional humorous quotes and witticisms attributed to Casey Stengel:

- Ability is the act of getting credit for all the home runs someone else hits.
- All right, everyone line up alphabetically according to your height.
- Being with a woman all night never hurt no professional baseball player. It's staying up all night looking for one that does him in.
- I feel greatly honored to have a ballpark named after me, especially since I've been thrown out of so many.

- I got players with bad watches—they can't tell midnight from noon.
- I love signing autographs. I'll sign anything but veal cutlets. My ballpoint pen slips on veal cutlets.
- The secret of managing a club is to keep the five guys who hate you from the five who are undecided.
- The trick is growing up without growing old.
- They say some of my stars drink whiskey, but I have found that the ones who drink milkshakes don't win any ball games.
- We're in such a slump that even the ones that are drinking aren't hitting.
- When you are younger you get blamed for crimes you never committed and when you're older you begin to get credit for virtues you never possessed. It evens itself out. (Creamer, 1984; workinghumor.com)

THE POLITICAL FRAME

Leaders operating out of the political frame clarify what they want and what they can get. Political leaders are realists above all. They never let what they want cloud their judgment about what is possible. They assess the distribution of power and interests.

Stengel began very early in his playing career to utilize political frame behavior, especially in dealing with upper management in salary negotiations. Even as a rookie, he began a pattern of negotiating the very most that he could get in his contracts. In 1912 at Brooklyn, dealing with owner Charles Ebbets, he was offered $250 a month. He wanted $350 per month. Stengel, only a rookie with three weeks of major league experience, held out all winter. Ebbets finally yielded, and Stengel agreed to $350 just as spring training started.

Stengel also used political frame behavior to establish himself as a model citizen and "employable commodity." In his first major league coaching job, with the Brooklyn Dodgers, Max Carey was the manager. Stengel was a good soldier. He worked hard under Carey, did all the things a coach should do and sublimated his character so as to not upstage the colorless, humorless manager. He also was careful not to be critical of management when he was fired, hoping that his restraint would lead to another job—and as we know, it always did.

Stengel again showed great restraint when Lou Perini, owner of the Boston Braves, watched an exhibition game and was bothered when one of the Braves bunted into a double play. After the game, he asked Stengel what had happened. Stengel was polite even though he bristled inwardly, as managers do when their baseball wisdom is questioned. But Perini was the owner, so Stengel went into one of his convoluted explanations, a wordy smokescreen designed to sound like an answer without imparting much specific information. Whether in frustration or because he was somehow satisfied with the explanation, Perini let the matter drop. Mission accomplished!

Another display of political frame behavior came when George Weiss, the Yankees general manager, wanted to trade Stengel's favorite son, Billy Martin. Stengel objected, but when Weiss insisted because he thought that Martin was a bad influence on the younger players, like Mickey Mantle, Stengel capitulated. Martin never forgave him, but Stengel, as a result, gained points with upper management.

His greatest audience regarding the use of political frame leadership behavior was the media—the sportswriters who covered his teams on a daily basis. Theirs was a symbiotic relationship. Stengel needed them, needed their attention, needed their admiration, and they needed him for copy. He used the press masterfully, sometimes even using it "to get to his players." The Stengel legend probably peaked on July 9, 1958, when he testified on behalf of baseball before the Senate Subcommittee on Antitrust and Monopoly. He both entertained and "snowed" the senators with Stengelese for almost two hours.

THE MORAL FRAME

The moral frame is my own contribution to situational leadership theory. In my view, the moral frame completes situational leadership theory. Without it, leaders could just as easily use their leadership skills for promoting evil as for promoting good. Leaders operating out of the moral frame are concerned about their obligations to their followers. Moral frame leaders use some type of moral compass to direct their behavior. They practice what has been described as servant leadership and are concerned with those individuals and groups that are marginalized in their organizations and in society. In short, they are concerned about equality, fairness, and social justice.

Casey Stengel did not seem to have a mean bone in his body. There are many instances in which he tried to do the right thing and few instances in which he did not. There is every indication that Casey Stengel had developed a moral compass that he used to guide his daily leadership behavior.

SITUATIONAL LEADERSHIP ANALYSIS

Situational models of leadership differ from earlier trait and behavioral models in asserting that no single way of leading works in all situations. Rather, appropriate behavior depends on the circumstances at a given time. Effective managers diagnose the situation, identify the leadership style or behavior that will be most effective, and then determine whether they can implement the required style.

As we shall see, Casey Stengel was a master at using situational leadership and balancing his leadership behavior among the four frames of Bolman and Deal. He used the symbolic frame to establish himself as "Stengel the Clown." Humor became an important component of his leadership behavior. He was known as a very funny man, a quick-witted wisecracker, a physical comic, a natural mime who was very facile at imitating others. Yet he was always serious about the game of baseball and about how it should be played. He moved from symbolic to structural leadership behavior in placing a great emphasis on having his players thoroughly schooled in the fundamentals of the game.

John McGraw, the Hall of Fame manager of the New York Giants in the early part of the twentieth century, was Stengel's hero. He patterned his managerial behavior after that of McGraw. Beyond winning, McGraw imposed his personality on his team and on the game. In his mind, he was the best, his team was the best, and he used symbolic frame leadership behavior to get everybody else to know it. He also used structural frame behavior, at times to excess, in being ill tempered, sneering, bullying, and unpleasant. His structural frame leadership behavior also established him as a baseball genius, a tactician whose sense of the progress of the game was uncanny, a strategist who could see impending strengths and weaknesses in his own and other clubs before anyone else. But at the same time, he was known to utilize human resource frame behavior in being warmhearted, generous, and even charming at times. And Stengel wanted to be just like him—and as we will see, to a great extent, he was.

An astute awareness of change helped make Stengel and his mentors great managers. Stengel came into baseball when it was a low-scoring, singles-hitting game. He was still a player when home runs and high batting averages took over. He managed three decades later, when it was a homeruns and low-batting-average league. Watching McGraw, Stengel learned about change at the same time he learned what was immutable. He learned, for example, that you not only have to have the players, you have to know how to handle them, to keep them motivated. In short, he learned that he had to utilize a variety of leadership frames in order to remain effective as the situation changed. When he was managing the Yankees, he used a much different approach than when he had managed the Brooklyn Dodgers and the Boston Braves earlier in his career. When asked about his lack of disciplinary rules for his Yankees, he responded: "If you have men who make you set rules, then you have rules. If they don't need rules, then you don't have to make rules" (Creamer, 1984, p. 223).

Phil Rizzuto, the great Yankee shortstop, took note of Stengel's changing leadership style in a less than positive way. He claimed that Stengel was a changed man after winning the pennant in 1949 with a flawed team. He became loud and sarcastic, took too much credit for the good things the team did, criticized his players when things went wrong, and got too chummy with the press. According to Rizzuto, the subdued Stengel who had patched up the underrated 1949 team and held it together to win the pennant was gone, and a garrulous, confident know-it-all had taken his place. Actually, it was Stengel practicing situational leadership—albeit in questionable fashion.

However, as astute as Stengel was as a situational leader in most cases, he was not able to reach the proper balance among the leadership frames with perhaps his most gifted pupil, Mickey Mantle. Stengel was never quite able to get Mantle to conform to his wishes. It was simply not in Mantle's nature to openly defy an authority figure like Stengel. Rather, the defiance came in the form of not listening, of not paying attention, of not doing, like a passive-aggressive and intractable teenager. On the other hand, Stengel knew what buttons to push with Billy Martin. Once, when Martin was fuming over Stengel pulling him for a pinch hitter, Stengel walked by Martin saying, "Widdle Bilwy mad at me?" (Creamer, 1984, p. 258). That kind of back-and-forth was impossible with Mantle. Stengel's anger toward Mantle subsided with the years, and they got along well enough after Stengel accepted the inevitable—Mantle wasn't going to change.

LEADERSHIP IMPLICATIONS AND CONCLUSION

Casey Stengel ultimately became a universally beloved figure in American life. He became so through the frequent use of symbolic frame leadership behavior, sprinkling in structural, human resource, and political frame behavior for good measure. He regaled the media and the American public with his colorful stories and flamboyant behavior, creating a language unto himself. However, he also established himself as "the Perfessor" by using structural leadership behavior in the drilling of his teams in the fundamentals of the game and in the unique strategies that he employed both in preparing for and during the games.

Although he did not overdo the use of human resource frame leadership behavior, he did employ it at appropriate times. He was especially successful in applying the human touch with his protégé, Billy Martin. He was so effective with Martin that Martin considered Stengel his second father, and Stengel became his coach on the field and in the locker room.

We saw how Stengel practiced political frame leadership behavior when appropriate. He was constantly trying to "win friends and influence people," which is emblematic of political leaders. He negotiated "sweetheart" contracts for himself and never burned any bridges when he was fired. He was particularly successful in applying political frame behavior with the media. As a result, he was quoted in and on the cover of virtually every major magazine of his time. Casey Stengel was an effective practitioner of situational leadership well before Bolman and Deal developed their model. In fact, it was through studying leaders like Stengel that situational theory was formulated. Leaders and aspiring leaders can benefit greatly from studying the leadership behavior of an exemplary and timeless situational leader like Casey Stengel.

Chapter Ten

Golda Meir

Don't be humble; you're not that great. —Golda Meir

BACKGROUND

Golda Meir was born in Kiev, Russia, in 1898 and immigrated to Milwaukee, Wisconsin, in 1905. She attended Milwaukee Normal School and upon graduation taught in the Milwaukee public schools. In 1915, she joined the Labor Zionist organization and immigrated to Palestine.

In Palestine she was elected to the women's labor council of Histadrut in 1928 and was later chosen as its executive secretary. In 1946 she served as president of the political bureau of the Jewish Agency. Remaining active in politics, Meir became Israel's minister to Moscow, labor minister, and, from 1956 to 1966, foreign minister. She served as secretary general of the Israeli Workers Party, and in 1969 she was chosen as prime minister.

Meir's administration became mired in controversy revolving around the occupation of the territories Israel acquired during the Six-Day War of 1967. She concurred with Defense Minister Moshe Dayan's plan to colonize and annex the territories. They were opposed by moderates led by Deputy Prime Minister Yigal Allon, who favored the return of the Sinai to Egypt and the Golan Heights to Syria, and permitting the West Bank of Jordan to become an autonomous part of the kingdom of Jordan. In 1970, Meir accepted a U.S. peace initiative whereby Israel would retain most of the occupied territories.

In the days leading up to the Yom Kippur War in 1973, Meir took the advice of her military officials that, in light of the disastrous results of the Six-Day War of 1967, Syria would not invade Israel. However, the experts were wrong, and an Arab invasion of Israel took place late in 1973. Israel's unpreparedness for the Yom Kippur War led to demands for new leadership, and Meir resigned as prime minister in April of 1974. Four years later she died of lymphatic cancer, at the age of eighty.

THE STRUCTURAL FRAME

We begin our analysis of Golda Meir's leadership behavior with the structural frame. Structural frame leaders seek to develop a new model of the relationship of structure, strategy, and environment for their organizations. Strategic planning, extensive preparation, and effecting change are priorities for them. They are often described as firm and direct by their followers. Golda Meir spent much of her time operating out of the structural frame.

Meir demonstrated her structural frame tendencies as a very young woman when, after growing up in Milwaukee, she joined the Zionist Party against her parents' wishes, and at the first opportunity after World War I migrated to Palestine. Even before leaving Milwaukee, she and her husband decided that they would make a full commitment to Zionism and live in a kibbutz (community living).

As a politician in the Jewish section of Palestine, Meir used structural frame leadership behavior in lobbying hard for a Jewish homeland. She realized early on that despite the contributions of the 600,000 Jews in Palestine, they would never be able to prevent something like the Holocaust unless they had their own state with their own sovereignty. The Jews in Palestine had to rely on Great Britain to protest the millions of Jewish deaths during World War II, and there were always excuses for not interfering. Meir wanted to be in a position to make her own decisions, and that could only be done through statehood.

Meir took a structural frame position in her relations with the surrounding Arab nations. She took a consistently aggressive stance when challenged by Arab hostility. "Apparently those responsible for these evil policies are unable to forgive us for one thing: that we are not a passive herd," she wrote. She was ultimately responsible for fighting three wars against Arab aggression in Palestine and Israel (Meir, 1973, p. 70).

In 1948, Meir engaged in structural frame behavior in shepherding the establishment of the Jewish state of Israel through the United Nations. She had no sooner accomplished this monumental goal than she was forced into again utilizing structural frame behavior in having to defend Israel from constant Arab hostility.

In 1956, as Israel's foreign minister, Meir was instrumental in the decision to take military action against the Arabs in the Sinai Desert. Her use of structural frame leadership behavior ultimately resulted in Israel occupying the Sinai Desert, the Gulf of Aqaba, and the Gaza Strip. "For eight years now," she declared, "Israel has been subjected to the unrelenting violence of physical assault and to an equally unremitting intent to destroy our country economically through blockade and through lawless interference with the development of our natural resources. Since Israel's effort to repulse the concerted Arab onslaught in 1948, my country has had no respite from hostile acts and loudly proclaimed threats of destruction. This needs to change or else" (Meir, 1973, p. 90).

For almost ten years following its founding in 1948, Israel had endured a sea blockade imposed by Egypt in the Suez Canal and in the Straits of Tiran. The United Nations Security Council confirmed time and again the illegality of this blockade, but to no avail. After trying to operate out of other leadership frames, Meir finally resorted to using structural frame behavior in the form of open warfare. She saw the futility of dealing peacefully with a country whose leader, Gamal Abdel Nasser, had declared that "every commander is to prepare himself and his subordinates for the inevitable campaign with Israel for the purpose of fulfilling our exalted aim which is the annihilation of Israel and its destruction in the shortest possible time in the most brutal and cruel battles" (Meir, 1973, p. 95).

After once again utilizing structural frame leadership behavior in conducting and winning the Six-Day War in 1967, Meir spoke at Madison Square Garden in New York, declaring: "Once again we have won a war, the third in a very brief history of independence. The last thing that Israelis want is to win wars. We don't want wars. We want peace more than all else. But our Arab neighbors and our neighbors' friends must learn this lesson. Those that perished in Hitler's gas chambers were the last Jews to die without standing up to defend themselves" (Meir, 1973, p. 155).

Meir responded with structural frame leadership behavior to the Soviet Union's selling of ground-to-air missiles to Egypt. She made it clear to both the Soviet Union and Egypt that Israel would forcibly defend any threat to its sovereignty, and that the cease-fire line that had been established would not be honored unless there was an immediate stop to the deployment of the Soviet-made ground-to-air missiles that Egypt was beginning to build adjacent to the cease-fire line.

After endlessly being provoked by terrorists operating out of bases in Lebanon, Meir finally gave into her structural frame leanings and retaliated against the Fatah bases in that country. Since the Lebanon government in Beirut was on record as not being "prepared on any account to act as a policeman guarding Israel," Meir decided that Israel "must do it ourselves" (Meir, 1973, p. 194).

Lastly, Meir did not limit her use of the structural frame to Israel's Arab neighbors. When Israel's labor unions engaged in their third strike of the year, Meir took action. "However recent an agreement is signed, a new round of claims is immediately submitted and even though there are claims of individual abuses, this situation does not absolve any side from the duty of honoring agreements. After these recent events, I must doubt my opposition to laws limiting strikes," she proclaimed.

THE HUMAN RESOURCE FRAME

Human resource frame leaders believe in people and communicate that belief. They are passionate about productivity through people. Golda Meir had a great respect for human dignity and thus acted out of the human resource frame quite frequently.

One of Golda Meir's most familiar quotes demonstrates her concern for humanity and her proclivity for operating out of the human resource frame: "Someday when peace comes, we may forgive the Arabs for having killed our sons, but it will be harder for us to forgive them for having forced us to kill their sons" (Meir, 1973, p. 14).

Because of her concern for human rights, Meir could not bear class distinctions. On the socioeconomic difference between the immigrant Jews and the established Jews in Israel, she had this to say: "If we must suffer for this sacred cause, then all of us will suffer. Let us not create two distinct groups of people among us. In the countries where such classes exist, we may be certain that immigration, absorption, and Zionism are not presented as desirable goals" (Meir, 1973, p. 83).

In reaction to Britain's limitation on the number of Jews who could immigrate to Palestine, Meir once again engaged in human resource frame behavior and declared: "I am authorized on behalf of the close to 160,000 members of our federation [Histadrut], to state here in the clearest possible terms that there is nothing that Jewish labor is not prepared to do in this country in order to receive large masses of Jewish immigrants, with no limitation and with no conditions whatsoever" (Meir, 1973, p. 55).

Meir donned her human resource frame hat in acknowledging how advanced the state of Israel was in considering social insurance legislation. She was proud of her young country when, in only its fourth year of existence, the Knesset was already preparing to debate a comprehensive state social insurance plan that would provide a safety net for Israel's poor and jobless and establish a federal health care system.

Meir's human resource frame sentiments not only applied to those in her homeland but also extended to those in other lands. "The cry that goes out from the African and Asian continents today is: Share with us not only food, but also your knowledge of how to produce it," she said. "The most frightening inequality in the world today lies in the gap between those that literally reach for the moon and those who do not know how to reach efficiently into their own soil to produce their daily necessities" (Meir, 1973, p. 122).

Meir's human resource frame tendencies often saw no bounds. "It is not enough," she said, "for education to be free and for schools to be accessible to all. We cannot ignore the difference between a child who leaves home with books, and returns after to a quiet room in which to prepare his lessons and a child with none of these advantages. A child whose father and mother can teach him and help him in his lessons is obviously not in the same situation as a child whose parents had no schooling" (Meir, 1973, p. 180).

Meir never let the immediate practicalities interfere with her human resource ideals. For example, she would not let the need to provide expenditures for military defense lead her to neglect the advancement of the lower socioeconomic levels. During her administration, she insisted on a balance between the funding of the military and the funding of social programs.

Further evidence of her frequent application of human resource frame behavior was her belief that Israel should continue to extend the peace branch and good neighborliness to all states around it and for the advancement of the entire Middle East. For example, when Egypt was engaged in civil war, it never occurred to Meir to exploit those difficulties and to attack Egypt in its moment of vulnerability to avenge its past sins against Israel. Of course, this quest for peace and prosperity for all became virtually unachievable at times because of the Arab position that Israel had no right to exist.

Meir's concern for humanity extended to the labor unions in Israel. She grew up in the labor movement and considered it an advocacy group not only for workers but also for leaders in the quest for social justice in all areas of society. As long as she was in charge, every component of government would include a social justice thrust in its mission. Such was her commitment to the human resource frame. For Meir this commitment also took the form of volunteerism. "Volunteering is the foundation for our entire renaissance movement," she declared. "Only through volunteering can we achieve the society which we all desire; only so shall we be faithful to the character and mission of the state of Israel" (Meir, 1973, p. 228).

THE SYMBOLIC FRAME

In the symbolic frame, the organization is seen as a stage, a theater in which every actor plays certain roles and the symbolic leader attempts to communicate the right impressions to the right audiences.

Meir engaged in the symbolic frame through her many speeches and writings. She used symbolic frame behavior in just such a way in reacting to the so-called Arab refugee problem whereby thousands of Arabs were leaving their war-torn homelands. Of course, the Arabs blamed Israel for creating the refugee problem, to which Meir's rather sarcastic response was: "I am sorry I cannot sympathize with the poor Arab states because they failed to exterminate us. The existence and independence of Israel are not negotiable. And if Israel now insists on secure and agreed borders according to the terms of the 1967 Resolution, it is partly because of the bitter memory of their acquiescence in the withdrawal of Israel from the Sinai and Gaza in 1957, only to have the terms of the agreement promptly broken by Egypt" (Meir, 1973, p. 14).

When Meir was criticized for being a "women's libber," she responded in true symbolic frame style. "In spite of the place which her children and her family take up in her life, her nature and being demand something more," she said in defense of women everywhere. "She cannot divorce herself from a larger social life. She cannot let her children narrow her horizon," she concluded.

Meir effectively used the symbolic frame in depicting the Israelis as a peace-loving people in contrast to the Arabs, who insisted on being warlike. Meir consistently maintained that the goal of the Israeli settlers was peace and prosperity. "From the outset," she declared, "they sought to achieve these goals in complete friendship and cooperation with the Arab population and with Arab laborers. It is significant that the first organization of Arab laborers in this country was founded by the Jewish workers who came at that time" (Meir, 1973, p. 53).

In speaking at a conference attended by the United States, Great Britain, and Israel, Meir reinforced her position by once again utilizing symbolic frame leadership behavior. She queried the conference delegates as follows: "I don't know, gentlemen, whether you who have the good fortune to belong to the two great democratic nations, the British and American, can, with the best of will to understand our problems, realize what it means to be a member of a people whose very right to exist is constantly being questioned" (Meir, 1973, p. 56).

Meir used symbolic frame leadership behavior to obtain arms for Israel. She argued that if the seven hundred thousand Jews in Israel were to remain alive, they would be a symbol for the next generation of Jews, showing that they were still a viable race that maintained its independence. However, they could not do it alone. The Jews' valiant spirit alone, she opined, could not overcome the Arab rifles and machine guns. "Rifles and machine guns without spirit are not worth very much," she said, "but spirit without arms can in time be broken" (Meir, 1973, p. 75). According to Meir, a comfortable decision had been made by the world that the Arab states would unilaterally enjoy the rights of war, while Israel would have the unilateral responsibility of keeping the peace.

Using symbolic frame language in a sarcastic tone, Meir continually pointed out that the Israelis did not fight for territorial expansion. Their boys were not sent into battle, as were the Egyptian soldiers in a "holy war," to destroy and annihilate, but out of necessity, so that their people could live in peace. She constantly pointed out the advantages of a country dedicated to peace rather than to war. The national income of her tiny Israel, she was fond of saying, was almost equal to that of Egypt, with a population ten times that of her country.

After winning the Six-Day War against Egypt, Jordan, and Syria in 1967 and restoring access to Jerusalem, Meir once again made use of symbolic frame leadership behavior by making a public display of visiting the Western Wall before leaving Israel to make a speech in the United States. Upon arriving in the United States, she emphasized that she had been able to pray at the wall for the first time in twenty years. She also reminisced about the first time that she had gone to the wall, some forty-six years before, when she first arrived in Palestine from the United States. The wall, she said, had stood for generations as a symbol of the great tragedy of the Jewish people: the destruction of the Jewish people, their independence, and their temple. But, ultimately, it stood as a promise of the eventual return of the Jewish people to their homeland.

When the Soviet Union arrested a number of Soviet Jews who had tried to immigrate to Israel, Meir defended them by using the symbolic frame once again. "Their sole guilt," she said of the Leningrad defendants, "is their wish to emigrate to Israel, their aspirations to be united with their people in their homeland" (Meir, 1973, p. 229). The attempt on the part of the Russians to depict it as some kind of Jewish plot against the Soviet Union was to Meir ridiculous and criminal, and a policy that was in direct violation of the basic rights of human beings. "Yesterday," she declared, "the members of the Cabinet went to the Western Wall to shake the hands of the immigrants who are keeping vigil there as a sign of protest. By this warm handclasp we sought to express our total solidarity with the innocent defendants and with every Jew in the Soviet Union who may stand in the dock for the crime of longing for Zion and Israel" (Meir, 1973, p. 231).

Perhaps Meir's most poignant use of symbolic frame behavior came with the following quotation: "Peace will come when the Arabs will love their children more than they hate us," she said. "When people ask me if I am not afraid that because of Israel's need for defense, the country may become militaristic, I can only answer that I don't want a fine, liberal, anti-colonial, anti-militaristic *dead* Jewish people" (Meir, 1973, p. 242).

THE SYMBOLIC FRAME AND HUMOR

Many times, effective leaders utilize symbolic frame leadership behavior in the form of inspirational quotes and humorous stories, jokes, and witticisms. Golda Meir was one such leader. Humorous and inspirational quotes attributed to her include:

- A teacher is one who has a program—arithmetic, reading, writing, and so on—fulfills it conscientiously and feels that he has done his job. An educator tries to give children something else in addition: spirit.
- (Asked if she felt handicapped by being a woman minister) I don't know—I've never tried to be a man.
- Being seventy is not a sin. It's not a joy, either.
- Do you think we're so particular whether we die by nuclear weapons or conventional weapons?
- Don't be humble; you're not that great.
- I don't want to have a bad influence on anybody, but there's no point in my giving up cigarettes now. I won't die young.
- I understand the Arabs wanting to wipe us out, but do they really expect us to cooperate?
- If Russia thinks it can prepare a peace plan acceptable to us, and has enough influence on President Nasser to get him to agree, then it has enough influence on him to say, "For God's sake, sit down with the Israelis and make peace directly."
- If we have to have a choice between being dead and pitied, and being alive with a bad image, we'd rather be alive and have the bad image.
- No people in the world knows collective eulogies as well as the Jews do. But we have no intention of going down in order that some should speak well of us.
- (Of the Soviet government) The most realistic regime in the world. No ideals.
- One of the first sights that shocked me, when I came to Israel in 1921, was an Arab turning over a field with a very primitive plow; pulling the plow were an ox and a woman. Now, if it means that we have destroyed this romantic picture by bringing in tractors, combines, and threshing machines, this is true: we have.
- Our secret weapon: no alternative.
- There should be some place on earth where there is a Jewish majority. As a minority we have quite a history.
- (To young volunteers who came to Israel during the Six-Day War, and were preparing to return home) You were ready to die with us. Why don't you want to live with us?

- We don't want wars even when we win.
- We have our backs against the wall. We don't even have a wall. We have a sea. The only friendly neighbor we have is the Mediterranean.
- We're told over and over again that Nasser is humiliated. Humiliated as a result of what: he wanted to destroy us and—poor man—he failed. Somehow I just can't bring myself to feel too sorry for him.
- (When her chief of cabinet suggested something for her to say to waiting journalists) You can't improve on saying nothing.
- When I came to Palestine in 1921, the heavy industry was chocolate. And when I asked, "Why does it taste so sandy?" I was told, "Sand is our only natural resource." (Meir, 1973; workinghumor.com)

THE POLITICAL FRAME

Leaders operating out of the political frame clarify what they want and what they can get. Political leaders are realists above all. They never let what they want cloud their judgment about what is possible. They assess the distribution of power and interests. Being a woman in a man's world, Golda Meir would not have survived, let alone flourished, had she not been adept at using the political frame when appropriate.

Initially, Meir was not accepted by the kibbutz because they doubted that an American girl would want to work hard enough to fit in at a kibbutz. But Meir used a little political frame behavior to disarm her skeptics. She casually mentioned that she had brought a phonograph along with her from America. Suddenly, she and her husband were welcomed with open arms.

Meir used political frame behavior in furthering the labor movement in Palestine. She was proactive in reaching out to the international labor movement for support. She affiliated with the British Labor Party and the Trades Union Congress in England and with the labor federations in the United States. She felt certain that these organizations would be in moral sympathy with Israel's labor union goals and be of help when and where they could.

Meir was not shy about using political frame leadership behavior to raise funds for her fledgling country. David Ben-Gurion described one of her trips to the United States to raise funds for arms in the following way: "Someday when history will be written, it will be said that there was a Jewish woman who got the money which made the state possible." Her message was clear. She expected worldwide Jewry to see Israel as the front line and do what the United States had done for Britain when Britain was on the front line in World War II. That is, "to give us the possibility of going on with the struggle" (Meir, 1973, p. 73).

When Meir first introduced her social program as prime minister, she engaged in political frame behavior in introducing it piecemeal. The program included health insurance, welfare, social security, and a myriad of other social programs. But with Israel's defense needs, the absorption of mass immigration, and increasing economic difficulties, she knew that it would be impossible for the country to support the total plan immediately and thus introduced it gradually.

Meir used political frame behavior with the United Nations, convincing them that if they did not intercede in support of Israel against their Arab enemies, the Middle East would continue to seethe and become the powder keg for others anxious to exploit its vulnerability. She wondered aloud if there were any other countries represented in the General Assembly that lived under the same conditions as Israel and whether there was a people in the world that would do what many were expecting of Israel: to take no action in its own defense.

Meir had to engage in political frame behavior in order for Israel to survive in the unfriendly Middle East. She was very astute in employing political frame behavior in every negotiated peace beginning with the first war with Egypt in 1956. Israel would agree to withdraw from its occupied lands of the Sinai Desert, the Gulf of Aqaba, and the Gaza Strip only if the United Nations established an arrangement whereby freedom of navigation through the straits and the gulf were permanently assured.

Meir was keenly aware that with the Arab world denying Israel's very right to exist, she had to make effective use of political frame leadership behavior at every opportunity. Thus, she was very suspicious that the so-called Arab refugee problem after the Six-Day War was a subterfuge to bring the Arab world to its ultimate goal, the dissolution of the state of Israel. "Now that the war on the battlefield is over," she proclaimed, "the battle in the United Nations has begun. On your television, on your radio, you hear falsehood and evil distortion. One would imagine that we were 40,000,000 who had attacked a poor little nation of 2,000,000. We are called criminals! Nazis! What crime have we committed? We won the war!" (Meir, 1973, p. 161).

When the Soviet Union came to Egypt's aid in its attempts to conquer Israel, Meir promptly engaged in additional political frame leadership behavior. She immediately pointed out the imbalance of power that was burgeoning. "When we asked to be allowed to buy more aircraft from the U.S., we based ourselves on the reality that the balance of power had been shaken by the enormous arsenals provided by the Soviet Union to Egypt free of charge," she charged. "Since the U.S. announced a deferment of the decision to sell Israel more weapons, it has become known that Soviet personnel are in

Egypt and Soviet pilots have been flying their planes. This adds a new and ominous imbalance, and the need to redress the equilibrium becomes more pressing and crucial," she argued (Meir, 1973, p. 192).

THE MORAL FRAME

The moral frame is my own contribution to situational leadership theory. In my view, the moral frame completes situational leadership theory. Without it, leaders could just as easily use their leadership skills for promoting evil as for promoting good. Leaders operating out of the moral frame are concerned about their obligations to their followers. Moral frame leaders use some type of moral compass to direct their behavior. They practice what has been described as servant leadership and are concerned with those individuals and groups that are marginalized in their organizations and in society. In short, they are concerned about equality, fairness, and social justice.

Perhaps Golda Meir's most poignant indication of the presence of a moral frame was in her reaction to the saga of illegal immigration to Palestine in the aftermath of World War II. In 1947 the SS *Exodus* was attacked as it brought four thousand Jews from death camps in Germany to the French port of Sète, from which they embarked for Palestine. The ship was boarded by the British navy and sent back to Hamburg, Germany. "Most shocking, perhaps, is not what happened to the thousands in the boats, the infants, the pregnant women, the young and old," she declared. "Even more shocking is the fact that not a single country, no statesman cried out in bitter protest against the world in which such events can take place. We have not yet heard of individuals other than Jews who joined in our fast for the men and women of the Exodus," she added (Meir, 1973, p. 67). She vowed never to turn such a cold shoulder to her people in the case of this type of injustice during her term in office.

In running her leadership behavior through a moral lens, Meir often referred to the fact that she was inspired by the historical aspiration of the Jewish people for a just human society. According to Meir, from their first appearance on the stage of human history, the Jews had, inspired by their prophets, fought for the rights of the poor and marginalized in society. These visions of social justice had left their mark on her and on all those interested in the cultural development of humankind. Suffice it to say that Golda Meir internalized a strong moral code by which she examined her leadership behavior.

SITUATIONAL LEADERSHIP ANALYSIS AND CONCLUSION

Situational models of leadership differ from earlier trait and behavioral models in asserting that no single way of leading works in all situations. Rather, appropriate behavior depends on the circumstances at a given time. Effective managers diagnose the situation, assess the readiness level of their followers, identify the leadership style or behavior that will be most effective, and then determine whether they can implement the required style.

Golda Meir was a prototypical situational leader. She was active in the structural frame and appropriately stood her ground when the safety, security, and welfare of her people were at stake. She showed her human resource side by constantly being concerned for all human beings, even her Arab adversaries. Her use of the symbolic frame through her many inspiring speeches, and especially through her keen sense of humor, was laudable. She was active in the political frame both as a politician and as a world leader. And it was quite obvious that she developed a strong moral compass to direct her leadership behavior.

We saw how effective Golda Meir was in balancing her leadership behavior among the five leadership frames and acting in moderation within each frame. We also observed how she took pains to understand and respond appropriately to the readiness level of her followers. Finally, we saw how she kept matters in perspective through the frequent use of symbolic behavior in the form of humor. We would all do well to model our leadership behavior after that of this admirable woman—Golda Meir.

Chapter Eleven

Ronald Reagan

But there are advantages to being President. The day after I was elected, I had my high school grades classified Top Secret. —Ronald Reagan

BACKGROUND

Ronald Reagan was born in 1911 and was the fortieth president of the United States. He made his way to the presidency with the help of his amiable personality, movie-star good looks, personal charm, and extraordinary sense of humor. He ran on a strict conservative platform of limiting the size of government and augmenting military capability.

Born and raised in rural Illinois, Reagan would spend the whole of his life pursuing his three favorite pastimes: sports, acting, and politics. After graduating from Eureka, a small Christian college, he took a job as a radio announcer in Iowa and graduated to sportswriter and broadcaster. His big break came when he was given a screen test and ultimately a contract with Warner Brothers Studios. He subsequently appeared in more than fifty films.

During World War II Reagan was assigned to narrating war training films. After the war he was elected president of the Screen Actors Guild, and his leadership proved effective in strengthening the union. Initially, Reagan was active in liberal politics, contributing to Democratic campaigns across the country. It was not until 1962 that he switched his voter registration to Republican. In 1964, he made a televised fundraising appeal for presidential candidate Barry Goldwater that raised more money than any other political endorsement in recorded history. Thus "the Great Communicator" came to be.

In 1966, Reagan won the governorship of heavily Democratic California. Two years later he lost the presidential nomination to Richard Nixon, but he was reelected governor in 1970. Reagan lost the 1976 Republican presidential nomination to Gerald Ford, but went on to defeat Jimmy Carter in 1980. He was reelected in 1984 by the greatest number of electoral votes in history. At seventy-three, he was the oldest man ever elected president.

Reagan made history when his negotiations with Mikhail Gorbachev resulted in a nuclear arms treaty, and he is given credit for ultimately settling the Cold War. On the other hand, it was revealed in 1986 that high-level Central Intelligence Agency and State Department officials had engaged in the sale of arms to Iran in exchange for the release of American hostages, and those monies from this illicit transaction had been turned over to guerrilla forces in Nicaragua and Honduras. The affair, labeled "Contragate" by the press, led to a number of administration officials being implicated, but Reagan emerged relatively unscathed. History has been kind to Ronald Reagan. He has been rated by many historians as one of the ten most effective U.S. presidents (D'Souza, 1997; Felzenberg, 2008; Taranto and Leo, 2004).

THE STRUCTURAL FRAME

Structural frame leaders seek to develop a new model of the relationship of structure, strategy, and environment for their organizations. Strategic planning, extensive preparation, and effecting change are priorities for them. Structural leaders are often referred to as "strong" and "no-nonsense" by their followers.

One glaring instance of Ronald Reagan's use of the structural frame can be seen in his handling of the Professional Air Traffic Controllers Organization (PATCO) strike in his first year in office. Initially, he used human resource frame leadership behavior and tried to collaborate with PATCO to find a solution. When that proved ineffective, Reagan used political frame behavior in the form of compromise. When even that did not work, he resorted to structural frame behavior and fired them, replacing them with new air traffic controllers.

Even when Reagan was using symbolic leadership behavior through his inspiring speeches, he made certain that those speeches were constructed in a structural frame way. "I wasn't a great communicator," he said quite modestly, "but I communicated great things" (Felzenberg, 2008, p. 141). In most people's opinion, he had it half right. What he said and how he said it mattered at a time when the nation—after a series of failed presidencies and years of high inflation, high unemployment, and repeated setbacks in the international arena—was ready to embark on a different course.

A self-made man educated at a small college in Illinois and then employed as an actor in Hollywood, he did not hobnob with intellectuals but worked out his own ideas. His lack of breeding earned him the contempt of many liberal intellectuals, including Clark Clifford, who typecast him as an "amiable dunce" (Taranto and Leo, 2004, p. 195). The reality was, in true structural fashion, he was a reflective man who chose among the ideas of his time without regard to convention or popularity.

Reagan's mother had taught him how to lower his voice, speaking barely above a whisper, in order to hold the attention of and establish intimacy with his audience, and then how to raise it in order to project the sincerity of his passion. As a boy and as a young adult, Reagan listened carefully to sermons and radio broadcasts, paying special attention to his then role model, Franklin D. Roosevelt. One journalist observed that if Reagan's voice was a gift, his delivery, which sounded so natural, was the result of hard work and careful preparation—both characteristics of structural leadership behavior.

In another indication of his appropriate use of structural frame behavior, one aide recalled watching Reagan "dive into the details of the federal revenue code," putting his mastery of memorization to good use in his negotiations with representatives and senators. "He only had five or six ideas," Margaret Thatcher said of him, "but all of them were big and all of them were good" (Felzenberg, 2008, p. 143).

Reagan did not merely follow the path of public opinion. Like a true structural leader, he worked hard to shape it, so that he could point out the best way for his country to achieve its ideals. Reagan defined transformational leadership as having "the vision to dream of a better, safer world, and the courage, persistence and patience to turn that dream into a reality" (D'Souza, 1997, p. 230).

What exactly were Reagan's ideas? Senator Daniel Patrick Moynihan said with nonpartisan insight in 1980 that the Republicans were the party of ideas even though not the party of the intellectuals. Reagan even challenged the thinking of the leading Republican intellectual, Henry Kissinger, in questioning détente as a policy in dealing with the Soviet Union. "Reagan was the first postwar president to take the offensive," Kissinger admitted (Taranto and Leo, 2004, p. 196).

Reagan was dissatisfied with the policy of détente because it depended on the mutual vulnerability of the Soviet Union and the United States. It equalized the two powers not only militarily but also morally, thus freezing the status quo. This meant, Reagan saw, that the United States was accepting the legitimacy of its adversary and could not assert the moral superiority of its own freedom. Reagan, in a famous speech in March 1983 that shocked the sophisticates of realism and relativism, did not hesitate to call America good and the Soviet Union an "evil empire"—structural frame behavior with a little moral frame behavior thrown in for good measure.

From the first, in a very structural frame way, Reagan began a deliberate campaign to raise the "costs of empire" for the Soviet Union, especially, but not only, by supplying the Afghans, who were defending themselves against the Soviet invasion of December 1979. In Europe he got an intermediate nuclear force installed over strenuous opposition from the left. Correctly discerning that the Soviet Union was weaker than it appeared and ripe for overthrow, Reagan determined to run an arms race that he thought Russia would lose.

His key measure was the Strategic Defense Initiative, which was both structural and symbolic, a program for missile defense dubbed "Star Wars" by critics who ridiculed it as science fiction. Fiction or not, it convinced the Soviet generals and leaders that they could not compete, and the evil empire began to disintegrate. Reagan, having originally rejected "summitry" but now turning diplomat, joined with Soviet leader Mikhail Gorbachev in a deal for arms reduction that proved to be the prelude to a Communist collapse in the beginning of the first Bush administration. When Reagan at Berlin in 1987 memorably called on Gorbachev to "tear down this wall!" it was no longer the vain hope it seemed to many.

There were a few times, however, when Reagan did not use enough structural behavior. He was a great delegator, and his lack of attention to detail sometimes cost him. A stain on his presidency was the scandal in Reagan's foreign policy, the Iran-Contra Affair, in which Reagan's lieutenants sought to evade a law forbidding U.S. aid to the contras, anticommunist fighters in Nicaragua. It showed the risks he would take and the perils of his system of delegation. But it also showed how far the Democrats in Congress would go in taking the side of the Communist government against counter-revolutionaries.

THE HUMAN RESOURCE FRAME

Human resource leaders believe in people and communicate that belief. They are passionate about *productivity through people.* Ronald Reagan was known as a "people person" and "the Great Communicator" in good measure because of his frequent use of human resource frame leadership behavior. Over time, he built up a good deal of social capital as a result.

One of many instances of his use of human resource frame behavior and an exploitation of his social capital was when congressional Democrats, who held a majority in the House, resisted Reagan's tax cuts—his highest domestic priority during his first year as president. Reagan made an appeal for public support in a nationally televised address. Representatives later complained that their telephone lines were tied up for hours with constituent calls. In this particular instance, along with human resource frame behavior, he incorporated symbolic and political frame leadership behavior.

THE SYMBOLIC FRAME

In the symbolic frame, the organization is seen as a stage, a theater in which every actor plays certain roles and the symbolic leader attempts to communicate the right impressions to the right audiences. One could easily argue that the symbolic frame was Reagan's strongest.

Perhaps the archetypical example of Reagan's use of symbolic frame leadership behavior came in his speech at the Berlin Wall. His goal, of course, was to defeat Communism, but in this case he went about it indirectly, using the Berlin Wall as a symbol of Communism and demanding: "Mr. Gorbachev, tear down this wall!" (D'Souza, 1997, p. 194).

Reagan made prolific use of symbolic behavior, especially in the form of humor. Through his mere countenance and body language, Reagan exuded command. Among the most enduring images of his time in office were of Reagan walking through the American cemetery at Normandy; reviewing caskets of fallen U.S. soldiers, victims of terrorist attacks in Lebanon; and singling out for praise, during his State of the Union addresses, ordinary Americans who had performed heroic actions. And, after having suffered a near-fatal injury during an assassination attempt, Reagan insisted on walking into the hospital emergency room, unaided and with his jacket buttoned.

As mentioned above, when congressional Democrats, who held a majority in the House, resisted Reagan's tax cuts, Reagan used symbolic leadership behavior and made an appeal for public support in a nationally televised address. Representatives complained that their telephone lines were tied up for hours with calls from their constituents. But Reagan got his way once again, and his tax cuts bill passed handily.

During the Iran-Contra arms for hostages scandal, Reagan was able to use his political capital. This, along with his reputation for honesty, his willingness to suffer embarrassment should those materials be made public, and the highly persuasive speech he delivered to the nation, in which he conceded that he had made errors even if he could not recall them, enabled him not only to survive the scandal but to end his presidency on the highest possible note by negotiating the beginning of the end of the Cold War.

THE SYMBOLIC FRAME AND HUMOR

Reagan was fond of engaging in symbolic frame leadership behavior in the form of humor. Humorous quotes and witticisms attributed to Reagan include:

- But there are advantages to being President. The day after I was elected, I had my high school grades classified Top Secret.
- Government is not the solution to our problem, government is the problem.
- Government's view of the economy could be summed up in a few short phrases: If it moves, tax it. If it keeps moving, regulate it. And if it stops moving, subsidize it.
- How do you tell a communist? Well, it's someone who reads Marx and Lenin. And how do you tell an anti-communist? It's someone who understands Marx and Lenin.
- Howard Baker told me on the steps of the Capitol, at the time of the inaugural, "Mr. President, I want you to know I will be with you through thick." And I said, "What about thin?" And he said, "Welcome to Washington."
- I am not worried about the deficit. It is big enough to take care of itself.
- I have left orders to be awakened at any time in case of national emergency, even if I'm in a cabinet meeting.
- (To surgeons as he entered the operating room after being shot in an assassination attempt) I hope you're all Republicans.
- I was going to make an opening statement, but I decided that what I was going to say I wanted to get a lot of attention, so I'm going to wait and leak it.
- I've noticed that everybody who is for abortion has already been born.
- Just to show you how youthful I am I intend to campaign in all thirteen states. (D'Souza, 1997; workinghumor.com)

THE POLITICAL FRAME

Leaders operating out of the political frame clarify what they want and what they can get. Political leaders are realists above all. They never let what they want cloud their judgment about what is possible. They assess the distribution of power and interests.

Of course, Ronald Reagan was a master politician, so using the political frame came almost naturally to him. One of his most famous uses of political frame behavior, along with a touch of symbolic behavior, was when he used the development of the Strategic Defense Initiative as leverage to convince the Soviets to sign a nuclear arms reduction treaty. Many liberals in the United States scoffed at Reagan for proposing such a laughable idea—but the Russians weren't laughing.

Reagan was always more Republican than conservative. Because he thought he could win Democrats to his ideas, he did not need the coherence of a doctrine—or wish for its inflexibility. Through his use of political frame behavior, what came to be known as the Reagan Revolution comprised major departures not only from the status quo but also from conservative orthodoxy.

Reagan used political frame leadership behavior masterfully in dealing with the Soviet Union. He did not agree with "arms control." Counterintuitively, he supported *increasing* the size and scope of U.S. nuclear power so that the United States could apply increased leverage once the Soviet Union conceded the weakness of its economy and inability to sustain an arms race.

THE MORAL FRAME

The moral frame is my own contribution to situational leadership theory. In my view, the moral frame completes situational leadership theory. Without it, leaders could just as easily use their leadership skills for promoting evil as for promoting good. Leaders operating out of the moral frame are concerned about their obligations to their followers. Moral frame leaders use some type of moral compass to direct their behavior. They practice what has been described as servant leadership and are concerned with those individuals and groups that are marginalized in their organizations and in society. In short, they are concerned about equality, fairness, and social justice.

Reagan was not a particularly religious man, but he had a strong sense of the Almighty and considered himself to be an instrument of God here on earth. This was especially true after he survived an assassination attempt when he "forgot to duck." When his friend Pope John Paul II indicated to Reagan that his own survival of an assassination attempt was a gift from God, Reagan was only too happy to go along with that thinking.

SITUATIONAL/TRANSFORMATIONAL LEADERSHIP ANALYSIS

Situational models of leadership differ from earlier trait and behavioral models in asserting that no single way of leading works in all situations. Rather, appropriate behavior depends on the circumstances at a given time. Effective managers diagnose the situation, identify the leadership style or behavior that will be most effective, and then determine whether they can implement the required style. Ronald Reagan was definitely a leader in the situational/ transformational mode.

Ronald Reagan believed that for a statesman whose ultimate objectives are not in doubt and who moves resolutely to achieve them, adapting to the situation as it develops, inconsistency of word and even action is not a vice. So, in effect, the situational nature of leadership was at his core.

Reagan made his reputation by operating out of the symbolic frame as the Great Communicator. As we have seen, he also had a highly developed sense of humor. But he was thought by some to be deficient in the structural frame of leadership. In examining his leadership behavior, however, a strong argument can be made to disarm these critics. Reagan did not merely follow the path of public opinion, for example. Like an effective structural leader, he worked hard to shape public opinion so that he could plan out the best way for his country to achieve its ideals. He defined leadership in a structural way: "to have the vision to dream of a better, safer world, and the courage, persistence and patience to turn that dream into a reality" (D'Souza, 1997, p. 230).

Vision, action, and the ability to convince one's followers are a combination of skills that is rare in one individual, but they were all present in Ronald Reagan. His structural leadership abilities, in particular, were tested in his first year as president by the PATCO strike. He took decisive action and ultimately fired the strikers and hired new air traffic controllers.

In contrast, Reagan utilized the human resource frame when appropriate. He was known to be a friendly man who had a "common man" persona, as witnessed by his ever-present jar of jelly beans at his White House meetings. He carefully cultivated his image as the nation's grandfather and, despite being a political conservative, was sincerely concerned about the plight of the poor.

Nonetheless, Reagan was most comfortable using symbolic frame leadership behavior, especially in the form of his eloquent and inspiring speeches, sprinkled with humor and witticisms. In addition, he was very adept at using catchphrases to make his points. For example, he declared that "there is no limit to what a man can do or where he can go if he doesn't mind who gets the credit." In his fight to defeat Communism, he said: "We meant to change a nation, and instead we changed the world." And of course, his famous demand, "Mr. Gorbachev, tear down this wall!" (D'Souza, 1997, p. 194).

He used symbolic frame behavior in developing the 1980 campaign question, "Are you better off today than you were four years ago?" (D'Souza, 1997, p. 45). Reagan "borrowed" that phrase from his Eureka College president's commencement address. Reagan understood better than most anyone since Charles de Gaulle the dramatic and theatrical demands of national leadership. Reagan once again utilized symbolic frame behavior, this time in the form of humor, when he described the liberal's approach to the economy: "If it moves, tax it. If it keeps moving, regulate it. And if it stops moving, subsidize it" (D'Souza, 1997, p. 53).

Reagan was also famous for using symbolic frame leadership behavior in the form of homespun stories. He loved to tell the story of two campers who were hiking and came upon a bear. One put on tennis shoes. The other said, "You can't possibly outrun a grizzly." The first camper replied: "I don't have to outrun the grizzly, I just have to outrun you."

Another of his favorite stories was about an American and a Russian encountering each other. The American said, "I can go into the President's Oval Office and say: 'Mr. President, I don't like the way you're running the country.'" The Russian replied, "I can do the same thing. I can go into the Kremlin and say: 'I don't like the way President Reagan is running the country'" (D'Souza, 1997, p. 188).

He also used symbolic behavior in more serious situations. For example, in clarifying his position on abortion he said, "If you don't know whether a body is alive or dead, you would never bury it. Until someone can prove the unborn child is not a life, shouldn't we give it the benefit of the doubt and assume that it is?" (D'Souza, 1997, p. 213).

Of course, being a politician by trade, Reagan was expert in using political frame leadership behavior. He would circumvent an uncooperative Congress by first winning over the people to his side on an issue. Then he would urge them to pressure their congressional representatives; then he would cut a deal that was very favorable to his policy priorities. His strategy in this respect was the classical one—he spoke in poetry and governed in prose.

Reagan believed that after negotiating with the bosses of the Hollywood studios when he was president of the Screen Actors Guild, negotiating with Gorbachev "was a snap." But in true political frame style, he also believed that you do better if you don't issue ultimatums but rather leave your adversary room to maneuver, and that you are unlikely to get everything you want.

Using political frame behavior, Reagan established a close personal bond with Pope John Paul II in addition to their mutual ideological anticommunism. The two men shared a bond because they both recently had been victims and survived assassination attempts. Reagan colluded with the Vatican to strengthen the Polish churches as a base of resistance to Communist tyranny—with the ultimate goal of defeating Communism in all of the Soviet Union.

Though not as strong as that of some presidents, Ronald Reagan had a significant sense of morality and used his personal moral code as a guide to his leadership behavior. His mother had taught him to see the best in people not because she rejected the reality of sin, but because she accepted the more powerful reality of redemption. "Looking back," Reagan recalled in 1981, his mother's stories as well as his early reading left him "an abiding belief in the triumph of good over evil"—in the case of the Soviet Union, "The Evil Empire" (D'Souza, 1997, p. 41). Reagan rationalized his mediocre performance in school by adopting the conviction that the most important truths are moral, not intellectual. He also believed it was immoral for a nation to preserve its security by threatening the mass destruction of another nation's civilian population—thus the development of the Strategic Defense Initiative.

Reagan's moral code was enhanced by an incident involving Mother Teresa. After he survived the assassination attempt, Mother Teresa said to him: "You have suffered the passion of the cross and have received grace. There is a purpose to this. Because of your suffering and pain you will now understand the suffering and pain of the world. This has happened to you at this time because your country and the world need you" (D'Souza, 1997, p. 187). Ronald Reagan was speechless and Nancy Reagan wept. Reagan used this incident as the inspiration for working with John Paul II in defeating atheistic Communism.

LEADERSHIP IMPLICATIONS AND CONCLUSION

We can readily see that Ronald Reagan adhered to the tenets of both situational and transformational leadership theory. He was a situational leader who was comfortable operating out of all five leadership frames and did so in pursuit of a transformational vision—defeating Communism in the Soviet Union and providing a better and safer life for all Americans. In examining his leadership, it is important that we emulate not his policies and ideologies so much as his flexible and situational leadership behavior. Many of us may have differing and even opposing ideologies and priorities to those of Ronald Reagan. But Reagan's leadership style, and especially his sense of humor, had a way of transcending these differences. He was able to place situational leadership theory into effective practice in a way that can be an inspiration and a model for leaders and aspiring leaders in any field of endeavor.

Chapter Twelve

John F. Kennedy

I think this is the most extraordinary collection of talent, of human knowledge, that has ever been gathered together at the White House, with the possible exception of when Thomas Jefferson dined alone. —John F. Kennedy

BACKGROUND

John F. Kennedy was the thirty-fifth president of the United States, serving from 1960 until his assassination in 1963. He was born in 1917 in Brookline, Massachusetts, and attended Harvard University. After graduating, he became a war hero while serving as commander of the Motor Torpedo Boats PT-109 and PT-59 during World War II. After being honorably discharged, he was elected to the House of Representatives, representing Massachusetts's eleventh congressional district. After four years as a congressman, Kennedy served in the Senate from 1947 to 1960. In 1960, Kennedy defeated Richard Nixon to become one of the youngest elected presidents in U.S. history.

During his presidency, the Bay of Pigs Invasion, the establishment of the Peace Corps, the Cuban Missile Crisis, the building of the Berlin Wall, and the Vietnam War occurred. In addition, Kennedy launched the first space program and introduced civil rights legislation that his successor, Lyndon Johnson, brought to fruition.

Kennedy's administration was brought to a premature end when he was assassinated by Lee Harvey Oswald on November 22, 1963, on a campaign visit to Dallas, Texas. He was only forty-six years of age.

THE STRUCTURAL FRAME

We begin our analysis of John F. Kennedy's leadership behavior with the structural frame. Structural frame leaders seek to develop a new model of the relationship of structure, strategy, and environment for their organizations. Strategic planning, extensive preparation, and effecting change are priorities for them. Their followers often describe them as being direct, authoritative, and hands-on managers. Although it was not his strongest frame, John F. Kennedy was very active in the structural frame.

Winning the presidency of the United States in 1960 was Kennedy's single most impressive display of structural frame behavior. It involved three years of labor and calculation. He even purchased a small house on his father's property where he could more easily collaborate with the ambassador. In early 1957, he began accepting hundreds of speaking engagements all over the country and compiling a list of potential contributors that eventually totaled over seventy thousand. After he won, it was generally thought that his victory had been inevitable. But that was not the case before the Democratic Convention of 1960. Few thought that a young, Roman Catholic Democrat could unseat the Republican regime of Dwight Eisenhower and his expected successor, Richard Nixon.

Nevertheless, after the success of his presidential campaign, Kennedy's very next use of structural frame leadership behavior backfired. During the Bay of Pigs Invasion planning, Kennedy allowed what became known as "group think" to influence his leadership behavior, and the decision to invade Cuba was a disaster. Still, his brother, Bobby Kennedy, considered it a positive development in that it prompted the reevaluation of how the elder Kennedy would apply the structural frame in the future. John F. Kennedy made key changes, bringing in his favorite general, Maxwell Taylor, as his military advisor and installing Richard Helms as Central Intelligence Agency director and Robert McNamara as Secretary of Defense.

Kennedy engaged in structural frame behavior in being the first president ever to sign a bill providing federal funding for elementary and secondary schools. The Elementary and Secondary Education Act, now commonly referred to as Title I, began by providing scholarships for needy college students and later provided auxiliary services to educationally deprived elementary and secondary school students and funded the first Head Start program.

The establishment of the Peace Corps spanned the leadership continuum, including the structural, human resource, symbolic, political, and moral frames. The idea of sending young Americans abroad to work on projects in third-world countries had been around for decades, but it took the creativity and ingenuity of Kennedy, with able assistance from Sargent Shriver, to bring it to fruition.

As with the Peace Corps, the idea of exploring the frontiers of space had long been discussed, but it took Kennedy's astute use of structural frame behavior to make it a reality. Of course, the Russian's launching of Sputnik 1, the first space satellite, in 1957 spurred the country on in its support of Kennedy's space program and the eventual moon landing.

As noted earlier, Kennedy learned the appropriate and proper use of structural frame leadership behavior from the futile Bay of Pigs Invasion, and used what he had learned in the decision-making process surrounding the Cuban Missile Crisis. Unlike the Bay of Pigs, where he allowed group think to dictate his decision, Kennedy used a more deliberate and discerning decision-making process in the case of the Cuban Missile Crisis and, later, in the establishment of the Alliance for Progress with South and Central America. These successes demonstrated just how much his structural frame thinking process had evolved.

Kennedy once again displayed his structural frame thinking in his efforts to negotiate a test ban treaty with Russia. Although he was not able to achieve this goal in his lifetime, in due course his initiative resulted in the Non-Proliferation Treaty and, later, the first Strategic Arms Limitation Treaty with Russia and China.

Due to Kennedy's effective use of structural frame leadership behavior during the first years of his presidency, the Kennedy administration achieved the largest peacetime expansion of the economy up to that time. With economic growth averaging 5.6 percent annually, unemployment at 5 percent, and inflation held at 1.3 percent, the administration's popularity grew. Kennedy continued to use structural frame behavior in establishing the aforementioned Peace Corps and the Alliance for Progress with South and Central America, along with laying the foundations for the space race, the War on Poverty, the Nuclear Test Ban Treaty, and the Civil Rights Act of 1964.

Kennedy's use of structural frame behavior started early on in his political career. In running for Congress in Massachusetts, he planned meticulously and worked diligently from the early morning to the late evening. "He got no more than four hours of sleep every night for four months," recalled Billy Sutton, Kennedy's campaign secretary. "And all the while he was fighting back pain" (Reeves, 1991, p. 78). By election day, he had covered all of the commonwealth's 351 cities and towns, and at a Springfield fire station, he had slid down two floors on a firepole, doubling up in pain when landing.

Another example of Kennedy's reliance on structural frame behavior was in his preparation for the Kennedy-Nixon debates. On the day of the first debate, Kennedy spent all day going over possible debate questions with his aides. In contrast, Richard Nixon spent the day alone, consulting only with his wife, Pat, from time to time.

Although we cannot predict whether Kennedy would have allowed the Vietnam War to expand to the extent that Lyndon Johnson did, Kennedy's use of structural frame behavior in this instance was less than satisfactory. After the Bay of Pigs fiasco, a confrontation with the Soviet leader Nikita Khrushchev in Vienna, and the construction of the Berlin Wall, pressure mounted on Kennedy to halt the domino effect and take a firm stand against Communist aggression in South Vietnam. Fortunately for his legacy, he declined to send combat troops there, settling instead for a massive weapons buildup and military advisors.

Again in 1962, Kennedy used structural frame leadership behavior, this time more successfully, in response to a pending United Steelworkers (USW) strike. With the threat of runaway inflation on the horizon, at Kennedy's urging the union agreed to a wage freeze for a year and an increase in fringe benefits of only 2.5 percent. After USW increased the price of steel to $6 per ton, four times the cost of the contract settlement, Kennedy again used structural frame behavior and intimidated the steelmakers into reversing their price increase.

In the area of civil rights, when Governor George Wallace made a publicity-inspired stand at the University of Alabama campus by not allowing several African Americans to register for classes, Kennedy demonstrated structural frame leadership behavior and immediately federalized several Alabama National Guard units to escort and protect the matriculating students. Despite some notable setbacks, it is fair to say that John F. Kennedy's use of structural frame behavior was for the most part effective.

THE HUMAN RESOURCE FRAME

Human resource frame leaders believe in people and communicate that belief. They are passionate about productivity through people. As we shall see, albeit later in his life, John F. Kennedy engaged in his share of human resource frame leadership behavior.

By all accounts, Kennedy demonstrated human resource frame tendencies in both his personal and professional life. He was always attentive to his children and became emotionally engaged in their lives. He enjoyed them, fretted about their well-being, and was concerned about their future. He displayed these same sentiments with his co-workers, generally being acutely sensitive to their needs and welfare (Reeves, 1991; Brown, 1996).

When their premature baby boy died a few weeks after delivery, a distraught Kennedy expressed human resource behavior and accompanied his wife, Jackie, to a Boston hospital and visited her several times a day. A friend of the Kennedy family, Cardinal Cushing of Boston, remarked: "It was an agonizing moment for a man never known to have had an emotional outburst" (Reeves, 1991, p. 400).

Kennedy and his wife became closer after the baby's death. Deputy Defense Secretary Roswell Gilpatric recalled: "There was a growing tenderness between them. . . . I think their marriage was really beginning to work at the end." It appeared that Kennedy's ability to empathize, to care and think about others, was growing beyond his earlier, more self-absorbed phase.

In 1956, as a senator, Kennedy demonstrated human resource leadership frame behavior in making headlines by calling on the Democratic Party to support unequivocally the Supreme Court's decision in Brown v. Topeka ending segregation in the public schools, even if it meant alienating many of his Southern Democratic colleagues.

As president, though he had to be prodded by Martin Luther King Jr., Kennedy demonstrated his human resource frame leanings once again by proposing civil rights legislation. Because of his death, his proposals had to wait to come to fruition until President Lyndon Johnson pushed them through Congress in the form of the Civil Rights Act of 1964 and the Voting Rights Act of 1965. Both pieces of legislation had lasting human rights implications and remain an important part of the JFK human resource frame legacy.

Kennedy engaged in human resource frame behavior in a more subtle and personal way when he established a committee to investigate the treatment and prevention of mental retardation and made recommendations for bills that would address the problem. He was motivated in this regard by the fact that that his older sister, Rosemary, was born with a mental disability. As it turned out, Kennedy agreed to every committee recommendation, and Congress passed the bills into law.

THE SYMBOLIC FRAME

In the symbolic frame, the organization is seen as a stage, a theater in which every actor plays certain roles and the symbolic leader attempts to communicate the right impressions to the right audiences. Many times, symbolic leaders express their leadership behavior in the form of stories, jokes, and witticisms. It was perhaps the symbolic frame in which Kennedy was most prolific. In fact, his critics charge that he spent entirely too much time in this frame, being more a man of form than a man of substance.

Kennedy was keenly aware of his image and frequently used symbolic frame leadership behavior to hone it. Although he had an image as a playboy in some circles, none of those who knew him well had ever mistaken him for a man of superficiality. His parents brought all their children up to attain the ideal of public service and insisted that they be serious about their education. To that end, Kennedy's senior thesis at Harvard was immediately revised for possible publication. It was titled *Why England Slept*, and it became a best seller. At age twenty-three, through the astute application of symbolic frame behavior, Kennedy already had a nascent national reputation. The book was symbolic in another way, having served as the vehicle to get him out from under his father's large shadow.

In another symbolic frame expression, Kennedy enlisted in the navy even before Pearl Harbor. As it turned out, his service enhanced his reputation; he found himself declared a hero when, as commander of a patrol torpedo (PT) boat in the South Pacific, he saved several of his men from drowning after the boat had been sunk. The perpetual promotion of the PT-109 story, especially in the book and movie that followed, positioned Kennedy as a person of genuine courage and bravery.

Later in his career, Kennedy once again practiced symbolic frame leadership behavior in the form of authoring a book. This time it originated from a magazine article that he had written depicting courageous stands taken by American politicians in the best interest of the public, but not necessarily in their own best interests. Ultimately, the article developed into a book titled *Profiles in Courage.* After it became a best seller, it helped catapult Kennedy into the national limelight. When the book earned the Pulitzer Prize for Biography it also helped to diminish Kennedy's playboy image, and replaced it with a reputation as a deep thinker and scholar. That image was further enhanced when Kennedy established his academic advisory committee consisting of such intellectuals as Archibald Cox, Arthur Schlesinger Jr., John Kenneth Galbraith, Walt Rostow, and Seymour Harris.

Perhaps one of his more ingenious uses of symbolic frame leadership behavior came in the form of his establishment of the Peace Corps, which was popular from the very beginning. What Kennedy and his Peace Corps really meant to the young people of his time can be illustrated by what happened after his assassination. The next day, the Peace Corps office was overwhelmed with applications, and within seven days it had reached its all-time weekly high of 2,500 volunteers.

Kennedy was known for his use of the symbolic frame in the form of his inspirational speeches. Perhaps the best example would be the one he gave to the American people in the midst of the Cuban Missile Crisis, when he rallied a concerned nation by pressing all the right buttons—"freedom," "surrender," "submission," and "peace." "This path we have chosen for the present is full of hazards, as all paths are," he said. "But it is the one most consistent with our character and courage as a nation and our commitments around the world. The cost of freedom is always high, but Americans have always paid it. And one path we shall never choose, and that is the path of surrender or submission" (Brown, 1996, p. 139).

Another of his speeches in which he used prototypical symbolic frame language was his brilliant inaugural address. Kennedy called for support in "a struggle against the common enemies of man: tyranny, poverty, disease and war itself." And his famous and memorable call for sacrifice followed. "And, so, my fellow Americans, ask not what your country can do for you; ask what you can do for your country" (Reeves, 1991, p. 1). It was not only the language of the speech that was symbolic, it was the whole picture. At the podium in below-freezing weather was this coatless, handsome, tanned, vigorous man expressing a message of hope for the future. In contrast, sitting nearby was the shivering seventy-year-old former president, Dwight Eisenhower.

In the aftermath of the Cuban Missile Crisis, Kennedy used his newfound popularity and engaged in some more symbolic frame behavior in promoting his civil rights agenda. He announced that he was going to send a major civil rights bill to Congress. What had seemed unthinkable and unattainable two years earlier was now a distinct possibility.

Kennedy was one of the first to take advantage of the mass media, especially television, as a means of engaging in symbolic frame leadership behavior. As early as his 1952 Senate campaign, Kennedy demonstrated his media savvy. The Kennedy publicity machine left his opponents gasping for breath as the rally launching the campaign and all his subsequent speeches were televised, and two teleprompters were always on hand, all to project the image of a young, vigorous, appealing man of warmth and humor.

Kennedy was also one of the first politicians to employ both a full-time speechwriter and public relations firm. Within one year of Ted Sorensen's employment as his speechwriter and the leader of his public relations team, Kennedy was on the cover of or had articles written about him in virtually every important national newspaper and magazine. Sorensen was so in tune with the image that Kennedy wished to project that he was moved to remark: "Our style and standard became increasingly one" (Reeves, 1991, p. 118).

The label "New Frontier" was another effective use of symbolic frame leadership behavior. In employing it, Kennedy had hoped that it would rank with Wilson's New Freedom and Roosevelt's New Deal. It was an appeal for public sacrifice to combat poverty, discrimination, and war. It was also a call to service, asking Americans what they could do for their country rather than what their country could do for them.

Kennedy used symbolic frame behavior in the selection of his cabinet. He wanted to project a young, vigorous, and scholarly image. Thus, he selected the youngest cabinet in the twentieth century, a full decade younger than his predecessor's. Ted Sorensen, Pierre Salinger, Larry O'Brien, Kenny

O'Donnell, and Walt Rostow were all in their thirties. As far as the scholarly image was concerned, one magazine counted sixteen Phi Beta Kappas, four Rhodes scholars, and a Nobel Prize winner among his highest-ranking appointees.

So adept was Kennedy in effectively employing symbolic frame leadership behavior that he managed to turn the disastrous Bay of Pigs Invasion to his advantage. Not only did his image emerge intact, but it was enhanced as he was perceived by the general public as at least trying to dethrone the Communist dictator Fidel Castro. Predictably, his popularity among Hispanics positively skyrocketed.

The Kennedy image was as positive overseas as it was in America. During the three days that the Kennedys were in France, for example, the couple's use of symbolic frame behavior rendered them the subjects of tremendous adulation. It began with the First Lady's reception at the Paris airport with chants of "Vive Jackie! Vive Jackie!" leading John F. Kennedy to exclaim, "De Gaulle and I are hitting it off all right, probably because I have such a charming wife." Later in the speech he famously commented, "I am the man who accompanied Jacqueline Kennedy to Paris, and I have enjoyed it" (Reeves, 1991, p. 298).

The Cuban Missile Crisis was a display of both effective structural frame behavior and productive symbolic frame leadership behavior. At the height of the Cuban Missile Crisis, when the Soviets were shipping nuclear weapons to Cuba, Kennedy went on radio and television to inform the American people. He announced for the first time publically that "a series of offensive missile sites" was being constructed by the Soviets in Cuba, the purpose being "none other than to provide a nuclear strike capability against the Western Hemisphere." He announced that he was imposing a quarantine whereby "all ships of any kind bound for Cuba from whatever nation or port will, if found to contain cargoes of offensive weapons, be turned back." Kennedy also threatened that if any Cuban missile was fired at the United States, we would react with "a fully retaliatory response upon the Soviet Union" (Reeves, 1991, p. 378).

In a symbolic way, Kennedy had drawn a line and left it to Khrushchev to decide whether to cross it. Early the next morning, word reached Washington that some Soviet ships had stopped dead in the water on the edge of the quarantine line. A few minutes later a second message confirmed that the ships were turning back toward the Soviet Union. A collective sigh of relief was heard from the American people. Kennedy's astute use of structural and symbolic frame leadership behavior had worked.

One final example of Kennedy's effective use of the symbolic frame was his famous "Ich bin ein Berliner" speech given at the city hall in West Berlin. Before a crowd of 150,000, Kennedy was deeply moved and gave a largely spontaneous anticommunist speech whereby he let the world know where he and the United States stood on individual freedom and the Berlin Wall. "Today," he declared, "I am a Berliner!" (Reeves, 1991; Brown, 1996).

THE SYMBOLIC FRAME AND HUMOR

John F. Kennedy was fond of engaging in symbolic frame leadership behavior in the form of humor. In the midst of the Cuban Missile Crisis, for example, he glanced out of the Oval Office window and said to Dean Acheson, "I guess I better earn my salary this week." His wry sense of humor seldom deserted him, even in a world crisis (Brown, 1996, p. 135).

During the James Meredith affair, in which Meredith was attempting to gain admission to the University of Mississippi as its first African American student and was being denied admission by segregationist governor Ross Barnett, Kennedy retained his sense of humor, commenting to his brother Bobby: "I haven't had such an interesting time since the Bay of Pigs" (Brown, 1996, p. 165).

One of Kennedy's staff members recalled his wit. "You could get away with anything if you could turn it into a witticism, somehow," she noted. His humor was mostly sophisticated, but could be quite earthy, like when he would say, "As the cow said to the farmer, 'Thank you for a warm hand on a cold morning'" (Reeves, 1991, p. 119).

Kennedy almost always utilized humor in his campaign speeches. In 1958, while on tour in Wisconsin, Kennedy opened his speech with a surefire gag: "Actually, I am not campaigning for votes here in Wisconsin. The Vice President [Nixon] and I are here on a mission for the Secretary of Health, Education and Welfare to test cranberries. Well, we have both eaten them and I feel fine. But if we both pass away, I feel I shall have performed a great public service by taking the Vice President with me" (Reeves, 1991, p. 155).

The following are more examples of John F. Kennedy's wit:

- "I know something about Mr. Khrushchev, whom I met a year ago in the Senate Foreign Relations Committee, and I know something about the nature and history of his country, which I visited in 1939. Mr. Khrushchev himself, it is said, told the story a few years ago about the Russian who began to run through the Kremlin shouting 'Khrushchev is a fool! Khrushchev is a fool!' He was sentenced, the Premier said, to twenty-three years in prison, three for insulting the party secretary, and twenty for revealing a state secret."

- "Ladies and gentlemen, I was warned to be out of here in plenty of time to permit those who are going to the Green Bay Packers game to leave. I don't mind running against Mr. Nixon, but I have the good sense not to run against the Green Bay Packers."
- "You remember the very old story about a citizen of Boston who heard a Texan talking about the glories of Bowie, Davy Crockett, and all the rest, and finally said, 'Haven't you heard of Paul Revere?' To which the Texan answered, 'Well, he is the man who ran for help.'"
- Question: Senator, you were promised a military intelligence briefing from the President. Have you received that? Mr. Kennedy: Yes, I talked on Thursday morning to General Wheeler from the Defense Department. Question: What was his first name? Mr. Kennedy: He didn't brief me on that.
- (Reaction to the criticism that he did not have enough experience to be President) "Ladies and gentlemen, the outstanding news story of this week was the story coming out of my own city of Boston that Ted Williams of the Boston Red Sox had retired from baseball. It shows that perhaps experience isn't enough."
- "I want to express my appreciation to the Governor. Every time he introduces me as the potentially greatest President in the history of the United States, I always think perhaps he is overstating it one or two degrees. George Washington wasn't a bad President, and I do want to say a word for Thomas Jefferson. But, otherwise, I will accept the compliment."
- "We don't want to be like the leader of the French Revolution who said, 'There go my people. I must find out where they are going so I can lead them.'"
- During his meeting with Russian Premier Khruschev in Vienna, President Kennedy noticed a medal on Khruschev's chest and asked what it was. The premier replied that the medal was the Lenin Peace Prize. "I hope you keep it," Kennedy commented.
- Barry Goldwater is an excellent photographer. He once took a good photograph of President Kennedy and sent it to him for an autograph. The picture came back with the inscription: "For Barry Goldwater, whom I urge to follow the career for which he has shown so much talent—photography. From his friend, John Kennedy."
- "I have just received the following telegram from my generous Daddy. It says, 'Dear Jack: Don't buy a single vote more than is necessary. I'll be damned if I'm going to pay for a landslide.'"
- "The last time that I came to this stadium was for a game with Stanford. In those days, we used to fill these universities for football, and now we do it for academic events, and I'm not sure that this doesn't represent a rather dangerous trend for the future of our country" (Adler, 1964).

The following quotes, jokes, and witticisms have been attributed to John F. Kennedy:

- A police state finds that it cannot command the grain to grow.
- Dante once said that the hottest places in hell are reserved for those who in a period of moral crisis maintain their neutrality.
- Forgive your enemies, but never forget their names.
- Do you realize the responsibility I carry? I'm the only person standing between Richard Nixon and the White House.
- I think this is the most extraordinary collection of talent, of human knowledge, that has ever been gathered together at the White House, with the possible exception of when Thomas Jefferson dined alone.
- Look at that, I have a total fiasco [Bay of Pigs Invasion] and my poll ratings go up. What am I going to do to get them up further?
- Mothers all want their sons to grow up to be president, but they don't want them to become politicians in the process.
- My brother Bob doesn't want to be in government—he promised Dad he'd go straight.
- The pay is good and I can walk to work.
- (On his reluctance in replacing Herbert Hoover as director of the Federal Bureau of Investigation) You don't fire God. (Reeves, 1991; workinghumor.com)

THE POLITICAL FRAME

Leaders operating out of the political frame clarify what they want and what they can get. Political leaders are realists above all. They never let what they want cloud their judgment about what is possible. They assess the distribution of power and interests. Being a career politician, John F. Kennedy became very proficient in the use of political frame behavior.

Kennedy had a predisposition toward political frame behavior. He was very much at ease in the world. Tending toward moderation, he refused both the smug self-righteousness of the conservative and the moralistic delusions of the progressive. He was above all pragmatic. In his book *Profiles in Courage*, he explored the comparative strengths and weaknesses of dictatorship and democracy and, in political frame style, concluded that neither was fully favorable in all given situations and circumstances. The book also revealed Kennedy's preference for the art of compromise. "Better to get half a loaf than to get nothing" became his philosophy.

An example of Kennedy's willingness to utilize political frame behavior in the form of compromise came in the wake of the Cuban Missile Crisis. The final agreement to have the Soviets remove their nuclear weapons from Cuba was based on the United States' promise not to invade Cuba and the removal of U.S. missiles from Turkey. Another example is the way he handled the civil rights issue. Kennedy had his own strategy for outflanking both the racists and the civil rights activists. While he was outwardly only tepid on the issue, behind the scenes he unleashed his brother, Bobby, and the Justice Department to litigate every case they could find where the Civil Rights Acts of 1957 and 1960 were being violated. He also had the Justice Department participate in a registration campaign for black voters.

Kennedy handled James Meredith's attempt to register at the University of Mississippi in a political frame way. He would not accept a Pyrrhic victory in Mississippi that would undermine his civil rights program in Congress and possibly cost the Democrats the 1962 and 1964 elections. So Kennedy tried to make a deal with Governor Ross Barnett for a peaceful solution. Although he was not successful, the southern politicians applauded his effort and the dire political consequences never materialized.

Despite having a predisposition toward the politics of compromise, Kennedy intensely disliked the handshaking, the backslapping, and the process of making friends and influencing people required in a political campaign. Nevertheless, he practiced political frame leadership behavior and did what was necessary, pretending to all but his trusted friends that he was enjoying the campaigning.

Kennedy used political frame behavior to help burnish his national image in 1954 when he abandoned a campaign pledge and gave a major speech endorsing the St. Lawrence Seaway. This stance was objectionable to his New England constituency, who feared the seaway's negative economic influence, but made him a national figure and helped him in his run for the presidency in 1960.

Like many of the politicians of the 1950s and 1960s, Kennedy tried to sidestep the controversy surrounding anticommunist fanatic, Wisconsin senator Joseph McCarthy. Complicating matters was the fact that McCarthy was a family friend of long standing. But Kennedy once again used political frame behavior and placated the liberals by opposing McCarthy from time to time on minor issues while refusing to support McCarthy's proposed censure. "I am not insensitive to the fact that my constituents perhaps contain a greater proportion of devotees on each side of this matter than the constituency of any other Senator," he admitted. Thus, he tried to be as noncommittal as possible (Reeves, 1991, p. 120).

Again using political frame behavior, Kennedy refused to call himself a liberal or conservative. "I'll stick to being a Democrat," he told the press. He was especially eager to avoid being labeled a liberal. He was embarrassed when the progressive political action group Americans for Democratic Action lauded his liberal voting record. He declared himself a moderate Democrat "who seeks on every issue to follow the national interest, as his conscience directs him to see it" (Reeves, 1991, p. 141).

Kennedy used political frame leadership behavior in traveling to Hyde Park, New York, to win over a reluctant Eleanor Roosevelt to his camp. Kennedy had to give his pound of flesh and grovel a bit, but eventually he secured her endorsement as the Democratic nominee for president in 1960. He did the same thing with Harry Truman, traveling to Independence, Missouri. When the reporters asked what had caused Truman to reverse his position and back Kennedy, Truman snapped, "When the Democratic National Convention decided to nominate him for President." Kennedy knew then that he was "the only game in town" (Reeves, 1991, p. 188).

In his first televised debate with Richard Nixon, Kennedy again used political frame behavior. Knowing Nixon's precise nature, he deliberately and casually strode into the studio only moments before the cameras went on in order to rattle his opponent. Larry O'Brien, one of Kennedy's aides, later wrote, "Kennedy had played the clock perfectly. He had thrown his opponent off stride. Nixon was ill at ease throughout" (Reeves, 1991, p. 194).

When Martin Luther King Jr. was imprisoned in Atlanta after a civil demonstration, Kennedy's aide Harris Wolford came up with the idea of using political frame behavior by having Kennedy make a personal telephone call to Coretta Scott King to express his sympathy and support. The telephone call was publicized in the mass media across the nation and helped garner for Kennedy the solid support of the African American community. King's father responded by saying: "I had expected to vote against Senator Kennedy because of his religion. But now he can be my President, Catholic or whatever he is. It took courage to call my daughter-in-law at a time like this. He had the moral courage to stand up for what he knows is right" (Reeves, 1991, p. 210).

Once in office, however, Kennedy used political frame behavior and showed great restraint on the civil rights issue. The opportunity to lead the country in a historic movement of social justice was bypassed in favor of political expediency. He was concerned about alienating Southern Democrats whose support he needed to pass legislation that had a higher priority on the administration's agenda. He also believed that a more moderate and deliberate approach would be more effective in ultimately passing civil rights legislation.

The Kennedy administration's deliberate approach was tested, however, when James Meredith attempted to gain admission to the all-white University of Mississippi. Kennedy telephoned Governor Ross Barnett six times in an effort to convince him not to interfere in Meredith's matriculation. At first, Barnett agreed. But later he succumbed to political pressure and reneged, whereupon Kennedy swept aside his moderate approach and threatened to go on national television and tell the nation what Barnett had done. Finally, the humiliated Barnett capitulated.

THE MORAL FRAME

The moral frame is my own contribution to situational leadership theory. In my view, the moral frame completes situational leadership theory. Without it, leaders could just as easily use their leadership skills for promoting evil as for promoting good. Leaders operating out of the moral frame are concerned about their obligations to their followers. Moral frame leaders use some type of moral compass to direct their behavior. They practice what has been described as servant leadership and are concerned with those individuals and groups that are marginalized in their organizations and in society. In short, they are concerned about equality, fairness, and social justice. Suffice it to say that John F. Kennedy was somewhat inconsistent in the use of the moral frame.

At least as far as his mother was concerned, Kennedy would mature to the point where he would develop a moral code through which he would filter his leadership behavior. As she watched him grow up, she observed the following about her son: "I said to myself, drawing on Cardinal Newman's words, 'he will do good, he will do God's work'" (Reeves, 1991, p. 234).

Kennedy demonstrated moral frame behavior in supporting racial justice as a matter of course and on his way to the presidency assured Roy Wilkins, president of the National Association for the Advancement of Colored People, that he could be counted on to support civil rights. But as we saw, once he gained office he was only moderately supportive, favoring the political frame over the moral frame.

Nevertheless, he consistently defined civil rights as a moral rather than a political issue. In a nationally televised speech on civil rights, he said:

> We are confronted primarily with a moral issue. It is as old as the scriptures and is as clear as the American Constitution. This is one country. It has become one country because all of us and all the people who came here had an equal chance to develop their talents. We cannot say to 10 percent of the population that you can't have that right; that your children can't have the chance to develop whatever talents they have; that the only way that they are going to get their rights is to go into the streets and demonstrate. I think we owe them and we owe ourselves a better country than that. (Brown, 1996, p. 170)

Kennedy demonstrated his awareness of the need for a moral code to direct one's leadership behavior when, between presidential debates, he gave a speech in Columbus, Ohio, in which he alluded to some minor scandals in the Eisenhower administration. He presented eight ethical guidelines to be followed by his administration and pledged to restore an atmosphere of moral leadership in the White House. The next president, he said, "must set the moral tone—and I refer not to his language but to his actions in office." Of course these platitudes seemed somewhat hypocritical when Kennedy allegedly continued his extramarital affairs while in the White House (Reeves, 1991, p. 201).

In his speeches and writings, Kennedy often alluded to Lincoln, Washington, the Roosevelts, Wilson, and Jefferson as presidents who in addition to engaging in the rough-and-tumble of politics nevertheless were men of great rectitude. Kennedy celebrated their integrity and intended to model his own behavior after these men. Character, he correctly declared, is the great wellspring of behavior. But unlike the nation's most admired presidents, it has been reported that Kennedy, at least as far as extramarital affairs were concerned, would at times stray from strictly adhering to his moral code. Nevertheless, it is generally agreed that by the time of the Cuban Missile Crisis, Kennedy's character had developed beyond the pursuit of power and pleasure and his political and behavioral instincts were predicated on a larger purpose (Reeves, 1991).

SITUATIONAL LEADERSHIP ANALYSIS AND CONCLUSION

Situational models of leadership differ from earlier trait and behavioral models in asserting that no single way of leading works in all situations. Rather, appropriate behavior depends on the circumstances at a given time. Effective managers diagnose the situation, identify the leadership style or behavior that will be most effective, and then determine whether they can implement the required style.

John F. Kennedy is a prototypical situational leader. We saw how he balanced his use of the four Bolman/Deal leadership frames and for the most part viewed his leadership behavior through a moral lens. He also operated in a balanced way within each leadership frame. Finally, we saw how he almost always seemed to be in sync with the readiness level of his followers.

He used the structural frame in preparing himself both educationally and experientially for the office of president. When he became president, he used structural frame leadership behavior in his handling of the Cuban Missile

Crisis and the establishment of the Peace Corps. His use of the human resource frame was evidenced by his being one of the first presidents to seriously advocate for civil rights legislation.

Kennedy's use of the symbolic and political frames was legendary. He
astutely utilized the symbolic frame to burnish the image of the president and
his family, which had an enormous and lasting impact on the nation. The
Kennedys were portrayed as young, vital, happy, warm, and caring. He consciously used the media to promote this image. Theodore H. White's best-
selling and influential book *The Making of the President*, published in 1960,
for example, praised Kennedy for high-minded ambition, energy, and intelligence. Kennedy's own book *Why England Slept* and the movie *PT 109*
further cultivated the image.

Kennedy was especially adept at using symbolic frame behavior in the
form of humor, coining many humorous quotes and witticisms. And his
disarming use of humor, especially in news conferences, along with his often
self-deprecating jokes and stories, endeared him to even his harshest critics.
He aptly demonstrated that the value of humor in leadership is indeed no
laughing matter.

We saw how Kennedy was almost always willing to utilize political
frame behavior in the form of compromise. He found equally repugnant the
smug self-deceptions of the archconservatives and the moralistic delusions of
the ultraliberals. He was not totally enamored with the deliberateness of
democracy, having seen its dysfunctional aspects bring the West to the brink
of destruction in 1939. Thus, he was a pragmatist at heart.

We also saw how over the years Kennedy developed a moral compass to
direct his leadership behavior. He agreed with Martin Luther King Jr. that
civil rights was a moral issue and worked perhaps more diligently than any
American president before him to pass civil rights legislation. As leaders and
aspiring leaders, we would do well to mimic the effective situational leadership behavior of John F. Kennedy.

Chapter Thirteen

What Have We Learned?

The greatest discovery of my generation is that man can alter his life simply by altering his attitude of mind. —William James

What do we learn about leadership from the ten leaders profiled in this study? First, as the title of this book implies, the importance of a leader possessing a keen sense of humor is indeed no laughing matter. Virtually all of these leaders were effective because, in addition to adapting their leadership behavior to changing situations, they all had an engaging sense of humor. They were all situational leaders and none of them was "stuck" in one paradigm. Some might be criticized for using one or another leadership frame too exclusively, but the reality is that, by and large, they were successful because, to a person, they were able to very effectively balance their use of the four leadership frames articulated by Lee Bolman and Terrence Deal.

More specifically, we have learned that there are four requisites for effective leadership:

1. A *knowledge* of, and *passion* for, one's field (competency)
2. An ability to engender mutual *trust and respect* with one's followers (moral frame behavior)
3. A knowledge of the organizational *culture* (readiness level) of one's followers
4. An ability to apply *situational leadership theory* to one's practice

As for having a sense of humor, it may not be a requisite for effective leadership, but it sure can't hurt!

LEADERSHIP BEHAVIORS

Lest one be confused about which leadership behaviors fit into which frames, here are some examples:

Structural Frame Behaviors

- developing a vision
- setting goals
- developing a strategic plan
- implementing the plan
- proposing and implementing change in the form of improvements
- closely supervising followers
- developing rules and regulations
- developing job descriptions and responsibilities
- striving for the magis (continuous improvement)
- demonstrating competency (knowledgeable, organized, industrious, passionate, committed)
- hands-on managing
- attending to detail
- lifelong learning
- meticulously preparing
- behaving authoritatively
- thinking analytically and logically
- mastering the technical aspects of one's profession

Human Resource Frame Behaviors

- developing a system of rewards to motivate employees
- giving praise for accomplishments
- empowering others
- showing concern for the individual (cura personalis)
- participative decision making
- team building
- acknowledging special occasions (e.g., birthdays, anniversaries, get-well sentiments)
- managing by walking around

Symbolic Frame Behaviors

- having concern for one's personal appearance
- providing leadership through motivational speeches and publications

- displaying inspirational quotes, slogans, adages, etc. (on letterhead/posters)
- displaying symbols of achievement in the workplace
- telling stories, jokes, witticisms, etc.
- being visible (leading by walking around)

Political Frame Behaviors

- negotiating a contract or covenant on compensation and working conditions
- lobbying for improvements
- fundraising and institutional development activities
- making compromises
- building political and social capital
- engaging in a force field analysis (neutralizing opposing forces) to effect change

Moral Frame Behaviors

- developing a personal moral compass to guide one's behavior
- modeling personal integrity and moral character (being honest and forthright)
- being sensitive to the human needs of all, especially the marginalized in the workplace
- being concerned about equality, fairness, and social justice in the workplace and in society

A SENSE OF HUMOR AND LEADERSHIP

The basic theme of this book is the importance of having a well-developed sense of humor in order to facilitate effective leadership. As we have seen, there is much empirical evidence that a sense of humor is a characteristic frequently associated with effective leadership and with a leader's ability to effect change in his or her followers. Many organizations, such as Southwest Airlines, Ben & Jerry's Ice Cream, and Sun Microsystems, attribute higher levels of employee commitment, cohesiveness, and performance to a leader's ability to use humor when dealing with his or her co-workers. In the field of education, Virginia Ziegler, Gerald Boardman, and Donald Thomas make the connection between humor, leadership, and school climate, indicating that a good sense of humor is the mark of a creative thinker who can stimulate others and create feelings of goodwill in a school.

We have put these research findings to the test by profiling ten proven leaders to ascertain whether their well-developed senses of humor helped them in their leadership effectiveness. We found that a sense of humor was indeed an asset to these leaders. Time and time again we saw how each of these ten leaders was made more effective by his or her ability to utilize symbolic frame leadership behavior in the form of humor, and that theory does, in fact, translate into effective practice in this case. Humor facilitates social affairs by providing perspective and bringing unexpressed attitudes and emotions into focus. It can also neutralize emotions, mediate impasses, and impart richness to contradictory events. A leader with a keen sense of humor contributes to the enjoyment of others and builds a sense of togetherness in the pursuit of strategic goals. We have found that a leader with a good sense of humor is invaluable to an organization's development—thus the title of this book, *The Value of Humor in Educational Leadership: No Laughing Matter.* We cannot go so far as to claim that a good sense of humor is the sine qua non of effective leadership, but we can assertively state that its importance is indeed "no laughing matter."

None of the leaders profiled was a professional educator, but we need only look at one of our own for evidence of the importance of humor in effectively carrying out our leadership functions. Take, for instance, Robert Hutchins, the historically famous former president of the University of Chicago and creator of the Great Books program. During his era, he was one of the few educators that was able through his writings and his many television and radio appearances to become a household name, largely because of his great wit and keen sense of humor. Although he was effective in all the leadership frames, he was particularly adept at utilizing symbolic frame behavior in the form of humor.

One such instance occurred in his early career when he humorously observed "that there was a world far from Oberlin, Ohio," where he attended college, "devoted to wine, women and song; but I was too well brought up to sing," he observed (Ashmore, 1989, p. 34). Projecting this sort of sardonic gaiety in his manner and his speeches led him to be dubbed "the Boy Wonder" by the press, a title he retained even after he was old and gray.

Another example of Hutchins's iconoclastic humor was when he met a venerable Supreme Court justice who said, "So this is the boy wonder. I understand you teach your students that the nine old men down in Washington are all senile, ignorant of the law, and indifferent to the public welfare." Hutchins replied, "Oh no, Mr. Justice, we don't teach them anything like that. We let them find it out for themselves" (Ashmore, 1989, p. 114).

Perhaps it would be appropriate to end this discussion of Hutchins's use of symbolic frame behavior in the form of humor by recalling his reaction to Henry Ford's recrimination of Hutchins's controversial speeches as director of the Ford Foundation. "I'm sure," he declared, "I have been guilty of bad judgment, but I didn't build the Edsel" (Ashmore, 1989, p. 362).

TEACHERS AS LEADERS

When we think of educational leaders we most often think in terms of administrators. While this is natural, I would argue that the classroom teacher is as much a leader in his or her own way as a principal or a superintendent. Certainly, every classroom teacher assumes the role of instructional leader and, if given responsibility for chairing a curriculum committee, or directing an extracurricular activity, also serves as a leader in those roles. So to some extent, we all serve in a leadership role in one form or another in some aspect of our personal and/or professional lives. Thus, what we have learned from the leaders profiled in this text should be applicable to all of us in one way or another.

I believe that the principles of situational leadership theory are constant and apply to all of us in our differing leadership roles. Using Bolman and Deal's situational leadership model, for example, one can easily see classroom teachers exhibiting structural frame leadership behavior by improving their classroom effectiveness by furthering their education, or by enforcing a strict code of conduct in their classrooms to create an atmosphere more conducive to learning. Those same teachers would do well to temper their leadership behavior with a modicum of human resource behavior by treating their students with the proverbial velvet glove at times.

To complete their use of situational leadership theory, teacher-leaders could engage in symbolic frame behavior by acting and dressing in a professional manner and by "showing the flag" in attending some of their schools' extracurricular activities. Political frame leadership behavior can be practiced by volunteering to direct the Sunshine Fund, getting involved in the school's fundraisers, or perhaps running for union representative. Finally, the moral frame can be operationalized by treating all students and colleagues equally, no matter their race, creed, ability level, class, or gender.

In order to be an effective situational teacher-leader, then, the classroom teacher needs to be introspective with regard to his or her role as an instructional leader. In other words, we have to think hard about what we say and do in the presence of our students and colleagues. The well-known psychiatrist and educational philosopher William Glasser suggests that in developing our daily lesson plans, for example, we consciously incorporate at least one or two activities that would address each of the four frames of leadership articulated by Bolman and Deal.

Therefore, attending to details like taking roll every day and strictly enforcing a classroom discipline code may be a way to cover the structural frame. Being sensitive to and addressing the needs of our special students in a creative way might be a way to satisfy the human resource frame. Varying one's teaching style according to the learning styles of the students by on occasion showing a video or making a PowerPoint presentation, engaging the students in some type of learning game (spelling bee) or cooperative learning activity, teaching through storytelling (case study method), and injecting humor into one's pedagogy would be examples of incorporating the symbolic frame into one's lesson plans. Finally, offering the students an occasional quid pro quo in the form of no homework for good behavior may be a way of incorporating political frame behavior into the classroom.

Another consideration for teacher-leaders is Paul Hersey and Ken Blanchard's idea of readiness. We are all familiar with Piaget's stages of development and the need to be aware of the instructional readiness level of our students, but we may be less aware of our need to accurately gauge our students' readiness for accepting our leadership behavior. As we have seen, Hersey and Blanchard's rule of thumb is to utilize structural frame or directing behavior with students who are at a low readiness level, while employing human resource, symbolic, and political frame leadership behavior or coaching and delegating behavior as the students' readiness level moves higher. Of course, we have to also be careful to account for both individual readiness and group (the entire class) readiness, which may be at different levels. Finally, in our application of these leadership principles, we should remember the slogan: "Everything in moderation, except moderation."

THE IMPORTANCE OF THEORY

We cannot underestimate the value and importance of theory in the field of leadership, and in any other field for that matter. As indicated in the fourth requisite for effective leadership, without theory we have no valid way of diagnosing, analyzing, and correcting failed practice. Without a theoretical base, we oftentimes revert to leading by trial and error, or by the proverbial "seat of your pants."

Theory is to leadership as the fundamentals are to athletics. For example, if a basketball player is suddenly shooting a lower percentage than his or her career average, something is obviously wrong. He or she has experienced "failed practice." What to do? Most athletes in this situation are coached to "go back to the basics or the fundamentals." The basketball player will review the fundamentals of shooting, like squaring oneself to the basket, keeping the shooting elbow in, keeping the guide hand off the ball upon release, snapping the wrist, and exaggerating one's follow-through. It is likely that one of these fundamentals is being violated and causing the shooting percentage decline, and when it has been corrected, the percentage will rise again to its most recent average.

If the athlete does not know the fundamentals of shooting, "shooting theory," if you will, he or she can only correct the problem through the very inefficient means of trial and error. The same goes for leaders who are losing their impact on their followers. If they have not adopted a leadership theory to guide their behavior, they can only correct the leadership decline by trial and error.

However, if the leader has adopted a leadership theory, the leader can review the tenets or principles of the theory and most likely diagnose the deficiency and correct it rather quickly. For example, the leader might find that his or her followers are no longer responding to the leader's friendly persuasion and active support (human resource leadership behavior). In analyzing the situation, the leader might conclude that he or she is using human resource frame behavior with the followers when structural frame behavior may be more appropriate. As a result of this analysis, the leader may decide to utilize a more structural approach and "lay down the law" to his or her recalcitrant followers. This rather simple example demonstrates the importance and value of theory in providing leaders with the wherewithal they need to be able to diagnose and correct failed practice in an efficient and effective way.

LEADING WITH MIND

Knowledge of one's field is a sine qua non for effective leadership. This quality usually manifests itself in one's structural frame leadership behavior. In sports terms, the leader must have a good command of the fundamentals of the game. In business terms, the effective leader must have a thorough knowledge of the technical aspects of how a business operates and a sense of how to develop a viable business plan. In education, the leader needs to know how schools and school systems operate and what the best practices in the field are in curriculum and instruction. In a family situation, the leader (parent or guardian) needs to have at least a modicum of knowledge of child psychology. In short, leaders in any field need to know that field and be able to apply that knowledge through the theory and practice of organizational development, which includes the following:

a. Organizational Structure: how an institution is organized
b. Organizational Culture: the values and beliefs of an institution
c. Motivation: the system of rewards and incentives provided
d. Communication: the clarity and accuracy of the communication process
e. Decision Making: how and by whom decisions are made
f. Conflict Management: how dysfunctional conflict is handled
g. Power Distribution: how the power in an institution is distributed
h. Strategic Planning: how the mission, vision, and strategic plan are developed
i. Change: how change is effectively implemented in an institution

I will not go into detail about these processes here. If the reader is interested in a comprehensive look at these processes, I would recommend an earlier publication of mine, *Educational Administration: Leading with Mind and Heart*, third edition. However, included at the end of this book is a pair of diagnostic tools, Heart Smart Surveys I and II, which I developed to help leaders assess the organizational health of their institutions and identify which of the factors listed above are in need of improvement.

LEADING WITH HEART

To recap, then, the effective leader needs to be *technically* competent. However, being technically competent is not enough. To be truly effective and heroic, leaders need to master the *art* of leadership and learn to lead with *heart*. In effect, leaders need to operate out of both the structural and political frames (science) and the human resource, symbolic, and moral frames (art) to maximize their effectiveness. This means that they should be concerned about the person (cura personalis). They should abide by the Golden Rule and treat others as they wish to be treated. As noted in chapter 2, truly effective leaders treat their employees like volunteers and empower them to actualize their true potential, thus engendering mutual trust and respect among virtually all of their colleagues.

In their book titled *Leading with Kindness* (2008), William Baker and Michael O'Malley share my views. They explore how one of the most unheralded features of leadership, basic human kindness, drives successful organizations. And while most scholars generally recognize that a leader's emotional intelligence factors into that person's leadership behavior, most are reticent to consider it as important as analytical ability, decision-making skills, or implementation skills. Such emotions as compassion, empathy, and kindness are often dismissed as unquantifiable, and are often seen as weaknesses. Yet research in neuroscience and the social sciences clearly reveals that one's physiological and emotional states have measurable effects on both individual and group performance.

In the jargon of the day, individuals who lead with heart or kindness are said to have a high degree of emotional intelligence. Most of us are familiar with the current notion of multiple intelligences; that is, individuals have a number of intelligences in addition to cognitive intelligence. Among these intelligences is emotional intelligence. Several theories within the emotional intelligence paradigm seek to understand how individuals perceive, understand, utilize, and manage emotions in an effort to predict and foster personal effectiveness.

Most of these models define emotional intelligence as an array of traits and abilities related to emotional and social knowledge that influence our overall ability to effectively cope with environmental demands; as such, it can be viewed as a model of psychological well-being and adaptation. This includes the ability to be aware of, to understand, and to relate to others; the ability to deal with strong emotions and to control one's impulses; and the ability to adapt to change and to solve problems of a personal and social nature. The five main domains of these models are intrapersonal skills, interpersonal skills, adaptability, stress management, and general mood. If the reader sees a similarity between emotional intelligence and what I term "leading with heart" and what Baker and O'Malley call "leading with kindness," it is not coincidental.

LEADING WITH MIND AND HEART

So the truly heroic leaders lead with both mind (science) and heart (art)—with cognitive intelligence and emotional intelligence. One or the other will not suffice. Only by mastering both will the leader succeed. For example, former President Bill Clinton was rendered ineffective as a leader because of the Monica Lewinsky affair and was nearly forced out of office. Why? Because he suddenly lost the *knowledge* of how government works (science)? No! He lost his ability to lead because he lost the *trust and respect* of much of the American public (art). He could still lead with his mind, but he had lost the ability to lead with heart. It is only recently, several years later, that he has begun to reestablish his integrity with the American public.

On the contrary, one could argue that former President Jimmy Carter lost his ability to lead because of a perceived lack of competency. Rightly or wrongly, the majority of the voting public did not believe that he had the knowledge necessary to manage government operations and effectively lead with mind. However, virtually no one questioned his concern for people, his integrity, and his ability to lead with heart. Absent the perceived ability to do *both*, however, he lost the 1980 election to Ronald Reagan.

I conclude, then, that effective leaders are situational; that is, they are capable of adapting their leadership behavior to the situation. They utilize structural, human resource, symbolic, and political behavior, when appropriate, with moral leadership being the constant. They lead with both mind (structural and political behavior) and with heart (human resource, symbolic, and moral behavior). They master both the science (mind) and art (heart) of leadership, and in doing so, they are transformational, leading their organizations to new heights. As Chris Lowney writes in *Heroic Leadership* (2003), such leaders are, in a word, truly "heroic."

ORGANIZATIONAL CULTURE

Effectively balancing the use of the five frames of leadership behavior assumes that the leader has a thorough knowledge and understanding of his or her organizational culture. In the words of Harold Hill in *The Music Man*, the leader needs "to know the territory." Knowing the territory, or knowing the organizational culture, means that the leader knows the beliefs, expectations, and shared values of the organization, as well as the personality of the individuals and the organization as a whole. Without such knowledge, the leader cannot appropriately apply the correct leadership frame to the situation.

As mentioned in chapter 1, Hersey and Blanchard contribute to our understanding of what it means to know the culture of the organization with their concept of *readiness level*. They define readiness level as the follower's ability and willingness to accomplish a specific task; this is the major factor that influences which leadership frame behavior should be applied. Follower readiness incorporates the follower's level of achievement motivation and ability and willingness to assume responsibility for his or her own behavior in accomplishing specific tasks, as well as his or her education and experience relevant to the task. So a person with a low readiness level should be dealt with by using structural frame behavior (telling behavior), while a person with a very high readiness level should be dealt with using human resource and symbolic frame behavior (delegating behavior).

At this point, the reader may be thinking that using leadership theory to determine one's leadership behavior is an exercise in futility. How can one be realistically expected to assess accurately and immediately the individual's or group's readiness level before acting? It seems like an utterly complex and overwhelming task. When confronted with this reaction, I relate the use of leadership theory to determine one's leadership behavior to riding a bike.

When we first learn to ride a bike, we have to concern ourselves with keeping our balance, steering, pedaling, and being ready to brake at a moment's notice. However, once we learn and have experience riding the bike, we seldom think of those details. We have learned to ride the bike by instinct or habit.

Having used situational leadership theory to determine my own leadership behavior, I can attest to the fact that its use becomes as instinctive as riding a bike after a while. At this point, I can almost always instantly assess the readiness level of an individual or group and apply the appropriate leadership frame behavior—and believe me when I tell you that if I can do it, so can you.

TRANSFORMATIONAL LEADERSHIP

We all aspire to be transformational leaders—leaders who inspire positive change in their followers. As we saw in chapter 1, charismatic or transformational leaders use charisma to inspire their followers. They talk to the followers about how essential their performance is and how they expect the group's performance to exceed expectations. Such leaders use dominance, self-confidence, a need for influence, and conviction of moral righteousness to increase their charisma and consequently their leadership effectiveness. A transformational leader changes an organization by recognizing an opportunity and developing a vision, communicating that vision to organizational members, building trust in the vision, and achieving the vision by motivating organizational members.

Virtually all of the leaders profiled in this book could be considered transformational leaders at some level. In every case they transformed their organizations in some meaningful and important way. Their effective use of leadership behavior reformed schooling, pedagogy, and the way we educate. They achieved this success by displaying the characteristics of a transformational leader. They all had a vision and had the personal charisma and ability to convince others to join them in achieving that vision.

Nevertheless, they achieved their visions in different ways by applying the appropriate leadership behavior to their differing situations. They were able to gauge the *readiness level* of their followers accurately and apply the appropriate leadership behavior, whether it be structural, human resource, symbolic, political, or moral frame behavior, or some combination thereof. Although this is easier said than done, studying these leaders' leadership behavior as depicted in this book should be helpful to anyone aspiring to become a transformational leader.

LEADERSHIP AS A MORAL SCIENCE

Left on its own, situational leadership theory is secular and amoral. As such, it is just as likely to produce a leader like Adolf Hitler or, in the modern era, Bernie Madoff as it is to produce a leader in the Abraham Lincoln or Albert Einstein mold. We have all seen examples of immoral and unethical leadership behavior. In education we have witnessed instances of this kind of behavior—examples ranging from the trivial, like stealing a box of paper clips, to the more serious, like fabricating standardized test scores, engaging in multimillion-dollar embezzlements, and stealing to support alcohol and gambling addictions. So, to ensure that leaders lead with heart as well as mind, I have suggested the use of the Ignatian vision as a moral lens through which one views his or her leadership behavior.

As recommended in chapter 2, asking ourselves whether our leadership behavior conforms to Ignatius's principles of the magis, cura personalis, discernment, service to others, and social justice will bring to completion our understanding and use of situational leadership theory and transform leadership into a moral science. In my view, using the Ignatian vision, or a similar model, as a moral compass to direct our leadership behavior will help ensure that history will witness more leaders like Abraham Lincoln and fewer like Adolf Hitler.

AN EFFECTIVE LEADERSHIP FORMULA

For the concrete/sequential thinkers among us, a complex theory such as situational leadership theory is oftentimes clearer and more understandable if it can be placed in mathematical terms. The following is my attempt to do so:

Effective Leadership Behavior = (is a function of)

$$\frac{St + Hr + Pl + Sy(Moral)}{Readiness}$$

where *St* stands for structural frame behavior, *Hr* stands for human resource frame behavior, *Pl* stands for political frame behavior, *Sy* stands for symbolic frame behavior, *Moral* stands for moral frame behavior, and *Readiness* stands for the maturity level (the ability and willingness to perform the task) of the follower(s).

Thus one would articulate this formula in the following manner: effective leadership behavior is the result of or the function of the appropriate application of structural, human resource, political, or symbolic frame behavior or some combination thereof, depending on the readiness level of the follower, with the moral frame being a constant.

Appendix: Diagnostics

THE HEART SMART SURVEY I AND II

Just as there are vital signs in measuring individual health, it is believed that there are vital signs for measuring the health of educational institutions. This survey (Heart Smart Survey I) will help to identify those vital signs in your school or school system. It, along with The Heart Smart Survey II, will indicate further whether the institution's leaders are leading with both mind and heart.

The Heart Smart Survey I

Please think of your *present work environment* and indicate the degree to which you agree or disagree with each of the following statements. A "1" is *Agree Strongly* and a "7" is *Disagree Strongly*.

Disagree Strongly	Disagree	Disagree Slightly	Neither Agree nor Disagree	Agree Slightly	Agree	Agree Strongly
7	6	5	4	3	2	1

1. The manner in which the tasks in this institution are divided is a logical one.
2. The relationships among co-workers are harmonious.
3. This institution's leadership efforts result in its fulfillment of its purposes.

4. My work at this institution offers me an opportunity to grow as a person.
5. I can always talk to someone at work, if I have a work-related problem.
6. The faculty actively participates in decisions.
7. There is little evidence of unresolved conflict in this institution.
8. There is a strong fit between this institution's mission and my own values.
9. The faculty and staff are represented on most committees and task forces.
10. Staff development routinely accompanies any significant changes that occur in this institution.
11. The manner in which the tasks in this institution are distributed is a fair one.
12. Older faculty's opinions are valued.
13. The administrators display the behaviors required for effective leadership.
14. The rewards and incentives here are both internal and external.
15. There is open and direct communication among all levels of this institution.
16. Participative decision making is fostered at this institution.
17. What little conflict that exists at this institution is not dysfunctional.
18. Representatives of all segments of the school community participate in the strategic planning process.
19. The faculty and staff have an appropriate voice in the operation of this institution.
20. This institution is not resistant to constructive change.
21. The division of labor in this organization helps its efforts to reach its goals.
22. I feel valued by this institution.
23. The administration encourages an appropriate amount of participation in decision making.
24. Faculty and staff members are often recognized for special achievements.
25. There are no significant barriers to effective communication at this institution.
26. When the *acceptance* of a decision is important, a group decision-making model is used.
27. There are mechanisms at this institution to effectively manage conflict and stress.
28. Most of the employees understand the mission and goals of this institution.

29. The faculty and staff feel empowered to make their own decisions regarding their daily work.
30. Tolerance toward change is modeled by the administration of this institution.
31. The various grade level teachers and departments work well together.
32. Differences among people are accepted.
33. The leadership is able to generate continuous improvement in the institution.
34. My ideas are encouraged, recognized, and used.
35. Communication is carried out in a non-aggressive style.
36. In general, the decision-making process is an effective one.
37. Conflicts are usually resolved before they become dysfunctional.
38. For the most part, the employees of this institution feel an "ownership" of its goals.
39. The faculty and staff are encouraged to be creative in their work.
40. When changes are made they do so within a rational process.
41. This institution's organizational design responds well to changes in the internal and external environment
42. The teaching and the non-teaching staffs get along with one another.
43. The leadership of this institution espouses a clear educational vision.
44. The goals and objectives for the year are mutually developed by the faculty and the administration.
45. I believe that my opinions and ideas are listened to.
46. Usually, a collaborative style of decision making is utilized at this institution.
47. A collaborative approach to conflict resolution is ordinarily used.
48. This institution has a clear educational vision.
49. The faculty and staff can express their opinions without fear of retribution.
50. I feel confident that I will have an opportunity for input if a significant change were to take place in this institution.
51. This institution is "people-oriented."
52. Administrators and faculty have mutual respect for one another.
53. Administrators give people the freedom to do their job.
54. The rewards and incentives in this institution are designed to satisfy a variety of individual needs.
55. The opportunity for feedback is always available in the communications process.
56. Group decision-making techniques, like brainstorming and group surveys are sometimes used in the decision-making process.
57. Conflicts are oftentimes prevented by early intervention.
58. This institution has a strategic plan for the future.

59. Most administrators here use the power of persuasion rather than the power of coercion.
60. This institution is committed to continually improving through the process of change.
61. This institution does not adhere to a strict chain of command.
62. This institution exhibits grace, style, and civility.
63. The administrators model desired behavior.
64. At this institution, employees are not normally coerced into doing things.
65. I have the information that I need to do a good job.
66. I can constructively challenge the decisions in this institution.
67. A process to resolve work-related grievances is available.
68. There is an ongoing planning process at this institution.
69. The faculty and staff have input into the operation of this institution through a collective bargaining unit or through a faculty governance body.
70. The policies, procedures, and programs of this institution are periodically reviewed.

The Heart Smart Survey II

Please think of your *present work environment* and indicate the degree to which you agree or disagree with each of the following statements. A "1" is *Agree Strongly* and a "7" is *Disagree Strongly*.

Disagree Strongly	Disagree	Disagree Slightly	Neither Agree nor Disagree	Agree Slightly	Agree	Agree Strongly
7	6	5	4	3	2	1

1. There is not much evidence of faculty and staff holding and espousing ethical values.
2. There is not much evidence of mutual respect and understanding among the faculty and staff.
3. There is not much of a sense of voluntarism and dedication among the teachers and staff.
4. There is not much indication that teachers and staff have committed themselves to the modeling of moral and ethical values.
5. There is not much trust and respect shared among faculty, staff, and administration.
6. There is little evidence that teachers encourage students to be concerned for the underserved in their communities.

7. There is not much evidence that the teachers are supportive of a moral or ethical code to guide one's behavior.
8. There are not many occasions when the faculty and staff get to interact with one another.
9. There are not many opportunities presented to students to develop an appreciation of and respect for cultures other than their own.
10. Teachers do not often bear witness to their values and beliefs through their daily behavior.
11. The faculty and staff do not seem to support one another in various events and activities.
12. There are not many occasions when faculty members accompany their students on community service activities.
13. There are no occasions when faculty and students discuss their values and beliefs.
14. There is not much in the way of promotion of justice and fairness among students.
15. There is not a culture that fosters service to the community at this institution.
16. The faculty does not seem to go out of its way to model their belief system to the students.
17. There is not much evidence of the promotion of justice and fairness among teachers.
18. There are not many occasions when teachers engage in community service by donating space, time, resources, and personal help.
19. There are not many times when the faculty and staff articulate or speak out on their values and beliefs.
20. There is not much evidence of the promotion of justice and fairness between teachers and administrators.
21. There are not many instances of faculty evidencing compassion and giving service to the needy, the disadvantaged, and troubled students and co-workers.
22. There are not many occasions when the faculty discusses teaching values and ethics.
23. There are significant barriers to effective communication at this institution.
24. The overall morale of the school is not very good.
25. The faculty and staff do not show much concern for world problems, like hunger, poverty, war, pollution, and social justice.
26. The faculty does not openly express its support of ethical and moral values.
27. The conflicts that arise among individuals and groups are not resolved very well.

28. The teachers do not encourage a sense of service and social justice in their students very much.
29. The faculty do not avail themselves of professional development opportunities to develop their skills in teaching values education.
30. The sense of trust and respect at this institution is not very high.
31. There is a tendency to merely "go through the motions" at this school.
32. There is a tendency for the superficial to be more important than the substantial at this school.
33. There is a dark tension that exists among key individuals at this school.
34. It seems that the attainment of short-term goals is preferred to the achievement of long-term goals.
35. There seems to be a loss of grace, style, and civility at this institution.
36. There is a tendency to do the minimal and not "go the extra yard" at this school.
37. The administration seems to use coercion to motivate employees here.
38. We do not ever seem to be able to find the time to celebrate accomplishments here.
39. The teachers and staff seem to treat students like customers or impositions here.
40. The employees feel manipulated and exploited here.
41. There don't seem to be many stories and storytellers to carry on the tradition at this school.
42. The leaders here seem to want to be served rather than to serve.
43. There seems to be a certain arrogance among the leaders at this school.
44. There seems to be a sense of competition here whereby one person or group's gain always has to be at another's expense.
45. Teachers here won't pick up a piece of paper because "that's the janitor's job."
46. When something goes wrong here, there is a tendency to want to cast blame.
47. Diversity and individual charisma are not respected here.
48. Teachers here seem to use up all their sick days even if they are not sick.
49. The administration seems to accumulate power rather than sharing it at this institution.
50. The climate in this school seems to encourage competition rather than collaboration.
51. Teachers seem to work solely for a paycheck here.
52. Teachers are asked to teach to the test to improve test scores at this school.

53. There is a tendency for the faculty rooms to be sources of malicious gossip and rumors.
54. There is a union mentality here whereby teachers do not want to do anything extra unless they are paid.
55. Administrators here seem to dwell on people's weaknesses rather than their strengths.
56. Individual turf is protected to the detriment of institutional goals at this school.
57. There is definitely a caste system here among the administration, the faculty, and the clerical and custodian staffs.

THE HEART SMART ORGANIZATIONAL DIAGNOSIS QUESTIONNAIRES

Just as there are vital signs in measuring individual health, we believe that there are vital signs in measuring the good health of organizations. These surveys will help us to identify those vital signs in your school or school system. The purpose of the Heart Smart Organizational Diagnosis Questionnaires, therefore, is to provide feedback data for intensive diagnostic efforts. Use of the questionnaire, either by itself or in conjunction with other information-collecting techniques such as systematic observation or interviewing, will provide the data needed for identifying strengths and weaknesses in the functioning of an educational institution, and help determine whether the leaders are leading with both mind and heart.

A meaningful diagnostic effort must be based on a theory or model of organizational development. This makes action research possible as it facilitates problem identification, which is essential to determining the proper functioning of an organization. The model suggested here establishes a systematic approach for analyzing relationships among the variables that influence how an organization is managed. The Heart Smart Survey II provides for assessment of three areas of formal and informal activity: moral integrity, a sense of community, and a dedication to service and social justice. The Heart Smart Survey I provides for assessment in ten areas of formal and informal activity (see diagram below). The outer circle in the following table represents an organizational boundary for diagnosis. This boundary demarcates the functioning of the internal and external environments. Since the underlying organizational theory upon which this survey is based is an open-systems model, it is essential that influences from both the internal and external environment be considered for the analysis to be complete.

The Heart Smart Wheel

Structure

How is this institution
organized?

Conflict Resolution

Is this institution functional or
dysfunctional?

Culture

What values and beliefs are
important here?

Goal Setting and Planning

Are the goals clear, accepted,
and operationalized?

Leadership

How effectively are the boxes
kept in balance?

INTERNAL

ENVIRONMENT

Power Distribution

Are the faculty and staff
empowered?

Motivation

Are the rewards and
incentives effective?

Attitude

Is this institution continually
improving?

Communication

Is the message being
transmitted clearly?

Decision Making

How and by whom
are decisions being
made?

EXTERNAL ENVIRONMENT   **EXTERNAL ENVIRONMENT**

HEART SMART SCORING SHEET I

Instructions: Transfer the numbers you circled on the questionnaire to the
blanks below. Add each column and divide each sum by seven. This will
give you comparable scores for each of the ten areas.

Structure	*Culture*	*Leadership*	*Motivation*
1_____	2_____	3_____	4_____
11_____	12_____	13_____	14_____
21_____	22_____	23_____	24_____
31_____	32_____	33_____	34_____
41_____	42_____	43_____	44_____
51_____	52_____	53_____	54_____
61_____	62_____	63_____	64_____

Total

_____   _____   _____   _____

Average

_____   _____   _____   _____

Communication	*Decision Making*	*Conflict Resolution*	*Goal Setting/ Planning*
5_____	6_____	7_____	8_____
15_____	16_____	17_____	18_____
25_____	26_____	27_____	28_____
35_____	36_____	37_____	38_____
45_____	46_____	47_____	48_____
55_____	56_____	57_____	58_____
65_____	66_____	67_____	68_____

Total

_____   _____   _____   _____

Average

_____   _____   _____   _____

Power Distribution	*Attitude toward Change*
9_____	10_____
19_____	20_____
29_____	30_____
39_____	40_____
49_____	50_____
59_____	60_____
69_____	70_____

Total

_____   _____

Average

_____   _____

Interpretation Sheet (Heart Smart I)

Instructions: Transfer your average scores from the Scoring Sheet to the appropriate boxes in the figure below. Then study the background information and interpretation suggestions that follow.

Background

The Heart Smart Organizational Diagnosis Questionnaire is a survey-feedback instrument designed to collect data on organizational functioning. It measures the perceptions of persons in an organization to determine areas of activity that would benefit from an organizational development effort. It can be used as the sole data-collection technique or in conjunction with other techniques (interview, observation, etc). The instrument and the model reflect a systematic approach for analyzing relationships among variables that influence how an organization is managed. Using the Heart Smart Organizational Diagnosis Questionnaire is the first step in determining appropriate interventions for organizational change efforts.

Interpretation and Diagnosis

A crucial consideration is the diagnosis based upon data interpretation. The simplest diagnosis would be to assess the amount of variance for each of the ten variables in relation to a score of 4, which is the neutral point. Scores *below* 4 would indicate a *problem* with organizational functioning. The closer the score is to 1, the more severe the problem would be. Scores *above* 4 indicate the *lack of a problem*, with a score of 7 indicating optimum functioning.

Another diagnostic approach follows the same guidelines of assessment in relation to the neutral point (score) of 4. The score of each of the seventy items on the questionnaire can be reviewed to produce more exacting information on problematic areas. Thus, diagnosis would be more precise. For example, let us suppose that the average score on item number 8 is 1.4. This would indicate not only a problem in organizational purpose or goal setting, but also a more specific problem in that there is a gap between organizational and individual goals. This more precise diagnostic effort is likely to lead to a more appropriate intervention in the organization than the generalized diagnostic approach described in the preceding paragraph.

Appropriate diagnosis must address the relationships between the boxes to determine the interconnectedness of problems. For example, if there is a problem with *communication,* could it be that the organizational *structure* does not foster effective communication? This might be the case if the average score on item 25 was well below 4 (2.5 or lower) and all the items on organizational *structure* (1, 11, 21, 31, 41, 51, 61) averaged above 5.5.

HEART SMART SCORING SHEET II

Instructions: Transfer the numbers you circled on the questionnaire to the blanks below. Add each column and divide each sum by 19. This will give you comparable scores for each of the three areas.

Moral Integrity	*Community*	*Service/Social Justice*
1____	2____	3____
4____	5____	6____
7____	8____	9____
10____	11____	12____
13____	14____	15____
16____	17____	18____
19____	20____	21____
22____	23____	24____
25____	26____	27____
28____	29____	30____
31____	32____	33____
34____	35____	36____
37____	38____	39____
40____	41____	42____
43____	44____	45____
46____	47____	48____
49____	50____	51____
52____	53____	54____
55____	56____	57____

Total

____   ____   ____

Average (Divide by 19)

____   ____   ____

Average (Divide by 3)

____

Interpretation Sheet (Heart Smart II)

Instructions: Study the background information and interpretation suggestions that follow.

Background

The Heart Smart Organizational Diagnosis Questionnaires are survey-feedback instruments designed to collect data on organizational functioning. They measure the perceptions of persons in an organization to determine areas of activity that would benefit from an organizational development effort. It can be used as the sole data-collection technique or in conjunction with other techniques (interview, observation, and so forth). The instrument and the model reflect a systematic approach for analyzing relationships among variables that influence how an organization is managed. Using the Heart Smart Organizational Diagnosis Questionnaires is the first step in determining appropriate interventions for organizational change efforts.

Interpretation and Diagnosis

A crucial consideration is the diagnosis based upon data interpretation. The simplest diagnosis would be to assess the amount of variance for each of the three variables in relation to a score of 4, which is the neutral point. Scores above 4 would indicate a problem with organizational functioning. The closer the score is to 7, the more severe the problem would be. Scores below 4 indicate the lack of a problem, with a score of 1 indicating optimum functioning.

Another diagnostic approach follows the same guidelines of assessment in relation to the neutral point (score) of 4. The score of each of the fifty-seven items on the questionnaire can be reviewed to produce more exacting information on problematic areas. Thus, diagnosis would be more precise. For example, let us suppose that the average score on item number 8 is 6.4. This would indicate not only a problem in the sense of community in the institution, but also a more specific problem in that there are not enough occasions provided for the teachers to interact with one another. This more precise diagnostic effort is likely to lead to a more appropriate intervention in the organization than the generalized diagnostic approach described in the preceding paragraph.

References

Adler, B. 1964. *The Kennedy Wit*. New York: The Citadel Press.

Aronson, S. 1997. *Fandex Family Field Guides*. New York: Workman Publishing.

Ashmore, Harry Scott. 1989. *Unseasonable Truths: The Life of Robert Maynard Hutchins*. Boston: Little, Brown and Co.

Auchincloss, L. 2001. *Theodore Roosevelt*. New York: Henry Holt and Company.

Baker, W., and O'Malley, M. 2008. *Leading with Kindness*. New York: AMACOM.

Biggart, N. W., and Hamilton, G. G. 1987. "An Institutional Theory of Leadership." *Journal of Applied Behavioral Sciences* 23(4).

Bolman, L. G., and Deal, T. E. 1991. *Reframing Organizations: Artistry, Choice, and Leadership*. San Francisco: Jossey-Bass.

Brown, H. 1996. *Kennedy*. London: Longman Publishing.

Chapple, C. 1993. *The Jesuit Tradition in Education and Missions*. Scranton, PA: University of Scranton Press.

Conger, A., and Kanungo, R. N. 1987. "Toward a Behavioral Theory of Charismatic Leadership in Organizational Settings." *Academy of Management Review* 12(4).

Creamer, R. 1984. *Stengel: His Life and Times*. New York: Simon & Schuster.

De Pree, M. 1989. *Leadership Is an Art*. New York: Dell Publishing.

D'Souza, D. 1997. *Ronald Reagan*. New York: Simon & Schuster.

Erickson, F. 1984. "School Literacy, Reasoning and Civility: An Anthropologist's Perspective." *Review of Educational Research* 54.

Ericson, D. P., and Ellett, R. S. 2002. "The Question of the Student in Educational Reform." *Educational Policy Analysis Archives* 10(31).

Felzenberg, A. 2008. *The Leaders We Deserved*. New York: Perseus Books.

Fiedler, R. E., and Garcia, J. E. 1987. *New Approaches to Effective Leadership*. New York: Wiley.

Foster, W. 1986. *Paradigms and Promises*. New York: Prometheus Books.

Glasser, W. 1984. *Control Theory: A New Explanation of How We Control Our Lives*. New York: Harper & Row.

Griffiths, D., and Ribbins, P. 1995. "Leadership Matters in Education: Regarding Secondary Headship." Inaugural lecture, University of Birmingham Edgbaston.

Hersey, P., and Blanchard, K. H. 1988. *Management of Organizational Behavior*. 5th ed. Englewood Cliffs, NJ: Prentice Hall.

House, R. J. 1977. "A 1976 Theory of Charismatic Leadership." In J. G. Hunt and L. L. Larson, eds., *Leadership: The Cutting Edge*. Carbondale: Southern Illinois University Press.

Hughes, L., and Avery, J. 2009. "Transforming with Levity: Humor, Leadership, and Follower Attitudes." *Leadership and Organizational Development Journal* 30 (Jan. 2009), pp. 540–62.

Institute of Jesuit Sources. 1995. *Documents of the 34th General Congregation of the Society of Jesus*. St. Louis, MO: The Institute of Jesuit Sources.

Isaacson, W. 2007. *Einstein.* New York: Simon & Schuster.

Kirkpatrick, S. A., and Locke, E. A. 1991. "Leadership: Do Traits Matter?" *Academy of Management Executive* 5(2).

Lowney, C. 2003. *Heroic Leadership*. Chicago: Loyola Press.

Loyola, I. 2007. *The Spiritual Exercises of St. Ignatius of Loyola*. New York: Cosimo Classics.

Lukacs, J. 2002. *Churchill*. New Haven, CT: Yale University Press.

McCullough, D. 1992. *Truman.* New York: Simon & Schuster.

McGovern, G. 2009. *Abraham Lincoln*. New York: Henry Holt and Company.

McGregor, D. 1961. *The Human Side of Enterprise*. New York: McGraw-Hill.

Meir, G. 1973. *A Land of Our Own*. Philadelphia: The Jewish Publication Society.

Mintzberg, H. 1979. *The Nature of Managerial Work*. 2nd ed. Englewood Cliffs, NJ: Prentice Hall.

Morgan, E. 2002. *Franklin*. New Haven, CT: Yale University Press.

Peters, T., and Waterman, R. 1988. *In Search of Excellence*. New York: Grand Central Publishing.

Priest, R., and Swain, J. 2002. "Humor and Its Implications for Leadership Effectiveness." *International Journal of Humor Research* 15 (June 2002), pp. 169–89.

Ravier, A., SJ. 1987. *Ignatius of Loyola and the Founding of the Society of Jesus*. San Francisco: Ignatius Press.

Reeves, T. 1991. *A Question of Character: A Life of John F. Kennedy*. New York: The Free Press.

Schein, E. H. 1974. *The Hawthorne Studies Revisited: A Defense of Theory Y*. Sloan School of Management Working Paper #756 74. Cambridge: Massachusetts Institute of Technology.

Senge, P. M. 1990. *The Fifth Dimension: The Art of Practice of the Learning Organization*. New York: Doubleday.

Solzhenitsyn, A. 1978. *A World Split Apart*. New York: Harper & Row.

Stogdill, R. M., and Coons, A. E., eds. 1957. *Leader Behavior: Its Description and Measurement*. Columbus: Ohio State University Bureau of Business Research.

Taranto, J., and Leo, L. 2004. *Presidential Leadership*. New York: Wall Street Journal Books.

Toner, J. J., SJ. 1991. *Discerning God's Will: Ignatius of Loyola's Teaching on Christian Decision Making*. St. Louis, MO: The Institute of Jesuit Sources.

Tripole, M. R., SJ. 1994. *Faith beyond Justice.* St. Louis, MO: The Institute of Jesuit Sources.

Willner, A. R. 1984. *The Spellbinders: Charismatic Political Leadership*. New Haven, CT: Yale University Press.

Ziegler, V., Boardman, G., and Thomas, D. 1985. "Humor, Leadership, and School Climate." *The Clearing House* 58 (April 1985), pp. 346–48.

About the Author

Robert Palestini is graduate dean emeritus and professor of educational leadership at Saint Joseph's University in Philadelphia. He is also the founding executive director of the Educational Leadership Institute at SJU. In almost fifty years in education, he has served as a teacher, principal, and superintendent of schools in one of the largest school systems in the United States. He has written more than a dozen books on various aspects of educational leadership.